# Juvenile Offenders and Guns

# Juvenile Offenders and Guns

*Voices Behind Gun Violence*

Diane Marano

palgrave
macmillan

JUVENILE OFFENDERS AND GUNS
Copyright © Diane Marano, 2015.

First published in 2015 by PALGRAVE MACMILLAN® in the United States—a division of St. Martin's Press LLC, 175 Fifth Avenue, New York, NY 10010.

Where this book is distributed in the UK, Europe and the rest of the world, this is by Palgrave Macmillan, a division of Macmillan Publishers Limited, registered in England, company number 785998, of Houndmills, Basingstoke, Hampshire RG21 6XS.

Palgrave Macmillan is the global academic imprint of the above companies and has companies and representatives throughout the world.

Palgrave® and Macmillan® are registered trademarks in the United States, the United Kingdom, Europe and other countries.

ISBN: 978-1-137-52013-5

Library of Congress Cataloging-in-Publication Data

Marano, Diane.
  Juvenile offenders and guns : voices behind gun violence / Diane Marano.
     pages cm
  Includes bibliographical references and index.
  ISBN 978–1-137–52013–5 (hardcover : alk. paper)
  1. Juvenile delinquents—United States. 2. Firearms and crime—United States. 3. Youth and violence—United States. 4. Firearms ownership—United States. I. Title.

  HV9104.M2647 2015
  364.360973—dc23                                             2015009988

A catalogue record of the book is available from the British Library.

Design by Scribe Inc.

First edition: September 2015

10 9 8 7 6 5 4 3 2 1

# Contents

Acknowledgments                                                                    vii

1   Introduction: Making Meaning from Guns                                           1

2   Consuming Violence, Constructing Masculinity                                    19

3   Consuming Guns: Pathways to Gun Acquisition                                     55

4   Producing Violence: "You Gotta Have a 'Don't Care' Attitude"                    87

5   Consumed by Violence: Negative Outcomes, Uncertain Outlooks                    127

6   Conclusion: "A Gun Is a Key to Anything You Wanna Do"                          149

Appendix A: Interview Protocol                                                     165

Appendix B: Demographic and Data Snapshot of Participants                          169

Appendix C: Background Information on Individual Participants                       171

Notes                                                                              185

Bibliography                                                                       195

Index                                                                              203

# Acknowledgments

I would like to express my gratitude to the young men who participated in this study for generously sharing their views with me, and to the staff of the New Jersey Juvenile Justice Commission for making the project possible. At the JJC, I would particularly like to thank Dr. Michael Aloisi for shepherding the project through the institutional channels and facilitating my contact with the superintendents of the programs I visited. I am grateful to Assistant Superintendent Cleophus Hendrix at the New Jersey Training School for all his work in helping identify potential participants, organizing the recruiting sessions, and introducing me to the residents in such a way that they would be receptive to my study. Likewise, the superintendents and assistant superintendents at the five other JJC facilities I visited graciously welcomed me and paved the way for my interviews, and I am thankful for their hospitality, without which my fieldwork could not have been as productive.

This book would not have been possible without the advice and support of the faculty at Rutgers, the State University of New Jersey, Camden. Daniel Thomas Cook and Lauren Silver of the Childhood Studies Department, and Michelle Meloy and Jane Siegel of the Sociology, Anthropology, and Criminal Justice Department generously gave their time and expertise and were always prepared to encourage and guide me at every step. Lynne Vallone, Childhood Studies Department Chair, and my classmates in the Childhood Studies Program created a stimulating environment in which to study children and childhoods.

Many thanks to my sister, Kathy Lusher, and my brother, Bob Lusher, for always cheering me on and cheering me up, and to my husband, Tom Marano, for sustaining and nourishing me for more than 25 years.

# CHAPTER 1

# Introduction

## Making Meaning from Guns

Why does a boy get a gun? To begin to answer this question, we must listen to those young men as they tell us about their worlds, their families, and how they see themselves. This book explores this question and others through interviews with 25 incarcerated juvenile offenders. The young men were selected to participate based on their juvenile offenses alone, yet all the participants in this study are young men of color. This circumstance itself suggests how childhoods may differ according to race and place.

In the United States, parts of many cities are viewed as "other worlds" where poor persons of color live apart from more privileged sectors of society. The combination of race, place, and absence of privilege[1] exacerbates the "otherness" of the boys and young men who live in these inner-city neighborhoods. When they are armed with guns, the young men come to represent an alien and fearsome group. The fact that they are in danger, as well as dangerous, often serves only to incline many to give both them and their surroundings a wide berth.

Much has been written about juvenile gun offenders, but few researchers have talked with them to learn about how they view themselves and their worlds. This study examines how young black and Latino men make, narrate, and conceive of their identities and life trajectories after they have been incarcerated for gun-related offences. Through the use of qualitative research interviews with these young men, and drawing upon symbolic interactionism, phenomenology and insights from criminal justice studies, this book investigates multiple ways in which guns, including the process of gun acquisition, have come to serve as an "actor" and symbol in their life worlds.[2] As the study is built around incarcerated young men and guns, it is both physically and theoretically situated in a juvenile delinquency context, thereby necessarily drawing upon the scholarship in this area, as well as research in victimology. Symbolic interactionism, as explained by Herbert Blumer (1969), emphasizes that an object may have a different meaning for different individuals. For this reason, in order to understand a person's views and the actions generated by those views, it is necessary to take a first-person perspective and "get inside of the defining process of the actor."[3] In recent years, criminologists have begun to make use of symbolic interactionism to theorize violent events. Yet the point at which the risk or potentiality for offending becomes an actuality in a given situation remains understudied.[4] What is missing from most accounts of gun acquisition and use is the perspective of the "offenders" themselves—that is, how and why they acquired guns, what they did with them and how "the gun," as a cultural-phenomenological object, resides in the relationships and social spaces of their lives.

For this reason, I chose to take a phenomenological approach[5] to the study that underlies this book—that is, I sought to obtain detailed descriptions of their experiences from the young men I interviewed in order to better understand their perceptions of their worlds.

## Talking about Guns

One reason for my interest in this area was that illegal gun users and observers alike seemed to agree that the most likely outcomes of juvenile gun possession and use were incarceration, injury, or death. Moreover, during the course of my 25 years as a criminal prosecutor in Camden, New Jersey, I saw many young men who had been released after a period of incarceration, intending never to return, who did in fact return to juvenile or adult facilities to serve another term for a similar offense. In view of the widely shared discourse concerning the negative outcomes often attending juvenile gun acquisition and use, I wanted to understand what had drawn these incarcerated young men to this type of activity.

This book aims to explore how participants experienced and viewed their worlds. While the study is focused on their nexus with guns, participants shared, sometimes obliquely, the shame of being poor, the discomfort of being a young man dependent on a struggling woman, and how they suppressed feelings of empathy in order to commit armed robberies. Thus feelings about money, family relationships, and interpersonal violence are also an important part of this story.

In pursuing this problem of youth gun acquisition, I ask the following questions: What were the circumstances surrounding the boy's first encounters with a gun? In what ways did guns figure into the everyday lives of the youths, both in family relations as well as in peer relations? How did the young men explain or narrate their experiences and feelings of using a gun or being confronted by somebody wielding one?

I discovered that there were many facets to participants' gun use. Indeed, for many of the problems that these young men faced, guns seemed to be the solution. Guns carried a broad range of meanings and uses that spoke to challenges the young men faced in their life worlds. Participants in search of a wide variety of different things—money, protection, respect, fun, and excitement—all looked to guns and found what they were looking for. I learned many of these realms were linked together and nested within each other, connecting in ways that reinforced the utility and symbolism of the gun in their lives.

In the economic realm, the support of fathers was generally absent, and children grew up in female-headed households that struggled to get by. This circumstance often pushed participants into the role of the man of the house, with the perceived obligation to provide financially that role traditionally entails. When combined with the paucity of legal jobs nearby and the modest returns from the jobs that were available, the wish to make money often drew young men into the illicit economy of the streets, especially selling drugs and committing robberies. A gun became a useful tool in these income-producing enterprises.

In the social realm, participants, like other young people, sought an acceptable social identity. Such an identity required that they have not simply clothes to cover their bodies but the right clothes and other accoutrements that would demonstrate that they were persons with dignity, despite—or even more because of—their impoverished setting. Participants were both income-producers and consumers who needed and wanted various things, including guns. They viewed guns not only as useful tools but also as sources of enjoyment in their own right and as powerful symbols in their presentations of self. Respect is a valuable asset in the streets, and guns often meant respect.[6] Guns thus functioned both as a means to something else and as an end in themselves, as consumer objects.

In addition, participants illustrated how people may occupy the same physical spaces and yet be living in totally different worlds.[7] These young men described a sort of parallel universe where boys not involved in street activities would have no need for a gun, while their neighbors who were involved in such activities would "need" one. Outside observers insensitive to the contexts and circumstances of these young men might view these neighborhoods as uniformly dangerous territories in a somewhat monolithic or undifferentiated way. Participants, on the other hand, tended to perceive and describe nuanced, varying levels of risk of violent victimization depending on their degree of involvement in delinquent activities.

It is not surprising that different research methods should support different kinds of inquiry and that the in-depth qualitative research interview[8] is one of the ways to learn how people account for how and why they did certain things and what world views support these accounts. A phenomenological approach and a symbolic interactionist stance make it possible to see how dissimilar interactions, associates, and activities constructed different life worlds for different young men, or even for the same young men at different times in their lives. The adolescent schoolboy who solely went about his daily home and school routine may have had little relevance to the boy in the streets, as they did not interact in any meaningful way. The meaningful actors for the boy in the streets were the others who were in the streets, and hence—due to his particular interactions, associations, and activities— the gun arose as a "need." Conversely, it was because of the absence of meaningful interactions with these street actors that the schoolboy would not feel the need for a gun, despite their sharing the same geographical space. Participants accordingly described how their perception of risk changed over time, resulting in a feeling that they needed a gun as they moved into the street lifestyle not merely because of "random" street violence, often touted in media accounts and everyday discourse, but rather to protect themselves from specific and often known and knowable others. Through detailed and sensitive attention to their views and life world, these young men arise not as undifferentiated young black male "others," but as active, actively engaged, and knowing social actors who assessed the increased risks that accompanied their street activities and adjusted themselves accordingly. It is this shift in perspective, from observer to actor, that I have strived to accomplish in this study so as to provide novel and important angles on and voices to the street violence and gun use.

Moreover, as the gun use of some participants evolved from defensive to aggressive uses, several felt themselves more and more likely to become victims of violence. These young men came to perceive that they were now targeted for violence in a more personal way, as they believed others might wish to retaliate against them. In this sense, a gun initially acquired for protection could contribute to making a participant even more vulnerable depending on how the boy used it, creating a cycle that provides its own momentum.

Because a phenomenological approach seeks an understanding of experience from the first-person perspective, it is also well suited to exploring the embodied experience and sense of self entailed by having or not having a gun. Participants described a range of views regarding how guns made them feel about themselves and their relationship to the world. Some embraced guns as central to their identities, while others problematized the nexus between their guns and their identities, explicitly rejecting any connection and emphasizing that a gun was nothing more to them than a tool. The pathways into gun acquisition and use were often understood by participants as a pathway out of various negative aspects of their environments, including material deprivation, feelings of powerlessness and dependence, and the tedium that accompanied inner-city poverty. At the same time, this pathway could also lead participants into a realm of even greater risks and grave consequences. Beyond gun use in particular, participants also described how violence in general had many meanings and functions in their lives.

## Consuming Violence

Throughout this book, I use an image of consumption, construction, and production to suggest the organic way in which these young men took in all their experiences to construct their view of their world, of themselves, and of their place in the world. Through these processes of interpretation and meaning-making, participants shaped and were shaped by their worlds.

Many young men described consuming violence not only during their adolescence but throughout their lives. I use the idea of consuming violence broadly to encompass not only direct victimization but also the boys' exposure to violence in their homes and neighborhoods. In tandem with their exposure to violence, these young men were exposed to varying degrees of poverty and felt economic pressures as they entered adolescence. As they frame their worlds, they recount how they entered "the streets" where they became consumers of guns. Some participants became producers of violence. For this subset in particular, the question arises as to whether they became or would become, in turn, consumed by violence and what this may mean for them.

## Constructing Masculinity

It is no accident that guns and gun violence are closely associated with men and boys, and it is important, in a book about young men and guns, to articulate what is meant by the idea of masculinity in general and how this relates to the role of guns in the lives of these particular young men. To frame such a discussion, it helps to recall that during the early decades of the women's movement in the 1960s and 1970s, the term *gender-specific* often suggested studies of women. As men constituted the traditional "default" category, the gendered nature of men's experiences was often left unexamined not merely in studies of crime and delinquency but in general. As Michael S. Kimmel put it, masculinity, as a status to be studied, was invisible.[9]

In the closing decades of the twentieth century and in the twenty-first century, more attention has been given to gendered studies of men "as men." Influential among these studies have been those that deal with the concept of hegemonic masculinity—that is, the type of masculinity that claims and sustains a leading position in social life[10] and is viewed as the most powerful. Depending on the social context, the hegemonic man may wield power economically, physically, politically, intellectually, or all simultaneously, although this omnipotent type of masculinity may be more frequently found in the abstract than in real life.[11] In our Western, consumer-driven society, the archetype of the hegemonic man is rich, white, and adult. The participants in the current study are thus positioned as the antithesis of the hegemonic man.

Moreover, studies of gender have attended to nonhegemonic masculinities as well as those of more privileged males. Viewing masculine gender as a socially constructed identity rather than as simply given by biology has proved to be a fruitful avenue for the analysis of differing gender patterns in delinquent and criminal behavior. Although males have long predominated both as victims and as perpetrators of adolescent gun violence, it could be argued that only in recent years have criminologists and sociologists begun to theorize the gender gap in criminal offending in a persuasive way. R. W. Connell (2005) argues that various "masculinities" are performed by men and boys, depending on their differing social backgrounds. Some boys in socially powerless situations respond to their circumstances with "a claim to the gendered position of power, a pressured exaggeration . . . of masculine conventions."[12] Connell singles out ethnic minority street gangs in the United States as a specific example of a collective form of this practice, where boys enter the gang milieu through the tensions "created by poverty and an ambience of violence." By means of this collective performance, an adolescent boy makes "a claim to power where there are no real resources for power." An adolescent's social context therefore will help to determine which of numerous "masculinities" he will enact.

## Male Gender and Gun Violence

According to the 2008 Uniform Crime Reports published by the Federal Bureau of Investigation, juvenile boys continue to be arrested approximately ten times more frequently for weapons offenses than do juvenile girls, roughly the same proportion as in 1998.[13] A study of self-reported weapon carrying by 12-year-olds found a proportion of eight to one, with boys again predominating.[14]

Male gender is clearly among the strong predictors for juvenile weapons offending. (Because this project focuses on the experience of boys, the masculine pronoun will be used throughout.) C. J. Pascoe (2012) argues that much adolescent male posturing entails the repeated repudiation of the specter of failed masculinity. Thus a young man may achieve his masculine identity by showing what he is not—by engaging in aggressive performances designed to distance him from anything remotely understood as "feminine." In that way, he attempts to dispel any doubts, on the part of himself or others, that he is a manly male.[15] In her discussion, Pascoe is careful to note that identifying typologies of male behavior, such as those she observed in the high school where she conducted her research, is not a substitute for analyzing power structures and relations. She emphasizes the need to avoid reified typologies that can distract researchers from developing a more nuanced view of masculinity.[16] Certainly, when studying young men of color who grew up in poverty, it is important to keep power structures and relations squarely in view. Moreover, in studying, as here, a group of incarcerated juvenile gun offenders who are all young men of color, it seems less important to identify typologies than to unpack those that are all too familiar.

Since a boy or young man must construct his masculine gender out of the social setting in which he lives, and with the resources available in that social setting, masculine gender identities will differ across class and race. Or, as James Messerschmidt (1993) puts it, "Boys will be boys, but differently."[17] Citing Erving Goffman to argue that gender is "done" and interactionally accomplished in situated ways, Messerschmidt maintains that crime may provide a way of "doing masculinity" for boys to whom other resources or avenues of success, such as school or careers, appear closed.[18] With regard to schools, education theorists have argued that urban school contexts may leave young men of color alienated, adultified, and positioned as "bad."[19] Engaging in delinquent activity may be one of the most readily available ways in which to construct maleness.

In addition to the traditional privileges that both hegemonic and non-hegemonic males have enjoyed, it is also critical here to focus upon the burdens that typically accompany manhood. Among the burdens that men are often content to bear as part and parcel of their masculine identities are those of protection and provision. For nonhegemonic boys and men such as those of color who live in poverty, these burdens are likely to be more onerous, particularly for those who assume them in their early teens.

In this book, I seek to attend to those aspects of the young participants' views and experiences that spring from a masculine identity, or perception of themselves and what they believe they should be as emerging men. Among other things, I found that this meant not to be "taken care of" but to take care of; not to be "protected" but to protect; not to be "provided for" but to provide. The participants in this study wished to see themselves as agentive and autonomous. Particularly when they found themselves being raised in a female-headed household characterized by material scarcity, their emerging masculine identities prompted them to cast off the dependency of childhood quite early in favor of self-sufficiency or even provision for others.

## Race and Gun Violence

Gun violence disproportionately affects young men of color, both as victims of gunshot injuries and as offenders. Elaine Cassidy and Howard Stevenson, citing statistics from the year 2000, point out that while African American male adolescents composed only 1 percent of the US population, those between the ages of 14 and 17 constituted almost 26 percent of all homicide victims that year. They also reported that an overwhelming percentage of African American males who die at young ages are killed by those who are also young, black, and male.[20] Juvenile facilities and adult prisons alike are notorious as sites where young men of color are disproportionately contained, and the public health community has recognized that gun violence constitutes a serious mortality threat to young black men. Latino youth, too, are frequent victims.

While race may be socially constructed, it has very real social meaning in America and influences, among other things, how children are viewed by the world, how they view themselves and the world, and of course, how children believe the world views them. The effects of racial discrimination in the United States are pervasive and systemic, often sending a variety of negative messages to children of color. The messages that many of these youth may absorb from growing up together in sites of urban poverty can lead them to believe that legal routes to success are not for them. Unsurprisingly, researchers have found that urban youth of color may be angry about what they perceive to be their life possibilities.[21] The combination of racial discrimination, anger, and guns constitutes a serious threat to young men of color, both offenders and nonoffenders.

## Poverty and Gun Violence

The criminal law, even when applied fairly to all offenders, has a very different impact upon children who live in poverty and those who do not. For young people who do not grow up in conditions of material deprivation, the motivation to engage in many types of delinquent activity is considerably diminished. Henry Giroux argues that it is important to "unravel how cultural differences have been constructed within the unequal distribution of resources,"[22] and there is little mystery in the higher rate of delinquency among poor children.

In addition to the vulnerability and anger that may arise from living in dangerous neighborhoods and experiencing the effects of racial discrimination, material deprivation itself can motivate adolescents toward offending behavior. Not only the need for basic necessities such as food and rent but also the desire to participate in our consumer society prompts youth to escape (or disguise) their visible material deprivation by acquiring the means to present a prosperous, or at least fashionable, façade. For young men living in poverty who engage in delinquency, a gun may be useful in numerous ways as will be discussed at length in the chapters that follow.

## Masculinities and Multidimensional Identities

The attributes of race, class, gender, and age all intersected as these young men made meaning of their lives and sought to find a place in their worlds. In the social contexts of these young men, masculinity was defined and manifested by protection, provision, capability, and efficacy. The condition of being powerless to protect himself or others, or unable to provide even for himself when his mother was struggling financially, was inconsistent with being a man. As a result, participants sought to remedy the feeling that they lacked agency and efficacy in their worlds. They tried to present, both to themselves and to others, the persona of a young man who could handle himself, his surroundings, and his circumstances. Their teachers, and even their parents, may have told them that this was the time for them to be schoolboys, but their experiences told them something different—that it was time to be a man—and a man must protect, provide, and present himself as one who has the ability, and the power, to do things.

In particular, this book explores the nexus of guns and, more generally, violence with such identity work—that is, how the idea of guns, the use of guns, gun knowledge, gun ownership, and the consumption and production of violence function in the construction of masculinity for these young men. The participants show us how constructing masculinity through guns and violence provides a way for young men in a Western, consumer-driven society to make a claim to power in contexts where they are otherwise relatively powerless.[23]

## Popular Culture and Guns

In a book about young men and guns, it is essential to consider the extent to which guns, and the idea of guns, are embedded in both US history and American cultural history. Popular culture testifies to the degree that America is, as Richard Slotkin (1992) wrote, a *Gunfighter Nation*.[24] From the time of the early settlers, to the nineteenth century and "the gun that won the West," to the newer immigrant gangsters of the early twentieth century and the "gangstas" of today, the man with a gun has been both a central part of American history and the basis of a national myth.

Actual guns and the symbolism of guns have long permeated US culture at many levels, often with special meaning among the dispossessed. Slotkin points out that the meaning of the gun as a tool for the "social bandit" who is unhappy with society's division of wealth and power has been a trope of popular literature for at least a hundred and fifty years.[25] Over the course of this long tradition, the myths of Jesse James and other Western outlaws gave way to the urban gunmen of the 1930s gangster films. These films suggested to Depression-era audiences that their criminal "quasi-heroes" were a "predictable, even a probable, product of modern American life."[26] Several outlaw Western films presented the same social critique, suggesting that the powerful elite placed the (often immigrant) poor in the position of committing economically based crime, often with guns. Slotkin cites the original 1932 film *Scarface* as an example of the urban gangster film genre, and its 1983 remake with Al Pacino portraying the lead character as a Cuban refugee illustrates the tendency of modern examples to focus on the experiences of young Latino or African American men. Indeed, participants in the current study referenced both *Scarface* (1983) and *New Jack City* (1991), featuring an African American protagonist, as relevant to their gun-carrying lifestyles, despite the fact that both films debuted long before participants could have viewed them in their original releases. Nonetheless, such films continued to provide both an interpretive frame and a mythic gloss to adolescents' gun-based activities. Citing rap music as evocative of their lifestyles, some participants seemed to position themselves within an outlaw or underdog discourse, though most hesitated to put it in explicitly race or class terms in their conversations with me. Rather, they tended to displace race or class references with references to place, speaking of their neighborhoods as the source of their lifestyles. In this discourse, guns often became not only symbols but, as Slotkin suggested, "fetishized" as material objects in much the same way as they were in Western films of the 1950s such as *Colt .45* (1950), *Springfield Rifle* (1952), *Winchester '73* (1953), and *The Gun That Won the West* (1955).[27] Participants thus drew, perhaps unintentionally, upon well-established gun narratives of American popular culture as disseminated in their contemporary iterations. The examples that resonated particularly with participants were those where powerless young men of color were able to prevail with the use of a gun.

## Contributions of This Study

The primary contribution of this study is to show how young gun offenders viewed their worlds and the place of guns in their worlds as explained by the young men themselves. This study provides a detailed description of the process of juvenile gun acquisition, illuminating not only how but also why these young men obtained guns. It shows that guns are multivalent objects for participants, and that the experience of gun possession includes an element of embodiment, which may give rise to the incorporation of the gun into the young person's view of himself. Through these processes, guns can become implicated in the young men's construction of masculinity. The study also demonstrates that participants experienced their environments not as places where everyone is equally at risk of violent victimization but rather as places where the level of risk is largely dependent upon whether one participates in what these young men call "the street lifestyle." This research contributes to our understanding of violent offending by juveniles, as participants who perpetrated crimes such as armed robbery described how they suppressed any feelings of empathy for their victims in order to accomplish their objectives. This study sheds light on family and community dynamics of vulnerability, interdependence, and responsibility to show how age, gender, and economic stress coalesce to push and pull participants into a place where gun possession seems sensible. At the same time, it reveals participants as young people who are interested in consumption, in having fun and excitement, and in presenting themselves to their peers in an acceptable way.

## Hearing Young Voices, Seeing Young Lives

By eliciting the narratives of the incarcerated young men who agreed to talk with me, I hoped to learn how, where, when, and why they first acquired and used guns. The objective of this inquiry was to better understand the place of the gun in relation to participants' views of themselves at the time of first possession and use, as well as their retrospective assessments of the activities and social worlds or contexts that prompted and enabled their actions.

### *My Own Background*

Reflexivity has a critical role in qualitative research, as the researcher herself is the research instrument.[28] Robert Emerson, Rachel Fretz, and Linda Shaw (1995) point out that what the researcher writes is her version of participants' version of their social worlds.[29] For this reason, foregrounding the basis for my interest and my possible biases is crucial for both the reader and me in considering the validity of my interpretations of the interview data. My interest in this subject arose out of my work for 25 years as an assistant prosecutor in Camden County, New Jersey. For the last 21 of those years I supervised the unit that prosecuted juveniles, who are defined in New Jersey as persons who have not attained the age of 18 at the time of the charged offense. The county seat, the city of Camden, is notorious as among the poorest and most dangerous cities in the United States, and a great deal of the violent crime in the city has consisted of gun offenses by juvenile boys.

As others have observed,[30] family court is a place where the judge, prosecutor, and defense attorney often feel more like social workers than attorneys, all struggling to find and craft a disposition (the juvenile court word for *sentence*) that could help to keep the juvenile from returning to court, either as a juvenile or as an adult. In the case of serious violent offenses, the safety of the community and the welfare of any surviving victim would weigh heavily in the balance for me in my role as a prosecutor.

In addition to issues of age and gender (virtually all gun offenders were male), issues of race and class were always salient. However, as many victims tended to be from the same neighborhoods as the juvenile gun offenders, the salient feature was not simply that the juvenile gun offenders were poor young men of color but that most of the victims as well as the offenders were poor persons of color. The participants in the current study reflected this racial/ethnic pattern—all the young men were African American, Latino, or both.

As an older, white, female professional, I was uncertain whether our differences would make participants less likely to discuss certain aspects of their experiences with me. Herbert Rubin and Irene Rubin (2005) refer to interviewing across demographic differences as "crossing boundaries."[31] I am certain that, in many ways, the young men did not talk to me as freely as they would a peer on the street, but they often seemed to welcome the opportunity to be the experts in explaining their environments and experiences to an "outsider." Moreover, they might not have felt the same obligation to act tough that they might have felt with another man, as Jody Miller (2010) has pointed out.[32] This circumstance may have resulted in an increased willingness on the part of participants in this study to discuss their feelings.

Although I did not disclose my background as a prosecutor, it was my impression that my familiarity with the intricacies of the juvenile and criminal justice systems served to put the participants somewhat at ease, and thereby facilitated our moving on to discuss issues relevant to the research project. In this area at least, we had a shared vocabulary and knowledge base, and what might be called "shop talk" served at some level as a bridge between us—we could both "talk the talk" of the juvenile justice system.

### Research Site and Selection of Participants

I interviewed 25 young men in the custody of the New Jersey Juvenile Justice Commission, visiting 6 different facilities. I wanted to talk with boys who had already been adjudicated delinquent—the juvenile court term for being found guilty or having admitted their involvement—so that they would not need to fear implicating themselves by discussing the matter for which they had been incarcerated. Since I was interested in researching juveniles with gun involvement, I attempted to identify participants with adjudications for offenses with a gun, such as gun possession, armed robbery, or aggravated assault. These criteria resulted in the selection of some participants who did not have an adjudication for a gun offense, such as those who had committed an armed robbery or aggravated assault with a knife, but these young men also described gun involvement that had not resulted in an adjudication.[33] Similarly, the young men with gun-related adjudications also discussed both other gun offenses for which they had not been adjudicated and other violent offenses. I conducted the interviews from November 2010 to June 2011.

The group of young people who agreed to participate consisted of 22 African Americans and 3 Latinos. Of these, 17 lived with their mothers, 3 with aunts, 1 with his grandmother, 3 with a mother and father, and 1 with his father. Thus 21 out of 25 participants lived in female-headed households. At least 5 participants already had children, and 2 more were expectant fathers. At least 6 of the young men had earned money legally at some point.[34]

## Voices

I assigned pseudonyms to each participant rather than asking them to choose their own in the hope of maximizing the confidentiality of what they shared with me. When participants' words are rendered in capital letters in quotations from interviews, this indicates that the participant placed special emphasis on those words. I did not "clean up" the texts of the interviews, but I sometimes omitted the names of particular towns, again in order to preserve confidentiality as much as possible. Where some brief portions of the recordings were inaudible, I indicated this in the transcripts.

The participants in this study were often eloquent, open, and insightful. I felt no need to tinker with their words in order to make their ideas more clear, as I believe their voices stand very well on their own. I am mindful of the frequency with which researchers are said to become overly sympathetic to their participants out of gratitude for making their research possible, and I hope that the methods employed in this project are sufficiently transparent that the reader can see past the grateful researcher and the judgmental prosecutor alike.

## Chapters, Pathways, and Directionality

Several concepts recur throughout the chapters of this book, including the familiar developmental oppositions of vulnerability and agency, dependence and independence, and irresponsibility and responsibility. In the life worlds of the participants, these domains, typically conceptualized as continua on the road to adulthood, become somewhat skewed. These adolescents responded to their perceived vulnerability by acquiring guns, a strategy that often succeeded, at least in the short term, in converting their feelings of vulnerability into feelings of agency. With one exception, however, the vulnerability that prompted participants' gun acquisition was born out of their illegal activities in the street, a form of delinquent agency that I argue was itself a response to various types of vulnerability that participants experienced in their environments. These young men often dealt with the discomfort of being dependent on financially stressed parents by seeking a measure of financial independence in the illegal economy of drugs, theft, or robbery. Sometimes they viewed this course of action as acting responsibly, albeit illegally, whether they were providing for many of their own needs and wants or contributing to the support of the household at large. The fact that their parents might accept these financial contributions could only reinforce such a view. In these ways, the participants' life worlds constrained and enabled their courses of action, permitting the creation of social and economic spaces in which they could feel competent, somewhat independent, and relatively responsible.[35] These young men were growing and learning in ways that they viewed, at the time, as adaptive, but they were hardly doing so along the conventional path to adult agency, independence, and responsibility. Rather, their pathways typically led first to the streets, then to gun possession, and then to aggressive gun use for some. Finally, each one's path brought him to a term of incarceration, where they paused long enough for us to meet.

## Ecological Systems Theory

Urie Bronfenbrenner's ecological systems theory (1979)[36] may be helpful in considering the influence of the environment on youth identity development as it unfolds in the chapters that follow. Bronfenbrenner described nested spheres of influence extending out from the individual child, from the microsystems of his daily interactions in the family, neighborhood, and peer group to the outermost reaches of the macrosystem, where broad cultural and media forces exert their influence on individual identity development. Rolf Muuss emphasized the phenomenological basis of Bronfenbrenner's theory, noting that it is both dynamic and mediated by the perceptions and perspectives of the individual at its center. Muuss pointed out that Bronfenbrenner viewed as an almost "immutable law" that "if men define situations as real, they are real in their consequences."[37] As Muuss put it, "What matters psychologically speaking are not the objective properties as defined by physical reality, but the significance attached to these properties by the individual in that environment." Therefore, when considering Bronfenbrenner's nested systems, ranging from proximal systems such as the microsystem and mesosystem to the more distal processes of the exosystem and macrosystem, it is important to consider not only the influences of these systems on each other and on the adolescent but also the differential impact of the environment on different individuals, and the influence that the adolescent can have on these systems and on their relationships. He thus incorporates George Herbert Mead's (1934)[38] idea that, in selecting among the possible responses to his environment, the individual constructs both his environment, and, ultimately, his identity.

This framework provides a way to consider the effects of participants' ecologies at all levels—from the most localized to the broadest cultural influences—on their identities and their actions. At the same time, it is a dynamic model that takes into account the influence of identities and actions upon each other and upon ecologies. As will be seen, the directionality implicit in the primary pathway to gun acquisition and use described in this study is also congruent with a life course perspective, as gun acquisition and some types of gun use can be viewed as significant life events that may mark transitions affecting participants' trajectories.[39]

## Chapter Outline

Chapter 2 describes the risks and challenges of participants' environments and some of the ways that they adapted to these challenges. In particular, it outlines how participants were drawn to the street life. Chapter 3 focuses on gun acquisition as a coping strategy employed by participants, generally in response to the challenges of the street lifestyle. It discusses how participants came to decide that they needed or wanted guns and how they acquired them. It also describes their embodied experience of having a gun and how participants viewed that experience as either influencing or not influencing their views of themselves. Chapter 4 describes how some participants moved from using a gun for protection to using a gun more aggressively, and discusses how these participants narrated their emergent identities as gun offenders. The chapter discusses the unfolding of several violent events, and explores participants' feelings about their violent offending. Chapter 5 considers several outcomes of the street lifestyle, including being shot. It thus conceptualizes embracing the street lifestyle as a coping strategy that may lead to specific negative outcomes. It also looks more broadly at how participants and some researchers have viewed the implications of gun involvement in particular and street activities in general, and examines what these incarcerated participants believed might have prevented them from taking this path. Chapter 6 concludes the discussion by reviewing some of the main findings and exploring several policy and intervention implications of these findings. Finally, I detail some limitations of the research and suggest directions for future projects.

The outcomes experienced by these participants, of course, are by no means inevitable or universal for young men from similar environments. This group of incarcerated adolescents, however, described their pathways as having a certain directionality that, while not chronological, included a series of contextually structured decisions that channeled their actions to a place where, as several put it, "We are having this conversation." Those contexts, decisions, actions, and conversations are the subject of the chapters that follow.

# CHAPTER 2

# Consuming Violence, Constructing Masculinity

I'm standin' in front of my house. It was a time back before I started doin' this. I was standin' outside in my helmet and shoulder pads, and I just hear gunshots . . . they just come down the street in a car and they shootin' and I, I just RUN . . . You know how people say, "Here today, gone tomorrow"—you could be here today, gone today . . . Tomorrow is not promised.

—Tim

Tim was describing a day back before he started selling drugs or carrying a gun, when he was dressed and ready to go to football practice. At that time, he was still a committed student-athlete, around 12 years old. Many of the boys described similar encounters with violence in their everyday lives. Three of them, more than 10 percent of the group, had been shot, 12 more reported having been shot at but not hit, at least 6 had been victims of one or more robberies, and at least 14 had friends or family members who had been shot. Direct and indirect victimization, poverty, and violence exposure of various kinds typically characterized their life worlds. In this sense, I view the participants in this study as consuming various forms of violence regularly; sometimes involuntarily through victimization, violence exposure, or the symbolic violence of poverty or structural racism, and sometimes more willingly, taking in violence in their neighborhoods or through media representations as entertainment. As they did so, they grew from boyhood to adolescence, constructing their identities as young men from all that they had consumed.

In this chapter I explore many of the challenges and threats faced by participants in their family and neighborhood spheres. Some of the ways in which they coped with these risk factors also form part of the context of their lives and experiences. The dynamic relationship among environmental risks, the individual adolescent's perceptions, and his coping responses is well illustrated by Margaret Beale Spencer's Phenomenological Variant of Ecological Systems Theory (2003).[1] Her framework, which acknowledges the subjective and interactive processes of identity development, helps to explain why some young men respond to their environments by becoming involved in illegal activities while others do not. Many children grow up in similar surroundings and do not become gun offenders. Therefore, in tracing participants' pathways to gun acquisition and use, it is important to consider how they described their experience of these environmental factors and how they related them to their identity development.

In addition, because the pathway to gun involvement described in this study tends to lead through a period of pre-gun offending, analyzing how participants began engaging in delinquent behavior arises as a critical dimension of the research. This chapter, then, focuses on the pathway into the illegal activities of the street lifestyle, which typically preceded gun acquisition and use among these participants. It highlights the environmental features described by participants as salient to their decision-making processes and their emerging identities as young men and juvenile offenders, rather than as students on the path to conventional achievement.

## Violence Exposure and Victimization

The most intimate sphere of a child's environment is his home, and while I did not ask participants directly about child abuse or domestic violence, several young men volunteered accounts of violence in their homes, and described what they believed to be its lasting effects upon them. Both Kevin, an 18-year-old Latino boy with a gun assault charge, and Thomas, a young African American who was over 18 and incarcerated for armed robbery, recalled being beaten by their mothers' boyfriends when they were little boys. As Kevin and I discussed the subject of angry feelings, he said his mother's former boyfriend used to beat both his mother and him. Now incarcerated for using a gun to beat another young man, Kevin listed the kinds of occasions when he would consider it appropriate to use a gun, including "if somebody, like, hurt my family, hit my mother or something like that." Similarly, Thomas said he had had a stepfather who would hit him frequently, and as he put it, "I grew up in an abusive home, and I just kept tellin' myself, one day when I get a gun, all this will stop." I asked whether he meant that he had wished he'd had a gun to defend himself on those occasions, and Thomas replied fervently, "I always did." For both Kevin and Thomas, a gun had meaning as an equalizer that could change them from helpless children in a dangerous, frightening situation into powerful actors who could stop the abuse. The power to protect was one aspect of the masculinity that these participants had felt they lacked as young boys in violent homes. They saw a gun as providing them with the ability to control these violent situations. However, as will be discussed in the next chapter, neither of them acquired a gun until after he had begun selling drugs.

Several young men described being introduced to guns in their homes, the guns' presence often attributed to older family members' involvement in the drug trade. Quinto told me he came from a drug-dealing family, and that guns were always hidden around the house, though not well enough to keep a curious child from finding them: "I was about four or five when I picked one up . . . a .357. That was my first exposure to a gun. And when I was about seven, I had picked up a rifle; it was wrapped around in a towel, a purple towel. I unwrapped it, and started playin' with it . . . When I heard my uncles comin' in, I just wrapped it up and put it back . . . behind the couch—that's where they had it."

The day rival drug dealers arrived and shot at his home, young Quinto was banished to the basement while his older family members returned fire. Eventually his uncles taught him how to hold a gun, and by the time he was eight or nine, Quinto was practicing his aim by using a BB rifle to shoot rats in the kitchen of his home:

> QUINTO: Yeah, we had rats inside the kitchen area, yeah. Rats, they would run through like on the stove, and then they would run across both sides . . . I'd be chillin' with the gun, waiting to shoot one of the rats. I'd see one come. I'd breathe . . . [demonstrates how he would inhale and then hold his breath] I'd go like that. And my hand would be shakin'. So I'd shoot.
> DM: For real?
> QUINTO: Yeah. I hit one of 'em in the head.

Any concerns that his account might have been embroidered or exaggerated were dispelled by my recollections of the rat traps deployed in the parking lot surrounding the office building where I had worked, only a few blocks from where Quinto grew up.

The detail with which Quinto recalled both his early discovery of a rifle in his home and his shooting of a rat in his kitchen suggests that he may have viewed both incidents as significant life events. Other participants, too, had vivid memories of their first encounters with guns as will be described in the next chapter.

## Participants' Victimization and Violence Exposure in Public Spaces

Thomas's childhood wish for a gun did not arise in a vacuum or simply from viewing glorified violence on television, but from lived experience. "You could walk through my door, there'd be bullet holes in there," he told me, describing his apartment building. What's more, when he was around nine years old, someone pointed a gun at him while he was in the building's elevator on his way to school. The elevator incident turned out to be a prank that had gone awry, but Thomas remembered being "in shock" when it happened. His shock quickly turned to fascination once the young man with the gun realized he had frightened the boy: "He seen the way I was lookin' and he said, 'Naw, little man, you're good.' So I'm lookin' at him like I'm upset, and he said, 'You can worry about it when you become a man.' And I said, 'Can I hold it?' He put it in my hand; it was a revolver . . . And then later, that whole day after I went to school, I was just thinkin' about it. Couldn't wait to get my own gun."

The complexity of Thomas's early feelings, combining gun fear and gun attraction in rapid succession, is apparent in this account. Incarcerated at the time of our interview for robbing drug dealers, Thomas recognized early that a gun could give him a measure of power and an accompanying feeling of safety. It is important to bear in mind that while I employ the linear image of a pathway to gun acquisition and use throughout this book, guns and violence often pervaded participants' lives whether they sought guns out or not. This means that these young men's contact with guns must be viewed in a more holistic way; consuming violence can encompass either involuntary consumption, such as violence exposure of various kinds, or more participatory types of consumption. With regard to the process of gun acquisition, what seems to be significant is what else was going on in a participant's life at the time of his various encounters with guns.

For example, Tim described finding two guns on the streets of his city. When he found the first one at around age 12, he was still committed to school and sports, and immediately turned the gun over to a local adult. By the time he came across the second one while in his teens, he had joined a gang and kept the gun for himself. The meaning of a gun for the same person changed from something that inspired fear or merely curiosity to a valued possession, depending on the broader context of the young man's life at the time. As Howard Becker, drawing upon George Herbert Mead, formulated the process, a person who makes meaning of an object or experience is interacting not only with others or the object but also with himself and must indicate to himself what the meaning of the object or experience is.[2] What a gun means to a young man therefore depends on how he is viewing himself and his life world at that particular time. For Tim the committed student-athlete, a gun had no relevance; for Tim the self-described gangbanger, it had obvious utility.

Another participant, Leon, talked about finding a job at around age 14 where he and his friend handed out fliers for an insurance company. As he put it, "I had a job, legal; I was tryin' to do the right thing." While working one day, he and his friend were robbed at gunpoint. When I asked him what that felt like, Leon answered, "Well it feel like, if you don't do what they want you to do, they just shoot you. And I wasn't gonna test they patience, because one thing you don't wanna do is test somebody with a gun's patience, 'cause you never know, you never know if they're really gonna shoot you, or not gonna shoot you . . . I didn't have pockets in my shorts. That's the good thing. They put the gun up to me, and they took it away. I told them, 'I ain't got no pockets!'"

Leon admitted that he had already begun committing robberies by the time he and his friend were robbed but, while the chronology is somewhat unclear, it appears that he had not yet begun doing armed robberies. Since Leon was wearing basketball shorts with no pockets, the robbers quickly turned their attention to his friend and coworker: "So they just went to him, and . . . I seen how it really is to have a gun. He did what he said, and . . . he started shakin' and stuff." Speaking of his own offending, Leon offered, "Yeah, I been doin' robberies since I was like 11 years old. It started off with just strong-arm robbery. But then I started seeing guns and stuff—that's when I realized that you could get it without having to fight. It would be easier, by stickin' 'em up. So that's the next part. That was the next thing."

As Leon said, in time he became an armed robber himself, ultimately wearing a bulletproof vest for protection against retaliation by his victims. At the time of our interview, he was incarcerated for an armed robbery of a liquor store. In listening to participants' accounts, I sometimes had the impression of a sort of feedback loop, wherein they both consumed violence and became consumed by the violence that surrounded them, taking it in until it overtook them and became a part of them. In this sense, their external surroundings became internalized.

Over time, participants typically learned how to be at home in violent surroundings. Sam described an incident that occurred when he was 14, walking from school with his cousin. A car came around the corner, followed by a man on foot chasing the car while firing two handguns. At first Sam couldn't believe this was really happening, especially in view of the reactions of the other bystanders: "And it's like, ain't nobody was runnin'! And it's like, it was NATURAL! Like it's a GAME or somethin' . . . When it first started happening, I was like, 'Think! Run!' I was like, 'Wow!' Then I saw my cousin's like, 'What you runnin' for? It ain't got nothin' to do with us.' 'What? You buggin'!' I mean, they're shootin', and ain't nobody runnin', ain't no babies cryin'. It just NATURAL! When the car got away, he just put 'em back in his pocket and walked away around the corner! Like ain't nuttin' happened!"

Asked about being in a violent neighborhood, Sam responded, "You know, you become used to it." Sam seemed eventually to take his cue from the nonchalant attitude modeled by his cousin and the other bystanders as neighborhood violence became normalized for him. If the violence had nothing to do with him, he learned to ignore it. Sam was incarcerated for an armed robbery of a man at a light rail station.

Murder, too, touched the lives of many participants, taking their family members or their friends. Naheem told of a friend being killed while he was nearby. The soon-to-be-victim's mother was visiting from down south, and Naheem, a guest at the gathering, had momentarily gone down the block with some other friends. They heard what sounded like a firecracker, but suspecting that it was not, ran back up to the house and found that their friend had been shot in the head three times. They waited for the police and provided some information, but according to Naheem, the homicide remained unsolved.

Significantly, Naheem appears to have withheld considerably more information about the possible killer than he provided to the police, believing the killer to have been someone the victim had recently robbed. While Naheem's summary of what he told the police about the deadly shooting was confined to what he observed that day, he told me, "I think he might have robbed somebody like that—that's probably the kid that came back to shoot him. But nobody found out yet though." As will be discussed in Chapter 5, much neighborhood street violence is viewed, by victims and witnesses as well as perpetrators, as retribution for previous offenses, and therefore not appropriate for police or court intervention. This is but one of several reasons participants gave for the practice of withholding information from the police. Naheem said he himself had committed only one robbery, and that was without a gun. He was currently in custody only for selling drugs, although he acknowledged keeping guns on his drug set for protection and once shooting a gun to chase away noisy children on the block who were interfering with business. While sorry to lose his friend, Naheem could not bring himself to provide the police with the information that might have connected the killer with his victim.

Like Naheem, other participants were alert to both the sound of gunfire and its meaning. Kyle said he had lost many family members, friends, and even enemies to gun violence. Hearing gunshots at night, he would think, "Somebody's gettin' shot, who is it now? Which friend am I gonna lose, which relative am I gonna lose? Which enemy am I losing?" He learned to cope with his dangerous surroundings by being careful not to walk beyond the corner store if he was out alone at night. Walking from his mother's house to his grandparents' house was thus something he felt unable to do. Kyle clearly perceived his movements to be circumscribed by the limits of a relatively small zone where he felt he could tolerate the level of risk, and this zone was even smaller at night.

Those who did venture out after dark were watchful for danger but still might not manage to avoid it. One participant drew on an account of his own street victimization to position himself as a knowledgeable actor sacrificing his safety to protect a friend, thus portraying himself as a sort of guardian even while acknowledging that he became a victim. Quinto provided a detailed description of an armed robbery that occurred while he and a younger boy were out walking one night. Quinto's 12-year-old friend had been smoking and wanted to buy some chewing gum before returning home so that his mother would not smell smoke on his breath. Quinto told me he had a bad feeling about two people who seemed to be following them, and as he recalled, "I told him. I knew it; I felt it . . . Like you can feel when there's about to be somethin' happening. You know something's wrong." Although he persuaded his friend to take the evasive action of crossing the street, the duo continued to follow them. At that point, Quinto recommended heading directly to his friend's nearby home, and reported that he argued with his companion when the boy still held to his plan to stop at the store first. He told the boy how foolish it was to risk being robbed rather than face his mother with smoke on his breath. When his friend insisted on continuing to the store, Quinto acquiesced, only "because I didn't want him to go by himself." Sure enough, the robbers approached. Quinto was about to turn and run, but saw that his friend still did not apprehend the situation. Once again, Quinto was loathe to abandon him. They were, as Quinto anticipated, robbed at gunpoint, both forced to lie facedown on the ground. Even then, Quinto attempted to school his companion, who seemed to be trying to peer up at the robbers: "I told him . . . 'Don't look up.' He looks up, and got pistol-whipped in the face." Quinto himself was kicked in the back of the head twice before the robbers left.

Throughout this account, however, Quinto positioned himself as the older, wiser actor who tried unsuccessfully to protect his less street-savvy friend, putting himself at risk to do so. Although he described himself as angry following the robbery, Quinto clearly relished telling the tale, dramatizing it with sound effects of footfalls by drumming on the table. Quinto was in custody for gun possession in connection with his drug-selling business, but described several instances of firing guns in a variety of circumstances—ranging from anger to celebration—as will be discussed later.

Participants thus explained how violence came to be incorporated into their everyday lives. Through exposure, violence became somewhat routinized, a part of their identities and expectations. Like Quinto, young men could construct a particular type of capable masculinity by knowing how to conduct themselves in their surroundings, and try to protect younger, less knowledgeable boys from familiar environmental risks.

### "What You Call Violence, I Call Excitement"

Street violence was also consumed (and produced) by adolescents as entertainment. While Thomas and Sam expressed some apprehension about their early exposure to guns and gun violence, Quinto expressed outright enthusiasm for watching a street fight unfold. He quickly reframed my question about witnessing violence in his neighborhood:

> **DM** [following up on a statement of his]: You felt, like, violence on your own block?
>
> **Quinto:** No. To me, I didn't see, I didn't look at it as violence. Like I don't look at that stuff as violence. I just look at it as excitement. I guess it excites me just to see two people arguing and not knowing whether they're going to start beating each other up. And then the other dude get beat all up, and he go grab his gun, go back around the block, just start shootin'. It's like something, I don't know, it's excitement.

Similarly, another participant, who had been incarcerated since he was 13 for an armed robbery with a knife, talked about being shot at by a rival gang member while he and his friend were sitting on a porch. They were about to beat the other boy up when their intended victim suddenly pulled out a gun and started shooting at them. I tried to get a sense of how Kenneth felt at the time:

> **DM:** Um, so was that scary?
>
> **Kenneth:** Yeah. It's scary but it's, still, it's fun in a way.
>
> **DM:** That's, yeah. So for you, it's sort of like excitement?
>
> **Kenneth:** Yeah. Yeah. It's [very slight pause] exhilarating.

While I was wary of leading Kenneth, I wanted to follow up on his suggestion that being shot at had been fun on that occasion, so I used Quinto's word. Kenneth's choice of the vivid adjective "exhilarating" satisfied me that he was not simply following my lead but rather expanding upon his own description of the experience as "fun."

Other scholars have suggested that many young men who live in poverty are bored, and violence and delinquency can provide excitement that relieves some of this boredom.[3] This seems to be true both for those who are participants in violence and for those who are spectators. What I, as a middle-class researcher, call violence evinces a different sort of meaning for many of these participants, framed as something that is fun and exciting— sometimes for watching, sometimes for participating in, and sometimes for just ignoring, as part of the everyday background of their worlds.

Quinto also described an incident that created problems for him in the neighborhood (scorching some siding on a local house with a cigarette lighter) as arising out of poverty-induced boredom: "I don't know, I was bored . . . There was really nothin' you could do. It just be boring . . . Most of the parents around here . . . they don't got enough money to go on trips, to take they kids somewhere . . . Niggers ain't got no money for no Wildwood and all that other shit."

Quinto, a very fair-skinned Latino boy, conflated race and class when arguing that the inability to take even a day trip to the Jersey shore resulted in his looking for excitement in the wrong places. Moreover, he was acutely aware that the poverty of his city contrasted markedly with conditions in the neighboring suburbs: "I don't come from a rich family . . . We do not live in no Pennsauken or Cherry Hill."

### The Structural Violence of Poverty: The Case of Quinto

Boredom, however, may be one of the less immediate threats to the welfare of these children in poverty. Some participants had little parental supervision, lived in rat-infested homes, and had to worry about what they were going to eat. Quinto's account of his home life provided glimpses of what some less forthcoming participants may also have experienced. He related that his mother lived in another part of town, and his father was usually at his girlfriend's house, leaving Quinto with plenty of opportunity to entertain friends at home. Home, however, was a place where Quinto could practice his aim with a BB gun by shooting a rat in the kitchen, as he told me with some pride.

Consistent with Erving Goffman's impression management theory (1959),[4] Quinto and other participants often seemed uncomfortable or evasive when our discussion threatened to uncover grave material deprivation or parental neglect. Quinto was hesitant about naming the only food that might be on hand:

QUINTO: Sometimes we might run out of food, or whatever; I'm hungry, like, since I don't eat certain stuff, and I WON'T eat it. 'Cause I just don't like it.

DM: Like what?

QUINTO: I would only eat it if I'm starvin'. Like some of the stuff that's there. Let's just say, if you don't got no chicken, no nothin', no none of that meat—we might not even have food or nothin'. We just got RICE. Just rice, that's it, just rice, so . . . I don't wanna eat rice.

Quinto spoke obliquely for a considerable time before finally naming rice as the hated food that he would eat only if he were starving. He was much more reticent about naming this food, which he evidently considered to be the emblem of his family's poverty, than he was about discussing his drug selling or violent offending. He seemed to feel keenly the stigma of being a poor teenager in a poor neighborhood of a poor city. Pierre Bourdieu has spoken of "sites of social relegation," "where the personal suffering of each is augmented by all the suffering that comes from coexisting and living with so many suffering people together—and, perhaps more importantly, of the destiny effect from belonging to a stigmatized group."[5]

Participants did not explicitly discuss the stigma of their positioning. Yet Quinto's evident embarrassment at revealing the scarcity of food in his home, and his generalization that the parents in his area could not take their children on trips, suggests that his "niggers ain't got no money" comment was not a casual one. Rather, his remark suggests that he believed himself to belong to a group and carry a social identity that was relegated to an undesirable state. Quinto was acutely aware of both his absolute and his relative poverty. He also seemed dubious about his ability to present himself credibly for the world of legal employment: "I didn't have the proper attire . . . Like, you got to have the proper attire to go to interviews. I didn't have that proper attire to go to the interviews, so why waste my time goin' in regular clothes when somebody else could go up in there with a dressy shirt and some slacks and some cone shoes, at least that's what I call 'em."

Without a nice shirt, slacks, and fashionable, pointed-toe dress shoes, Quinto could not even envision himself stepping out beyond his neighborhood and being taken seriously in the "legitimate" world. Moreover, something about the tenor of his speech hinted that his lack of confidence, despite his usual bravado, extended beyond simply not having the right clothes. The "destiny effect" Bourdieu described seemed to function like an invisible fence, keeping Quinto confined within his site of social relegation. As uncomfortable as his surroundings were in many respects, they seemed to constitute a comfort zone within which he felt capable of making a successful presentation. He had followed in the familiar path of his uncles and become a drug dealer.

## Welcome to My World: Narrating Capability

As I listened to Quinto relate his experiences of being robbed at gunpoint, shooting a rat in his kitchen, and sometimes having nothing in the house to eat except rice, his accounts struck me as harrowing instances of victimization, neglect, and vulnerability. Nonetheless, his demeanor was quite cheerful as he recounted these things; perhaps he even enjoyed the opportunity to shock a presumably naïve listener with his tales. I realized he had constructed and narrated himself as a capable, resourceful person who knew how to negotiate his life world.

He framed his account as something like an adventure story, wherein he heroically battled each foe. However, he ruefully granted that his agency was sometimes limited to knowing the procedure for surviving armed robbery, as when recounting how he guided his younger companion through the victimization experience with as little harm to them both as possible. His poverty featured in his narrative primarily as an explanation for why he sold drugs and why, out of boredom, he found excitement in risky ways.

He also explicitly, if haltingly, defended his parents, who seemed to have left him largely on his own as a young teenager. At the same time, he seemed defensive about having to do so: "So I needed some money, so whatever . . . They, it's not, if they had money, they'd give it to me; it's not like they stingy with it. And then they just, I mean, sometimes, they don't have the money. They don't got money, whatever."

I inferred from his account that on those occasions when there was little food to be had at his father's house, his efforts to find something to eat at his mother's apartment were not very productive either: "She had some food at her crib, but it wasn't like, I mean, the stuff she had there, it wasn't, she had food, whatever, she, she had it, but it would go—it would be gone."

A voluble young man who happily talked with me for an hour and a half, Quinto only stumbled when discussing his severe material deprivation. His evasion and hesitation when speaking of his difficulty in obtaining food suggested that he was engaging in what others have called *shamework*—an effort to save face when exposing an area that would position him as "lesser" in some way.[6] What Quinto sought to highlight for me was his resourcefulness in meeting his many challenges, not the fact that his parents had failed to provide for him. In short, he attempted to manage my impression of him by accentuating the positive, his agency, while downplaying what he plainly considered to be the negative, his vulnerability. In Chapter 4, Quinto will provide an example of how shamework is performed with a gun.

With his mother and father living separately and his older brother "locked up for a long, long time," Quinto said he began selling drugs because he needed some money, and I believed him. His living situation recalled what Laurie Schaffner described as "empty families."[7] Although Quinto had a roof over his head, he seemed to be missing many of the other material and emotional supports that nonoffending children may take for granted. He was the only participant to explicitly cite food insecurity as a reason for selling drugs, though many participants said they would use the proceeds from their drug sales to buy food. I wondered how many other participants, less forthright than Quinto, likewise worried about what they were going to eat. When telling me how they spent their money from selling drugs, almost all participants listed food or clothing first.

## Man of the House: At the Intersection of Masculinity, Poverty, and Race

The accounts of these young African American and Latino men demonstrate that it was not only when experiencing or performing violence but also when dealing with shortages of money and creating their place in a female-headed household that they sought to construct their identities in terms of masculine competence and capability. They tended to view themselves as providers, protectors, and in control of their situations to the extent possible, even while they labored under severe constraints upon their agency.

The degree of financial hardship among the different participants' families no doubt varied. However, secondary only to all the participants being young men of color, the outstanding common demographic feature among them was that the vast majority, more than 20, lived in female-headed households. Of that majority, 17 lived with their mothers, 3 with aunts, and 1 with his grandmother. Only 3 lived with a mother and father, and 1 lived with his father, although according to the participant, his father spent little time at home.

Much has been written about the multiple ways in which growing up without a father in the house affects boys. Often the focus is on the absence of male guidance or discipline in the household as the boy becomes a young man.[8] The most salient feature of the female-headed household as discussed by the participants in this study, however, was the shortage of money. Many described the experience of living with their struggling mothers as impelling them to seek income. Over and over, participants reported that they believed they should, at the very least, provide for their own needs rather than drain their mothers' limited resources. They seemed intensely aware that their mothers were under a financial strain, and felt that it was incumbent upon them, as young men, to do something about it. They experienced the dependent status of being supported by a struggling woman as incompatible with their emerging masculine identities.

Unlike middle-class adolescents who may be purely reacting against the dependency relation of age when they seek employment, these young men described feeling called upon to relieve their mothers of part of the burden of supporting them, in view of the family's straitened circumstances. Their accounts suggest that one criminogenic aspect of fatherless homes may be that a young man, whether or not his mother is genuinely poverty stricken, may feel the need to be financially self-sufficient. Some participants reported contributing to the support of their households through their criminal activity, whereas others simply provided for their own needs, stating that as a consequence of having an "independent" source of income, they didn't have to take money from their mothers. Ernie said he used the money he obtained from drug dealing and robberies for "anything I wanted. Like clothes, food, whatever. I ain't gotta ask my mother for nothin'." Several participants did have legal employment at various times, but either lost or left those jobs, eventually falling back upon the drug trade, the default employer in the inner city, or other types of delinquent activity such as robbery or automobile theft. In addition to the participant who had distributed fliers for an insurance company, one boy had worked at a university food court, one at a chicken restaurant, and one at a women's clothing store. Several others reported applying for jobs without success, and still others, like Quinto, seemed to consider such efforts futile.

As Prudence Carter (2005) and James Messerschmidt (1993)[9] have discussed, young people who reside in the inner city often have very limited
networks for connecting with legal employment, and the connections they
have may be fragile, leaving these young men with less-than-robust identities as legal workers. Thus after Ernie lost his job at a women's clothing
store, he became demoralized and decided that he would return to selling
drugs: "I was just, like, just screw it. I just did not care about a job no
more . . . I can't get a job . . . I'm, like, I couldn't do nothin'—I just felt like
the best thing I was good at was sellin' drugs."

Xavier, an 18-year-old African American, described a similar experience,
except that he never succeeded in finding a job. Both a drug dealer and a
robber of drug dealers, Xavier moved back and forth between his mother's
and his aunt's homes and said, "I had tried fillin' out job applications; I
didn't get no response. So I guess I just gave up on that." In addition to
buying clothes and other things for himself, he said he would buy things
for his aunt. He acknowledged that both his mother and his aunt could use
help with the bills, "'cause I understand that they were strugglin'."

Likewise Kevin, an 18-year-old Latino, recalled that as soon as he made
his first drug sale and saw how fast the money came, he "stopped askin' my
mom for dollars here and there; I had a bunch of dollars in my pocket." With
five more siblings at home and his father incarcerated, Kevin felt pressure
to bring in some money. He said of his siblings, "They were younger than
me. I'm the oldest. So it was like, old take care of the young." Although still
too young to get a legitimate job, he said he helped his mother by buying
her a car and fixing things around the house. Many young men described
similar scenarios, wherein they would use the proceeds from their dealing
or robberies to provide for themselves or to help support their mothers, to a
greater or lesser degree. At the very least, as David, also an 18-year-old African American, said of his mother in a comment that typified those of other
participants, "She has priorities, too," and he felt that whatever money he
did not have to obtain from his mother would leave more for her own needs
and priorities.

Thomas, who was temporarily living with his girlfriend, explicitly declared
that after he began to make money through his illegal activities, he felt his
masculine identity had been forged: "When I started doin' stuff, like, when
I started bringin' food home and I started bringin' money home—that's

when I felt as if, like, I'm a man."[10] Raewyn Connell (2005) conceptualizes gender, like race, as socially constructed. Young men construct their masculinity from the resources available to them in their environments, and those in poverty do not have the same avenues for the construction of masculine identities as do those who grow up in more affluent surroundings.[11] Messerschmidt (1993) likewise argues that middle-class young men, who have their youth culture and other material needs met by their parents, usually construct their masculinity from resources such as the school context and, sometimes, minor misbehavior, generally of a nonviolent nature. He points out that white working-class boys, if not focused on school, often have access to part-time employment or summer jobs, and when they engage in criminal activity, tend to engage in sporadic property crime and hate crime in order to obtain extra money and forge bonds with their peers, respectively. He argues that, for some lower working-class and poor racial minority boys, neither school nor legal work presents a sufficiently absorbing site for the construction of their masculine identities. Legal work may be unavailable, or if available, menial.[12]

Naheem worked for a time in a chicken restaurant: "I served chicken and stuff like that. Workin' there, you get good money, too. You're always gettin' paid; they didn't know that I was still sellin' drugs. [smiles] Yeah, and I would open the store in the morning. But . . . I had quit that job; I was wastin' time in the morning. That's what I thought."

Naheem seemed to like several aspects of this legal job—getting paid "good money" regularly, the responsibility of opening the store in the morning, and as he put it, "I didn't have to worry about bein' locked up or nuttin'." Yet the money he could have been making by selling drugs, and perhaps, the increased freedom of the street, convinced him that he was wasting his time at this job.

Similarly, Keith found work at a university's food court while he was being supervised on an electronic bracelet, but he later decided to leave that job: "When I got off the bracelet, I stopped workin' there." Keith lived with his mother and two little brothers and had been selling drugs in order not to be financially dependent on his mother. He was incarcerated for gun possession when I met him but told me that when he is released, he hoped to just work and help his mother. In *American Project* (2000), Sudhir Venkatesh argued that "doing the right thing" may force these young men to confront their social position of weakness and impotence. Instead, they find the resources to construct their identities in the street, where they can feel some power and relative autonomy.[13] The ubiquitous opportunities in the illegal drug economy can make the menial legal jobs that are available to these participants seem less appealing.

As participants described their own experiences of these structural constraints, they emphasized their own agency in either ignoring or responding to various aspects of their circumstances. Regarding matters over which they viewed themselves as having no control, such as where they lived, participants generally adopted a stoic attitude. Where they perceived a space in which to maneuver, which often consisted of a way to increase their material resources, these young men seized their opportunities, legal or illegal.

What they emphasized in their accounts were often relational aspects of their experiences; how they interacted with others, took care of others, presented themselves to others, and imagined they were perceived by others. As will be seen, it was practicable in their world for a young man in his teens to display his ability to take care of himself and others by getting a car, clothes, jewelry, and some consumer goods for the family home, but not for him to provide the family or himself with a better home in a more tranquil neighborhood. Neither the helpless child victims described by Alex Kotlowitz (1991) in his book *There Are No Children Here*,[14] nor the successful older gangsters who could move to the suburbs, these young men were capable of marginally improving their lives, in situ, in material ways. Before being incarcerated, they had found that they could act to impact some things in their worlds, if not to change the worlds they lived in.

## Fathers

Participants' relationships with their fathers were generally nonexistent, intermittent, or strained. As discussed in the previous section, this circumstance often propelled the young men into a provider role, to varying degrees, and to assume the de facto role of "man of the house." Xavier, however, was the only participant explicitly to tie his economically motivated offending to his having been repeatedly disappointed by his father. He said, "My father, he wasn't really there. I mean, he'd pop up every once, he wasn't regular." Xavier had been a boxer and said his father would sometimes come to watch him box: "[He] would watch, and leave. And then I wouldn't see him for a couple months. From there, it just taught me the main thing, like, he ain't coming. I wouldn't know the next time he was gonna come." Xavier explained that his father could not be relied upon to support him emotionally or financially, even for "something simple, like shoes." He never knew whether or when his father was going to "pop up" to cheer him on in the ring, or come through with a little money when it was needed: "So if I don't know, then, that's all right, I'm gonna get it myself, and went to get a job. That's when I filled out job applications, didn't get hired," and then eventually began making money in the street. Xavier's description suggests that he would have been happy to be a dependent, supported child for a while longer, but that he began to become financially independent when he felt his needs, even for "something simple, like shoes," were not being met. He offered the aforementioned account in response to my question about what might have kept him from going down the path of delinquency, saying that "things would have been better" with a father who provided both material and nonmaterial support.

Thomas, who said he had been hit a lot by an abusive stepfather, acknowledged that his own theory about a real father making a difference might not be valid, since he couldn't really imagine what it would have been like to have such a father:

> Mmm, I always say this, but I don't know if it's true, if I could ever put myself in the situation. But I say that if my real dad was there for me, then I don't think we would be sitting here having this conversation. So I think if my dad would have been there, or somebody, if any male would have been there for me positively, I wouldn't have been here. I wouldn't have felt the need to look up to somebody who I thought was doing right if I could have looked up to somebody who I know was doing somethin' right.

The imagined "good father," and good father-son relationship, remained powerful ideas that continued to inspire some participants. Naheem was hoping to repair his relationship with his father. Naheem had been on juvenile probation for a robbery when he turned 18 and incurred a new drug arrest. He spent some time in the county jail on the adult charge and then was transferred to a juvenile facility to serve additional time for violating his probation on the robbery charge. Naheem said,

I had a father figure in my life, but we had an argument when I was in the program. After that I didn't really talk to him. But I was getting ready to go home [abscond] from the program and, like, yeah! He came to get me, to tell me to go back, but I ain't listen to him. I felt as though, like, he locked up for five years of my life, so I was like, you wasn't there, so, why should I listen to you now . . . I been thinkin' about it, lately, when I was in the county doin' my time or whatever. He always told me, "You ain't gonna like it when you get to the county" . . . and I went, and I didn't like it . . . I'm gonna go home and tell him, like, "You was right." Leave all that stuff we got in the past. Try to get a little connection, like, back again. [smiles] That's how I was gonna start off, 'cause I, like, there was a CO [corrections officer] in the county jail who I used to talk to sometimes. He, uh, helped me out, like, I used to talk to him, whatever. I had to figure out how to start a conversation with my father—that's how I find it. That's how I'm gonna start over.

As Naheem's account illustrates, the authority of some fathers is undermined not only by their having been absent from their sons' lives but also by their having been incarcerated. In Naheem's case, conversations with a supportive corrections officer in the county jail helped Naheem to see both that his father's perspective could be useful and that candidly acknowledging this to his father could provide an opening for a conciliatory conversation with him. I did not ask participants whether their fathers or father figures were criminals, but more than half a dozen of them volunteered that the significant male adults in their lives either had been incarcerated or were drug dealers.

Kenneth, too, hoped his father might reenter his life in a supportive way. He first mentioned his father when describing his initial gun exposure. Kenneth said he was about seven or eight years old when he was cleaning his father's kitchen and came across a gun behind the breadbox. Kenneth recalled that his father walked in while Kenneth was handling it, took the gun from him, and told him not to touch it again. In the years between that event and the period of Kenneth's incarceration, their relationship had suffered a break, and Kenneth said he hadn't seen his father in four or five years. Further complicating the family picture, Kenneth said he had numerous siblings, most of whom lived with his father. Kenneth would visit them, but only when his father was out because, as he said, "I don't talk to him . . . I just don't like him." Kenneth's story of his troubled and intermittent bond with his father ended with a surprise twist. Kenneth was scheduled to be released in 20 days, just after his sixteenth birthday. Despite their long estrangement, Kenneth had just heard from his father: "So I'm gonna get a job, 'cause my dad, my dad just recently wrote me a nice letter. He just recently wrote me, and he said that he doin' good now, and he own his own construction business. He said that if I'm gonna try to stay out of trouble, I could come work for him, and so I could probably do that."

As with so many participants in this study, Kenneth's father seemed a tantalizing phantom who was sometimes in and sometimes out of Kenneth's life. Participants believed they had been adversely affected as a result of being let down by absent, undependable fathers or fathers who were poor role models. Leon, whose father was a drug dealer, replied when I asked what could have made a difference in his life, "Maybe if I was brought up around better people. If I didn't see any of this stuff happening . . . it's like, all I know was to do it." Leon's father, after being asked to leave the house by Leon's mother, had given Leon a gun and a box of bullets so that Leon could protect the rest of the family. Leon was about 14 years old at the time.

Some participants were already fathers themselves. I did not routinely ask whether participants had children but the topic occasionally arose in the course of our interviews, usually in the context of hopes and plans for the future. At least five participants were fathers, and two more were expectant fathers. Kevin, who had both a daughter and a son, expressed a typical sentiment: "I don't want them to do what I did, to follow in my footsteps; I don't want them to grow up like me. I hope they be nerdy or something." Since Kevin himself had begun selling drugs to contribute to the support of his household during his father's period of incarceration, he was no doubt aware that his hope to raise nerdy children might depend on his staying out of trouble in the future. Nevertheless, he was currently incarcerated for beating another man over the head with a gun because the man was selling fake drugs in front of Kevin's house, which was Kevin's own drug-selling territory. Kevin had also been shot some time earlier in retaliation for another assault he had committed. He clearly hoped that his children would escape the delinquency, criminality, and violence that had already ensnared both him and his father. In Kevin's mind, the best way for his children to do so was to embrace the opposite of the street lifestyle, which Kevin dubbed the "nerdy" lifestyle.

Having or not having a father, as well as being a father, affected participants' relationships among dependence and independence, responsibility, developing masculine identities, money, and even violence, as Leon's receipt of a gun from his departing father illustrates.

## Dangerous Adaptations

Researchers have consistently found that exposure to violence has negative consequences for youth.[15] Learning to ignore "extraneous" violence around them, or even to enjoy it, appeared to be one way in which these young men internalized a sense of control over their environments. Early researchers of children's violence exposure expressed concerns that such accommodations to their dangerous life worlds might lead to problem behaviors as boys entered adolescence. For example, John Richters and Pedro Martinez (1993) found that, as boys exposed to violence grew older, they tended to downplay their fears and engage in boastful behavior despite living in dangerous surroundings.[16] This finding gave rise to a concern on the part of the researchers that the boys might develop maladaptive behaviors as a way of coping with their fears. Yet the failure to develop such coping mechanisms hardly suggests a better prognosis.

For the boy who cannot get away from his violent, materially deprived neighborhood as he transitions from boyhood to adolescence, adopting an identity as a capable young man who has found a way to come to terms with his environment, downplaying his fears if need be, does not seem maladaptive in itself. As Richters and Martinez intimated, however, the accommodations that accompany this adaptive masculine identity may be problematic. Moreover, young men who felt themselves thrust into the role of man of the house could engage in economically motivated street crime with ultimately disastrous results for themselves.[17]

## Negotiating the Lure of the Good Life:
## Popular Culture and Consumption

Living in a consumer-driven world where popular culture continually presented the image of the successful man as having money and lots of "stuff," participants sought not only to remedy their lack of the minimal material items necessary to sustain life but also to obtain the kind of consumer goods that would sustain a successful presentation in the eyes of those around them, and in their own eyes.

In Quinto's case, the combination of money, excitement, and family tradition drew him both to the drug trade and to the gun violence of the street. Additionally, popular culture offered reflected images of the same type of excitement, arising from similar activities, and provided a mythic gloss to the street life. During our interviews, Quinto and other participants sought to bridge the cultural divide between our worlds by referencing films or music that were meaningful for them. As Quinto explained, with regard to the context for his gun carrying, "There's always a beef, like, if you watch hood movies, you would understand. Like *New Jack City.* If you watch certain movies like them, you would understand how it is in the hood more. Like, I can tell you, but you're not gettin' a visual picture of the story."

Another participant asked whether I listened to rap music, saying that was what his world was like. Although many participants earnestly tried to translate their perceptions and experiences into terms that I would understand, one observed that "somebody who not actually doin' it, I don't think they can ever figure it out . . . It's hard to figure out somethin' that you're not doin' . . . You're not actually doin' it, so you would never know—positively, 100 percent, you'll never know." These and other participants held the view, shared by many educational theorists, that concrete experience was essential to gaining an understanding of any subject. They believed that simply telling me about their lives would not suffice to provide me with a full "picture of the story."

While correctly pointing out that I could never have a "100 percent" understanding of his life world, Tim provided a nuanced description of his drift from good student and enthusiastic football team member to full-time gangbanger and drug dealer, noting that for a time he tried to straddle both worlds: "It's hard to do both things. To try and stay positive and do negative things. See, you can't play both sides of the fence. See, I was tryin' to play football, but then I decided to get some money. So I started doin' what I wanna do, sell some drugs, you know what I'm sayin'? And I still had my mother to provide for me, but at that stage, there were just things that I saw that I wanted that my mother couldn't provide for me . . . So that was the reason behind me sellin' drugs."

He expanded on the reasons he provided for his own needs and wants, rather than relying on his mother: "I think I just felt a little proud issue in myself. I always was like this—I don't like for a person to feel like I NEED them. Do you know what I'm saying? Even though that's my mother, she have her own needs, too. I don't ever want her to feel that I NEED her. Plus, she worked but she couldn't give me what I wanted."

Tim cited what he called pride and the desire to be independent, as well as consideration for his mother's needs and her modest income, as reasons he began selling drugs. His developing view of himself as a person who should be self-sufficient, and his material wants that exceeded his mother's limited means, seemed to mutually reinforce each other in drawing him into the street. Tim wanted money not only to go shopping for the sweatshirts, pants, and sneakers he spoke of but also to take his girlfriend out to dinner and clubs, and to buy cars. For example, he said he wanted a Mercedes automobile and did not want to wait for it, saying, "See, I was in the fast lane, and I, it was, 'Listen, I want this and I wanna get it now.'" Tim said his mother's slower-paced approach to expensive purchases, where she might say, "Oh, baby, we can wait, and like I can put a down payment," was not for him.

Participants' desire for expensive consumer goods, especially cars, as well as for more everyday needs, was important to their presentation of self and their enjoyment of life. As a young African American male living with his mother in a dangerous area of his city, Tim's making a show of affluence could have profound meaning for his identity processes, serving to offset, to some extent, the obvious structural disadvantages of his position. As Allison Pugh (2009) argued in *Longing and Belonging*, young people's wants may be constructed as needs when they seem necessary to keep up one's dignity with peers, or even to "reshape the powerful social asymmetries that order our experience."[18] One participant, who lived with both his mother and father, said he would "help out as needed" with the bills at home, as well as buy himself clothes, cars, and jewelry with the proceeds from his drug sales. He would pay an adult to go to a legitimate car rental company and obtain a car for him to use. For Vernon, the "fast money" on the street was the attraction. Another young man, who preferred not to specify how he obtained money but said he didn't use a gun to do so, clearly distinguished between "wants" and "needs" when I asked whether he had felt a pressing need for money. "Um, [pause] not a pressing need, you know, but everybody has wants, so, that's about it." He said the things he wanted, but did not feel comfortable asking his mother and grandfather for, included clothes, shoes, and if he had the money, a car. As David put it, "It got to the point where I'm sayin', like, well, I'm getting this old, and I shouldn't be askin' my mother for money to live my life with. I mean, she has priorities to take care of, too. I know she can't always give me what I want. If she can, she will. So it got to the point where I said I gotta get myself some income."

Xavier listed some of the things that made his street lifestyle fun: "It brought a lot of females, a lot of attention, a lot of, like, cars. It brought me a lot: clothes, keep my fashion in step, cell phone . . . Yes, I liked it. I had a car, I stayed up to date with fashion . . . and I had money and everything." Xavier said he also was helping his aunt, with whom he lived, to "pay some of the bills."

In addition to helping with household bills and buying themselves things they needed, such as food and clothing, participants reported buying things that they seemed to consider luxuries, such as jewelry and cars. The line between wants and needs, however, was not at all clear, and several young men seemed to acknowledge this by characterizing themselves as "greedy," as Luke did:

> **DM:** Okay. Um, and what was your mom's financial situation?
> **LUKE:** [quietly] It, there was no problem.
> **DM:** [quietly] Okay.
> **LUKE:** Um, she works at a hospital, so.
> **DM:** Okay. So would you say, would she be in a position to buy you your clothes?
> **LUKE:** [quietly] Yeah.
> **DM:** Okay.
> **LUKE:** I just was plain greedy.

Once again, the subject of family finances seemed to be very sensitive for the participant, who redirected the discussion toward what he claimed to be his own shortcomings and away from his mother's level of ability to provide for him.

Xavier, too, claimed greed as the reason for both selling drugs and robbing drug dealers, despite the fact that he was also helping pay the household bills. As he put it, "I mean, like robbery both and sellin' drugs, it just meant more money. Basically I was greedy. Money. Just bring in more money." Xavier was enjoying a free-spending lifestyle and having fun, as well as buying what he needed and helping support the family.

Finally, Naheem said he saw his friends who were selling drugs with two new pairs of sneakers each week, and wanted what they had. He said he himself had new sneakers, but started selling drugs because he wanted the fast money to buy more "of the stuff that I want. I didn't really need it, 'cause I had it, I just wanted more." Yet he also said he would give money to his mother because she was struggling. In these participants' accounts, it is sometimes difficult to tell where provisioning leaves off and consumption begins.

The young offenders who called themselves *greedy* seemed to be saying, at least in retrospect, that they had failed to limit their consuming to what was really needed, instead insisting upon obtaining for themselves those things that their mothers could not provide.[19] In addition to feeling ashamed of what they could not afford, these participants seemed to feel ashamed of wanting more than their families could give them. The exact location of the line between wants and needs may have been viewed differently by the youth and the parent, with the parent defining "needs" in terms of what she could afford.

Consistent with this interpretation, a social worker at one of the facilities I visited shared her view of the source of participants' use of *greedy*. She opined that some of their mothers may have called their sons greedy in an effort to limit their desires to what the mothers could buy them. (In the same conversation, the social worker also alluded to the opposite dynamic, recalling mothers who had given birth when they were 15 or 16, viewed their teenage sons as the man of the house, and virtually thrust their sons into the streets to make money.) The boys who used the word *greedy* when speaking with me may also have been engaging in another sort of shamework, preferring to call themselves greedy rather than acknowledge that their mothers were unable to provide for them. Several participants described their mothers' objections when they saw their son wearing clothes that she had not bought. They recalled their mothers saying, "Take that off!" or "Don't be coming into this house with two-hundred dollar pants!" The numerous meanings of money and consumer goods created a complex dynamic in terms of material possessions and identity. Among the young offenders' reasons for wanting jewelry, cars, or two new pairs of sneakers per week may well have been that money, autonomy, success and manhood were all connected for them. Helping out at home by purchasing their own things was likewise part of this autonomous masculine identity. The extent to which they were caught up in a consumerist ethos, or consumed by consumption, was difficult to tell.[20] In the worlds experienced by these young men, where money meant autonomy, autonomy meant masculinity, and money, therefore, defined masculinity, the ability to spend or provide was much of what being a man was about. Participants' mothers no doubt exhibited a range of parenting styles, and while the study design did not permit me to determine whether some mothers in fact encouraged their sons' illegal income-generating activities, participants did discuss different ways in which this income was or was not addressed.

### Talking, or Not, about a Juvenile Son's Illegal Economic Contributions

The ways in which parents, usually mothers, and sons negotiated the issue of the son's illegal income was complex, and varied both among the participants and also over time for individual participants. Some maintained that their mothers did not know that they had illegal sources of income; others described a *sub rosa,* or unspoken, understanding about these monies; and one participant said he and his mother talked about it openly. The latter participant said he and his mother had more or less come to an understanding to disagree, since she could not stop him from making money in the streets. Several participants said, "Mom's from the hood so she understands." Those who said their families did not know about their offending were careful not to be conspicuous about their spending, as in Leon's case. Leon, who both sold drugs and committed armed robberies, said that after his father left the family, he decided to obtain money illegally, primarily for his own upkeep:

> LEON: I didn't wanna put too much strain on my mom, so I had to do what I had to do.
> DM: You felt that you were kind of costing her money, in a way?
> LEON: Yeah, also I feel as if I go get it by myself, that's less I need to get from her . . . I gave her more money back. I always see how she be like talkin' about not havin' that much money for herself, so I just let her have her money and I did what I did for my money.
> DM: Did you bring money to her also?
> LEON: Well, I, she wouldn't like me makin' money like that. So if I tell her, she would wonder why, how I got money like that, so, so I would, sometime here and there, I would buy somethin' from the store, for the house.
> DM: Like food and stuff?

**Leon:** Yeah, I'd buy food.
**DM:** So basically, so she would not have approved of what you were doing?
**Leon:** Oh, no!

While Leon says his mother would talk about not having much money for herself, he maintains that she would not have approved of his illegal activities, and so he mainly used his money for his own needs, only infrequently buying food for the house in order to keep his delinquent activity somewhat "under the radar." This "don't ask, don't tell" method of dealing with the subject was alluded to by other participants. In Leon's case, he related that his father had been a "big-time drug dealer" who moved out because Leon's mother didn't like what he was doing. It is difficult to imagine that Leon's mother could have been unaware of his delinquency, but by tacitly agreeing not to discuss it, they could maintain the fiction that she did not know. Vernon, who was one of only three participants who lived with both his mother and father, said that, in addition to spending money on himself, he would "help out as needed" with the household bills. Vernon was incarcerated for conspiracy to distribute crack cocaine and gun possession, although he said it was his codefendant who had the gun. When I asked Vernon whether he thought his parents knew the source of the money he was contributing, he answered in the affirmative:

**DM:** And um, do you think your parents had an idea where the money might be comin' from?
**Vernon:** Yeah.
**DM:** They knew you were sellin' drugs, I guess?
**Vernon:** Not for a fact, they just assumed it.
**DM:** Right. So it was not spoken of, really, but they appreciated the help, I guess.
**Vernon:** Yeah.

Lara Riley (2005), as well as Cheryl Meyer and Michelle Oberman (2001), has discussed the family dynamic of group denial in the context of "concealed" pregnancies that ended in infanticide.[21] They pointed out that the expedient of parents "seeing but not seeing," and "knowing but not knowing," might be used to avoid the topic of a child's unwanted pregnancy, which was too disruptive to acknowledge or discuss. What the authors referred to as family collusion, in not acknowledging what everyone knew, led to tragic consequences for the pregnant mothers and their unborn children. In the case of the young male offenders in the current study, the issue of needed but illicit income seems likewise to have been a source of discomfort, sometimes for both mother and son. In the following excerpt from Naheem's interview, both his uneasiness in discussing the matter with me and the sensitivity of the issue in his relationship with his mother can be inferred:

**DM:** Okay. So once you got this money, what did you spend it on?

**NAHEEM:** Clothes, gave some, some to my mother, some weed [smiles].

**DM:** You think your mother knew where it was comin' from?

**NAHEEM:** Yeah. See, my mother, she grew up, she grew up in the hood, so she know how, she knew what I was doin', and she couldn't really say nuttin' to us 'cause—I always listen to my mother, but at the same time, like—she [inaudible], like, she can't do nothin'. We, she got three boys. There's three of us. So she really can't do nothin' about a problem that we be doin', and sometimes she strugglin' on her own, so.

**DM:** So she had money problems.

**NAHEEM:** Yeah.

**DM:** So she wouldn't mind taking some from you.

**NAHEEM:** At the same time she was, she was [inaudible] take it from me. I know she feel like she wouldn't want it.

**DM:** She wouldn't be wanting it.

**NAHEEM:** Yeah. She might not like what I'm doin', but she can't, she can't stop me.

**DM:** Right, she can't stop you, and also, you think she needed money so she would also take it.

**NAHEEM:** [pause, and seems a little reluctant to concede this] Yeah.

Although it was Naheem who first introduced the point that he would give some of his drug money to his mother, when I followed up on it he suggested that he and his brothers were doing something against his mother's will. Yet he acknowledged that because she was "strugglin' on her own," she would accept money from him, even though "she feel like she wouldn't want it," and didn't like what he was doing. He narrated himself both as the good son and as doing something his mother didn't like, and he described his mother as both disapproving of his activities and accepting the proceeds. There seems to be a certain ambiguity, or even queasiness, in Naheem's discourse about the provider role that he and his brothers patently played in the family. He, and other participants, seemed at the same time to be proud of providing, and ashamed that there was a need for them to do so.

In Naheem's account, perhaps one can discern as well his mother's shame that her boys were placed in this position. Once again I sensed that it was much more difficult for participants to discuss their family finances than their violent offending. They seemed to be trying to save the family honor by minimizing the extent to which the adult family members were aware of the son's illegal income. Certainly Naheem's sense of shame in disclosing his mother's needs and her understanding of where the money came from is evident.

Another participant, Tim, outlined a gradual evolution in his relationship with his working mother, from his unsuccessful concealment of his income to her acceptance of the fact that she could not do anything about his activities:

> **Tim:** I shouldn't have to keep askin' my mother for money. Even though she would ask me, "Oh, you want some?" "Nah, I'm good."
>
> **DM:** Now, I take it at some point she became aware that you had more than what she was providing for you.
>
> **Tim:** Mmm.
>
> **DM:** Did she know specifically what was going on, or what?
>
> **Tim:** Well, it started, like I used to bring like sweatshirts home, like I'd go out shopping and I'd say to my mother, like, she like used to question, like, "Where you get that from?" . . . "Oh, I bought it." "Oh, you bought it." Or I used to lie, "Oh, my friend bought this." Or "My girlfriend bought this." [inaudible] Know what I'm saying? So I lied. But basically, she catch on, said, "Don't come in the house with two hundred dollar pants and sneakers." . . . Know what I mean? Twenty-five, twenty-five hundred dollar watch . . . you know, ain't no average friend just buy you all this stuff. Plus, she's from the hood, too. She knows what goes on.
>
> **DM:** So you think that, eventually, she figured it out, but it was just something that wasn't discussed?
>
> **Tim:** No! We discussed it [inaudible]. She talked to me about it. But it's really nothin' nobody can do . . . All they can do is talk to you and try to persuade you into doin' what they want you to do . . . Takin' a positive outlook. She can't just shackle me down and keep me in the house for the rest of my life.
>
> **DM:** So she would give you advice, but you would disregard her advice.
>
> **Tim:** Basically.

As in Leon's case, the distress of Tim's mother's was likely exacerbated by the fact that his stepfather, according to Tim, had been a high-level drug dealer who had been shot and killed when Tim was 13. One can only imagine his mother's feelings as she watched her son take a similar path, powerless to do anything beyond insisting upon a limit to his displays of ostentation.

Not surprisingly, participants and their families negotiated this delicate morally and financially mediated territory, which implicated dimensions of dependence and independence, responsibility and irresponsibility, and vulnerability and agency in a variety of ways. Since almost all the participants still lived with their families, they remained dependent on adults for their housing needs, but there were diverse degrees of interdependence with regard to other requirements, going in both directions. In this sense, concepts of adultification, the parentified child, and mutuality are all involved. Both Tobias Hecht (1998) and Mary Lorena Kenny (2007) explored similar themes in the context of poor Brazilian children who brought income into their households. Kenny discussed a young girl who began to have "more of a say in things" and to undermine her mother's authority as a consequence of bringing money into the household.[22] Hecht discussed children who nurtured their families, gaining favor with their mothers through the income they contributed.[23] For the young men in the current study, some erosion, inversion, or subversion of parental authority may have accompanied their increased financial power. As they became the "man of the house," the balance of power may have been shifting, often with their mother's consent or acquiescence, as in Hecht's and Kenny's studies.

The relationships of these provider-children with their parents, usually their mothers, were characterized by a form of economic interdependence in some ways similar to that found among families in the global South.[24] Unlike middle-class American adolescents who work part time in legal jobs, participants' income was more than symbolic of their evolving independence. Whereas middle-class teenagers are traditionally viewed as working while in high school in order to build their character, constructively fill their free time, learn the value of a hard-earned dollar, and have some pocket money, participants were often an integral part of the family economy, whether contributing to the support of the household at large or simply relieving their parents of much of the burden of supporting them. Like Kenny's income-producing children, participants at times seemed to approach being "hidden heads of households." What participants called the "fast money" of the streets, however, often convinced them that the low-paying legal jobs available to them were a waste of their time, as Naheem said when explaining why he quit his job at the chicken restaurant. In this sense, participants, at least prior to their arrests, were learning a very different lesson from the one middle-class American working teenagers are assumed to learn.

### Emotional and Social Attractions of Gangs and the Street

Clearly, what these young men described as wants, needs, and helping out with household expenses all factored into the financial lure of the streets. Beyond the money, however, was a social draw that blended fun and excitement with companionship or, as one participant said, "the love." When I asked Luke what had attracted him to his gang, the Bloods, he answered, "The love, the money, the drugs, the love." He felt that this group, the Bloods, was the best place for him to find the atmosphere of loyalty that he was looking for.

Keith, another former student-athlete who had been proud to play varsity football as a high school freshman, described the process of drifting from being a full-time student, to cutting half of the school day, to not going to school at all during his sophomore year: "Once I start hanging back with the old friends, and seein' how much fun I could have, and like, I felt welcome, like, I felt that was where I should have been, instead of doing everything else, and I told you like . . . I was just having a lot of fun, so that's what I stuck with." The fun that Keith described included going to parties, spending time with girls, and smoking marijuana. He also sold drugs and belonged to a gang, and the companionship of this group that made him feel welcome and feel that this was where he belonged seemed to provide a strong nonmaterial inducement for him to stay with the gang and in the street.

Tim, also a member of the Bloods, stressed the importance of having loyal friends when explaining the difference between a friend and an associate: "A friend is somebody who's loyal to you, somebody who cares about you, somebody who's by you whether you are right or wrong." Tim made the same distinction between friends and associates that Nikki Jones discovered while studying African American inner-city girls in *Between Good and Ghetto* (2010)—a friend was expected to stand by you in a crisis.[25]

Participants found loyalty, friendship, fun, and feelings of welcome and love, as well as money and drugs, in their street associations or gangs, as

Luke explained. It has also been pointed out that unpleasant conditions in their homes, whether material, emotional, or physical, could make hanging out in the streets seem a more attractive alternative. While we did not discuss bad home lives except when participants offered accounts as historical background, the desire to escape painful experiences of home may also be significant here. In the introduction to *Fugitive Cultures: Race, Violence, and Youth,* Henry Giroux (1996) described a pertinent experience in his own youth, after the departure of his mother and his sister left him feeling "homeless in [his] own home." Giroux felt that his experience was similar to that of many working-class youth in that "home was neither a source of comfort nor a respite from the outside world." As a result, the neighborhood became his home, and his friends, his sanctuary.[26] For a variety of reasons, many of the participants in this study seemed to find feelings of home and sanctuary in their street associations.

## The Lure of the Streets

A combination of forces seemed to both push and pull these young men to the streets. Elijah Anderson (1999) wrote of children being "sucked up by the streets,"[27] and these incarcerated participants likewise seemed to view the streets as having a Venus flytrap quality that drew them in, held onto them, and could devour them. One young man, Nate, had moved to a nice neighborhood when he was ten, but continued to return to the projects in the worst part of his city to get in trouble. Nate said his deceased father had been a drug dealer, and his mother had had an alcohol problem and a nervous breakdown, resulting in her abandoning Nate and his younger brother when Nate was ten years old. He went to live with his aunt in a nice, quiet area of the same city. His aunt had two older sons, both "good boys," as Nate said, and a good job that enabled her to give Nate plenty of money. As Nate put it, "It was perfect!" Yet he persistently went back to the projects, where he began to smoke and sell marijuana, rob, sell heroin and crack, steal cars, and join the Bloods. The only explanation Nate could offer was that he had grown up in that section of town, had always seen drugs and guns, and was accustomed to it. Later he added, "Trouble was fun to me! It still is fun to me!" Moreover, Nate was not the only participant who sought out the "trouble" of the streets even though he was not living nearby. David said he appreciated the quiet atmosphere of his home town but went into the city where his relatives lived to hang out and make money illegally.

This "stickiness" of the streets continued to be a concern for participants as they contemplated their release back to their home communities. More than one participant expressed the worry that it would be difficult to stay away from the same friends and activities he had known. Mark said he believed he would need to live in a different area because he doubted his ability to find a different circle of friends with whom he would feel the same bond in his home town. "You gotta feel trust," he said, and he believed his old group, those with whom he got into trouble, was the only group with whom he could experience this type of mutual loyalty. As Mark put it, "If I called them, they'd be right there," and likewise, "they could count on me."

### A Place to Construct an Acceptable Social Identity

Many explanations for the attraction of gangs and similar groups have been put forward, but it is easy to understand why the participants in this study might want to construct a social hierarchy in which they are not on the bottom. In describing the attraction of what Jack Katz (1988) called "street elites," or groups of adolescents who engaged in fighting or other forms of illegal behavior, Katz argued that these young men were trying to construct an elevated platform for themselves, an identity in which they could take pride by placing others who were in social proximity to themselves "beneath them in social disrepute."[28] By virtue of their race and class, participants had reason to feel socially marginalized. Yet in addition to joining with peers to construct an "elite" social identity, some of the young men explicitly designated others as more marginalized than themselves, or beneath them, as Katz wrote. Participants who sold drugs, for example, often made a point of distancing themselves from their customers, calling them "crackheads, dope-fiends, crack-fiends," or just plain "fiends," and emphasizing that they themselves never used the crack or heroin that they sold. One participant described "fiends" as "dirty," "low," and wearing "old clothes." Another, clearly proud of his fit appearance, laughed when I asked whether he had used crack, retorting, "Do you know anybody who uses crack and looks like me?" In contrast to those they disparaged as "fiends," participants, by presenting a clean and fashionable appearance, could show that they had sufficient money to be viewed as credible consumers, or persons with dignity. The street was where the money to keep up appearances could be obtained readily. The salient fact that all the participants in this study are young men of color in the United States no doubt influences the way in which we, and possibly they, frame their identity work.

## Financial Capability, Street Vulnerability

The passage from childhood through adolescence to adulthood is often viewed along several dimensions; as movement from vulnerability to agency, dependence to independence, and irresponsibility to responsibility. These participants, in what many would view as vulnerable circumstances, constructed themselves as capable agents, although their agency was not always viewed as positive, by themselves or others. While still dependent on their families for housing, the young men often sought to be financially independent for many of their other needs. In doing so, they tried to act as responsible young adults in some ways, making money to take part of the financial burden off their mothers' shoulders. Despite forays into the world of legal employment, several of these teenagers found that the menial jobs available to them either did not last or did not hold their interest when compared to the myriad attractions of the streets.

This chapter has sought to lay a foundation for the argument that will be developed further in the chapters that follow. The participants described many environmental stressors and few protective factors, or supports, that most law-abiding children would take for granted. Primary among these stressors were violence exposure and poverty, usually within the context of a female-headed household where participants felt that they should cease to be provided for and should instead assume, to a greater or lesser extent, the role of a provider as they entered adolescence. These many challenges, along with the paucity of supports, shaped the young men's movement to the street, where they constructed a type of capable masculinity that permitted them to survive, and even thrive, in many ways. These adaptations, however, presented them with new challenges.

A surplus of violence and a shortage of money were among the most salient features of participants' life worlds prior to the time of their gun acquisition. While participants viewed most of their responses to their circumstances as adaptive—at least at the time—I will suggest in the next chapter that some responses, such as selling drugs and joining gangs, propelled them into even riskier contexts that made gun acquisition seem sensible. The courses of action that participants forged in order to reduce their material vulnerability and to meet other, nonmaterial, needs were soon perceived by these actors as increasing their physical vulnerability.

## Chapter Summary

This chapter explored some of the challenges faced by participants in their environments, and explained how they coped by learning to normalize violence and to address many of their needs in the streets. Participants, all young men of color, described growing up in violent, poverty-stricken neighborhoods, and sometimes in violent families. Most participants lived in female-headed households, usually with their mothers. As they entered their teens, many participants began to experience their financial dependence on their mothers as both burdensome to their mothers and inconsistent with their emerging masculine identities. They responded to this perception by entering into the illicit street economy, sometimes after disappointments in, or in conjunction with, employment in the legal job market. While some participants used their income primarily to provide for their own wants and needs, many contributed to the support of the household in varying degrees. The illegal source of this support was sometimes openly acknowledged and sometimes not, seemingly constituting a source of ambivalent feelings on the part of both parent and child. Participants also found nonmaterial rewards in their street associations and activities, including excitement, fun, and the companionship of peers. As these young men consumed multiple types of violence, they constructed masculinities and ways of dealing with their worlds that laid the foundation for their gun acquisition and use. Although the streets held many attractions for these young men, the most frequently cited was money, because "you gotta be that man and provide." Guns came to be viewed as vital tools in these and other identity-making projects, as will be seen in the next chapter.

# CHAPTER 3

# Consuming Guns
## Pathways to Gun Acquisition

When I started gettin' into the streets, I started gangbangin', I started hustlin' and things, and then, eventually, it just come. It's not like a specific time when you decide it come, you just come across it, like one of your homies give you one, your friends give you one, you find one, or you get you a connect that sell guns and you just buy it.

—Tim

As Tim described the acquisition of his first gun, it simply came into his hands at the appropriate time in his life—when he started getting "into the streets," being active in a gang, and selling drugs. At the same time, he suggested that his own, almost organic, experience of getting a gun could be generalized to that of other similarly situated young men.

### Pathways to Gun Acquisition

In this chapter I examine the process of gun acquisition, which encompasses the factors that prompted participants to acquire guns and how they did so. I also examine their changing experiences of normality and embodiment in their environments, first without and then with guns, as well as participants' enjoyment of guns and how they say guns made them feel. In exploring their experiences of normality, I discovered that a geographical space that may have felt "normal" or "regular" to participants before they began to engage in illegal activities was experienced as requiring the protection of a gun once they became involved in the "street" lifestyle. Moreover, gun possession was often experienced in an embodied way, sometimes changing the way participants felt about both their environments and themselves. I identified one primary pathway to gun acquisition and another less typical one, but both can be characterized as coping strategies for these young men.

Just as Tim says in the previous quotation, the guns often came to the boys as often as the boys sought out the guns. While some participants acquired guns as gifts from peers or older men in the neighborhood who introduced them to guns, others simply found guns or purchased them from a variety of intermediaries, often referred to as "connects." Yet in view of the high levels of violence exposure and victimization described by participants in the previous chapter, as well as their early fascination with guns, it seems appropriate to consider at the outset why they were not motivated to acquire a gun sooner.

## Juvenile Offenders Frame Their Worlds

When I asked participants to describe their neighborhoods, they typically responded as follows:

> **KEITH:** Well, it's basically the same thing that you see anywhere—the drugs, gangs, when you go outside, crackheads everywhere. That's what I'm used to, so I don't really know anything different, so that's regular to me.
> **ERNIE:** Rough . . . Like that's the only place I really grew up at, so I don't know other cities, but to me it's like, a bunch of gangs, and everybody sells drugs, and almost everybody got a gun . . . I always feel safe because I grew up there, know everybody, so I really didn't care about being harmed or anything.
> **TIM:** Yeah, I would feel safe—no, I wouldn't say "safe," actually, because there's stuff that go on around there, but to a person like me, that was normal to me. People shootin' at each other, people gettin' shot almost every day, people sellin' drugs—that was normal. So I was so immune to it. I, that's what I adapted to, so that wasn't really like, um, fearful of this because this is what I see every day.

Participants said they felt their surroundings to be "regular" or "normal" because that was what they were used to and what they had always known. Most participants considered a neighborhood with high levels of gang activity, drug activity, and gun violence to be the taken-for-granted background of their daily existence.

They were clear on another point, however, which was that if you are "in the streets," you need a gun. It was not the high ambient level of violence that seemed to occupy their minds but rather the increased level of vulnerability that attended their "street lifestyle." They also asserted that it was entirely possible to live in their neighborhoods and not need a gun. As several put it, "It all depends on their lifestyle."

What participants sometimes referred to as their "lifestyle," they most frequently simply called "being in the streets." Although they resided in houses or apartments, these young men, much like the Brazilian street children described by Tobias Hecht (1998) in *At Home in the Street,* "speak of the street not as a mere physical place but as a way of life."[1] To these young gun offenders, the idea of being "in the streets" encompasses all the things that they acknowledge to increase their exposure to violence, such as staying out late at night, socializing in venues where violence is likely to erupt, dealing drugs, joining gangs, and committing both property and violent crimes. While other adolescents from their area might confine themselves largely to spaces such as school, home, church, and organized activities, these young men feel themselves both pushed and pulled to take another path. They exemplify Herbert Blumer's concept (1969) that a person—albeit within certain constraints—selects and thereby creates his own environment, because although they and many others may live together in the same violent neighborhood, these young men have selected, while not freely, the most dangerous activities, hours, locations, and associates to constitute their personal ecology. As Blumer puts it, "People may be living side by side yet be living in different worlds,"[2] and participants told me that a young man from their same neighborhood who did not share their "lifestyle," and who therefore was not what they considered to be "in the streets," would not have the same need for a gun as they felt they did.

For example, Kilal, when asked why he wanted a gun when he was 15, explained, "I was in the streets real thick, so, for protection." He explained why other young men could live in his neighborhood and not need a gun: "It all depends on how they live their lifestyle." As for those in the neighborhood who did have guns, he said, "I don't give them any thoughts. It's just their lifestyle; they're obviously in the streets, and they need protection from something." When I asked Keith, who had described his neighborhood as full of drugs, gangs, and crackheads, whether he had felt the need for a gun before he joined a gang, he explained why he had not: "Not really, 'cause I wasn't really into the streets; I wasn't really out like that. If I was doin' anything it was like sports or school or out with friends." Following up again later, I asked whether he believed he would have wanted a gun if he hadn't been involved with that group. Keith responded, "I think I still would have been involved with sports. And my time would have been occupied, so I wouldn't have been in the streets, and I wouldn't need the gun."

One may argue that the "normal" environment of their dangerous neighborhoods did not signal danger to these young men in a particularly notable way, but the enhanced danger presented by the circumstances of their lives "in the street" was sufficiently noticeable that they felt the need to arm themselves against it.[3] Taking the statements of the participants at face value, one must conclude that they did not fear their neighborhood itself but rather the particular threats they had encountered and expected to encounter. The young men described these threats as arising from their lifestyle in the streets, and generally said that these particular encounters had prompted their initial gun acquisition.

In Keith's particular situation, he and members of his gang had attended a party where a fight broke out between his group and another group, and someone from the other group pulled out a gun. Keith then decided that he should get a gun so that he would not feel as vulnerable if he were in a similar situation again. He anticipated that this might happen because his gang and the other one shared the same neighborhood, and he believed his gang would be likely to "bump heads with them any time." Before his gang involvement, he did not perceive such a threat, and viewed the usual background of gun and drug activity in his neighborhood as "regular." Similarly Ernie, who joined the Crips at age nine, said he was in seventh grade when his gang was having repeated fights with members of a rival gang. He reported that it was this intergang violence that prompted his gun acquisition. He said he had always felt safe in his drug- and gun-infested neighborhood because he grew up there and knew everybody. It was the fights that accompanied his involvement with the gang that made him believe he should get a gun. This amplified level of risk arising from involvement with the streets stood out, or signaled, something different from the background of neighborhood drug and gun violence to which participants were accustomed. Although they rarely used the word *fear*, these young men now felt a want or need for a gun.

## Peer Influence or Sphere Influence

Participants never referenced the idea of peer pressure, whether to get into the streets in the first place or to acquire a gun once there, except to deny its relevance. Quinto, for example, spontaneously introduced the term into our discussion only to reject it after I suggested that his friends were telling him he had to join in a particular fight. He responded, "Naw, they didn't peer pressure, they just asked me, like, 'Yo, bro, these guys over there, they talk shit about you,' and all this." Perhaps in this case it would be more accurate to say that his friends played the role of instigators.[4]

Rather, participants said they were drawn to the street by its attractions such as seeing others with money when they themselves had none, and were motivated to get a gun in response to specific threats that they faced. In this sense, their accounts support Sheldon and Eleanor Glueck's conclusions that, instead of peer pressure, a desire to be around other young men who are participating in the same type of activities that interest them (the "birds of a feather" theory) is the dynamic that brings these actors together.[5] After conducting a new analysis of the Glueck data as well as considering more recent research, Robert Sampson and John Laub reached the same conclusion—that self-selection and the group nature of delinquency were more important than the influence of peers.[6] More recently, although Jan Kornelis Dijkstra and colleagues' quantitative study of friendship networks (2010) found that juvenile males' weapon carrying tended to more closely resemble that of their friends over time, they also found that the perceived attractiveness of weapon-carriers as friends, as well as respondents' prior aggression, played a role.[7] Based on the current participants' reports that the situational threats in their new circumstances were the impetus for their gun acquisition, I would suggest that the chronological sequence identified by Dijkstra and colleagues signifies not peer pressure, but if you will, sphere pressure. The many risk factors pervading the worlds in which these young men lived, from home stressors to neighborhood features to macro-level influences, created spaces that drew these young people together and prompted both their social and economic courses of action.[8] I would argue that participants' circumstances and surroundings created the pressure for these young men to join together in ways that advanced their shared interests. The context provided by the interview data supports the interpretation that the milieu in which the participants were moving provided the impetus to have a gun, although new, armed, associates may also have come along with participants' immersion in the street lifestyle.[9]

From the perspective of the young men themselves, however, perhaps another factor in these participants' inclination to downplay the role of peer pressure or influence is the importance they attach to identifying themselves as strong and independent young men. Nonetheless, once the participants have selected their peer group, the interview data suggest that these chosen peers are likely to influence the young men's actions, as will be discussed more fully in Chapter 5. For now, two brief examples should suffice. Thomas said he fired toward another group when he was showing off his gun and his friends then pointed out that their enemies were right across the street. He reflected that he sometimes was not certain whether he was trying to prove to himself or to his friends that he was a "gangster," but he did feel that he was trying to prove something. Another participant, Ernie, reported shooting at rival gang members who were taunting him and two of his fellow gang members. He did not make explicit the influence of his peers, although it seems reasonable to infer that their presence was a salient factor. As Deanna Wilkinson and Jeffrey Fagan (2001) argue, the social and situational nature of adolescent violence highlights the influence of third parties—for good or for ill—as these others can act either as "instigators" or as "peacemakers."[10] The current study, focused on violence rather than its avoidance, provides examples of the former, and participants often supplied considerable detail when explaining the interactional aspects of violent events.

The institutional ethos, wherein residents are encouraged to take responsibility for their own conduct, may also contribute to participants' tendency to focus on their own reasons for their actions. Just after completing my field research, I had the opportunity to observe a focus group of detained youth discussing what types of programs and interventions they would consider helpful in preventing future offending. When one member of our group of visitors asked what challenges the young men faced out on the street that could lead to further involvement in the juvenile justice system, a white resident who had attained the highest level of privileges in the detention center offered that "people you hang with" could pose a challenge. At this, an African American young man who had been previously incarcerated and was about to return to the Juvenile Justice Commission to serve a term for a new offense, made an animated rebuttal. He derided the other resident's response as something that "they," indicating our group of adult visitors, should say, not the young men. Rather, he maintained that "you choose the people you hang with, and if you want to get into trouble, you will hang with the people who are going to get into trouble." He argued further that everyone on the street knows who those people are because it is obvious to all. His forceful rejoinder that one chooses one's associates with eyes wide open, however, does not refute the argument that those associates, once chosen, are likely to influence one's actions. My suggestion is that young men growing up in environments such as those typical of the study participants are influenced to engage in illegal activities by multiple stressors in multiple spheres, and that peer pressure is hardly the most important one.

## Initial Gun Acquisition

Participants had little difficulty recalling and recounting their reasons for acquiring their first guns. Ernie was a member of the Crips, and said he was tired of seeing his friends beaten up by the older and bigger members of a rival gang. He decided to employ a gun when members of his gang made a preemptive strike against the other group. He felt this action would deter the rivals from further predations against the members of his gang. At that point, Ernie purchased a gun for his fellow gang member to wield during the attack. As Ernie put it, "You know, you can't beat everybody, so I bought a gun." The details of how Ernie acquired this first gun are explored later in this chapter.

Several of those who sold drugs felt that this made them more vulnerable to violent attacks, and this sense of vulnerability prompted them to obtain a gun. Kevin, who sold drugs for his older brothers, said he felt that it was important to have a gun if you were selling drugs "because people envy you. Like, people just see that you got somethin' they don't got, and they want it, so they try to take it from you . . . Money, drugs, chains, jewelry, anything. They'll try to take it." Kevin obtained his first gun from one of his brothers. Kilal, too, said that once he "started being in the streets more" at around age 15, he began at first to handle friends' guns, and eventually to acquire his own. While he never officially joined a gang, his friends were members of the Crips, and a friend gave him his first gun because "we had a lot of 'beef' goin' around." At the same time, Kilal was selling heroin and crack cocaine, and this eventually made him feel even more vulnerable: "I started makin' a lot of money, and for some reason I started bringin' a lot of attention to myself because of the money that I was makin', and a lot of people started . . . they started hatin' on me, people try to—like, people try to rob me a couple of times, and from then on I knew I needed to keep my gun on me."

Kevin and Kilal knew the dangers of visibly having more money or material possessions than many of their inner-city neighbors. For Kilal, who was a partisan of the Crips, these dangers were compounded by his involvement in ongoing gang hostilities. For both young men, being drawn in by the street's magnetic attractions also meant being exposed to elevated levels of risk, prompting their acquisition of guns in order to survive life in the streets and avoid being ripped off.

For them, it was neither the general nature of their neighborhoods nor the threat of random or anonymous violence that drove their wish for a gun, even though they may have conceptualized their motivations as falling under the rubric of "protection." Rather, within their dangerous environments, particular interpersonal threats arising from their activities and associations appeared salient. Other, more nonspecific, dangers seemed to constitute simply the backdrop of neighborhood life.

This pathway seemed to constitute the typical avenue to gun possession. Participants who grew up in urban neighborhoods felt relatively comfortable in their surroundings, not perceiving the need for a gun until they entered the realm of gang fighting or drug dealing.

### Tony's Story: Not "Normal" for Him

There was only one participant, Tony, who said he had obtained a gun simply for protection from random street violence. Tony, however, had lived in the suburbs until he was ten years old. It was "much better" there but, as he put it, "My mom just moved!" Tony's experience highlights the powerlessness of children to choose their own environments. Like the other participants, he described his current neighborhood as a place where murders, robberies, assaults, thefts, burglaries, and a lot of drug activity, including outdoor sales, took place. Once he stepped outside of his home, even in the daytime, he did not feel safe because "anything could happen," like a "drive-by shooting" or "somebody just walk up and try to rob you." While the other participants said this was the only environment they had ever known, and that they were "used to it," Tony seemed unable to get used to it. Even though his own illicit activities were limited to smoking marijuana, drinking alcohol, and being outside after curfew—what teenagers might do with some regularity in many urban and suburban communities in the United States—he felt he needed a gun in order to feel safe in this neighborhood. Tony defined being "in the streets" differently than other participants. For him, "in the streets" just meant literally being out at night, visiting friends, hanging out, smoking cigarettes and marijuana, and drinking. Once he had saved up the 50 dollars he needed to purchase his first and only gun, he felt that he could "walk anywhere, don't really have to watch my back and worry about somethin' happenin' . . . I felt safe."

For Tony, the background level of violence pervading his city neighborhood never came to feel like just the "field" upon which the daily events of his life played out as it did for those who had been born and raised there. He was never able to take his new surroundings for granted, and they continued to elicit signals of fear.[11] Tony had had no charges prior to being arrested with a loaded nine millimeter handgun at two o'clock in the morning. Also, atypically, he had never even tested the gun because he did not know a safe place to do so. In this group of participants, Tony was the sole representative of a second pathway to gun acquisition, one where the motivation to obtain a gun arose from a severe sense of discomfort in his neighborhood, unconnected with street fighting or drug dealing, and simply due to not being "immune" to his environment, as Tim had put it.

Tony said he had no gun exposure in his home, but was first exposed to guns when he was 15 or 16 and saw the movie *Scarface* (the 1983 remake with Al Pacino). Tony had particularly noted one element of the plot relating to the protagonist's gun use—that "when they tried to come in his house, he used it to protect himself," and Tony thought this type of defense might work for him, too. He then began asking around in order to learn something about guns; how they were used, and where one could be obtained.

Tony was not in a gang, did not sell drugs, and did not have "beefs" with others to worry about. Though he had never been shot at or robbed, he said he imagined being the victim in such a scenario "all the time." People he knew—older, younger, and his own age—had been shot or robbed at gunpoint. It was because of these crimes that he felt he needed a gun for protection. He explicitly stated that he would feel "unsafe" if he were walking around at night without a gun: "You could just be walkin' somewhere, and just get caught in a crossfire or somethin'." For this reason, he "didn't walk around a lot; just go to a friend house, and then we used to walk to a store, and stuff like that."

Yet with a gun in his possession, Tony's experience of his life world was completely different. He now had a new ability to travel through the space around him and, in a sense, a new relationship to the world. To use Nancy Lesko's example, just as when one learns to swim, a lake changes from being perceived as something that could not be crossed to something to which one has access;[12] once Tony had a gun, he ceased to feel unsafe in the streets, and felt that he could walk anywhere without worrying. In this way, an instrument or tool can enable someone to "incorporate" or embody a new ability that derives from the object, such as when a person learns to drive a car.[13] From the point of view of the person who is experiencing it, the phenomenon of walking around the street has changed; Tony's embodied experience can be understood as having been transformed from one of perceived vulnerability to one of perceived agency. He now "can walk anywhere." Unfortunately for him, once he is released and returns to the same neighborhood, he must face the decision whether to resume carrying a gun. He acknowledged that this prospect has caused him considerable concern.

Although Tony reported that the majority of people he knew sold drugs, he explained that he didn't do it because "I felt as though I'd be a follower if I just did it because they was doin' it." He declined to sell drugs despite being invited on several occasions to do so, providing an illustration of a young man who did not respond to peer pressure, or at least peer invitations. In response to my questions, he acknowledged that he didn't need the money and that his mother was able to provide what he needed. Not perceiving an acute need to obtain income, he did not find the sale of drugs to be irresistibly attractive.

While this study cannot address the question of how many other relatively law-abiding young men like Tony may be carrying guns for "pure protection" from random street crime, Daniel W. Webster, Patricia Gainer, and Howard Champion (1993) found that, in a population of junior high school students in Washington, DC, gun carrying tended to be associated with highly aggressive delinquency, rather than purely defensive behavior. Among their sample, all the boys who had been arrested on drug-related charges also carried a gun, and many of them had social networks that were involved in violence. The authors explicitly stated, "Our findings are not consistent with the image of otherwise law-abiding youths carrying guns solely for protection."[14] Tony, however, did not obtain a gun until he was 17 years old, and as Webster, Gainer, and Champion acknowledged, "less deviant and aggressive adolescents may later decide to start carrying guns purely for reasons of self-defense." Not only may such low-profile gun carriers often manage to avoid arrest, but a young man without a history of delinquency arrested for simple gun possession could frequently receive a noncustodial disposition and would therefore not appear in a sample drawn from incarcerated youth. In short, this study cannot shed light on how many more young men like Tony may acquire guns through a pathway that does not include other types of offending.

The obverse of Tony's move at age ten from a safe suburban neighborhood to one perceived as dangerous is the previously discussed situation of Nate, who moved from the rough projects to a "nice, calm neighborhood" at the same age. Just as Tony never felt at home on the crime-ridden streets of his new city, Nate could not accustom himself to the quiet atmosphere of his aunt's area, returning again and again to the projects.

### Getting Guns: Old Heads, New Heads, and "Connects"

Aside from Tony, every participant who acknowledged gun involvement related his gun acquisition to his lifestyle, as they often called it, of being in the streets. As Tim, the young man whose quotation leads off this chapter, said, "When you're in the streets, all around you is . . . guns, drugs, money, and it's just a combination of everything." As he outlined the process, a gun just comes into a young man's life when the circumstances seem to call for it. Another young drug dealer likewise described his first gun being put into his hand when he was 15 by an older person who saw that he was getting into the street. Owen recalled, "My man had gave it to me," saying to him, "Cuz, you're gonna need this.'"

Yet another gun carrier, who eventually became both a drug dealer and a robber of drug dealers, reported receiving his first gun when he was 14. After someone pointed a gun at him late one night, Xavier told a friend who was already selling drugs about it, and the friend gave him a loaded .357 magnum revolver to keep. According to this participant, the gun donor's motivation was probably a combination of friendship and recruiting.

Many participants received guns from "old heads" in the neighborhood. Victor, incarcerated for armed robbery, had been primarily stealing cars and getting into lots of fights when he decided it was time for him to get a gun. He talked to one of the older guys, or "old heads," as he said, who had previously shown him guns, and this man gave him a new .32 revolver, still in the box, as a gift. Another participant, Sam, asked his cousin to get him his first gun when the cousin traveled to Virginia; his cousin likewise did not charge him for the gun, but provided it as a gift. Finally, Kevin, whose father was incarcerated, acquired his first gun as he joined his older brothers' drug-dealing business. When I asked whether it was routine to issue drug-selling novices a gun as part of their work equipment, Kevin said that it was not if "they too young . . . dumb, trigger-happy. But somebody older, like my age or somethin', like 15, probably if they got, like, common sense, then if that person ask for it, they'll give them something small, nothing big."

Only one participant reported receiving his first gun from his father. Leon was not the first participant to preface his response to one of my questions with, "Well, actually, you won't believe it when I tell you," but when I encouraged him to continue, he responded that he received the gun when "my father gave it to me." Leon, incarcerated for armed robbery, said his father was a drug dealer who departed the family home at the request of Leon's mother, who did not approve of his activities. Shortly after his father had moved out, Leon was living with his mother, his older sister, his younger brother, and his stepfather. According to Leon, his father gave him the gun, a .380 revolver, "just so I could protect myself and my little brother and my family." His father had previously given Leon BB guns, to which his mother had also objected, but this time he gave him a revolver in a bag, along with a box of bullets. While a number of participants seemed to have been adultified by their mothers in the absence of another man in the house, this was the sole example of a young man having a gun thrust into his hands by a parent and being charged to protect his family. Leon carried that gun until he was arrested with it. After it was confiscated, he acquired a series of other guns until he was arrested for his current offense, an armed robbery of a liquor store. The receipt of guns from family members, here a cousin, brothers, and a father, is consistent with findings by Philip J. Cook, Jens Ludwig, Sudhir Venkatesh, and Anthony A. Braga (2007). During the course of their study of underground gun markets, Venkatesh interviewed non-gang-affiliated youths aged 18 through 21 who had owned guns, and found that 40 percent of them reported obtaining their gun from a relative.[15]

Some participants did not feel the need to purchase their own guns, as guns were readily available for use within their social networks. Nate, who said he had committed numerous armed robberies with guns (although he was currently incarcerated for an armed robbery with a knife), said that from the time he was 14, guns were always available to him: "Like, everybody in my project had guns . . . Like if you needed a gun, if you needed it, like to go rob somebody, you was like, give me the gun, and they'd give it to you." Nate said the first gun he handled was a two-shot derringer that was useful for armed robberies despite its small size: "I never really bought it. It's just like any time we needed it I knew where to get it from . . . It would be stashed, or it would be with somebody, and then, after like the small guns, started using big guns." When I asked whether he had ever purchased a gun, Nate replied, "No, I don't need to. Why buy it when I can go down the block and go use it?"

Similarly, Xavier, who was incarcerated for an armed robbery with a sawed-off shotgun, said this shotgun was always stored under a porch on the corner where he sold drugs. He said he had no idea where it originally came from and did not consider the gun to be his; rather, "different people in the area use it, I mean, everybody had access to it"—more specifically, "the people I was with." Other participants who sold drugs described shared guns or "stashed guns" that would always be somewhere on their drug corner. Like Xavier, another participant spoke of such guns as though they belonged to the landscape, as always having been there:

**DM:** Where'd you get the shotguns?
**NAHEEM:** I don't know . . . It was like passed down to us. It was the block's.

Naheem said he, his brothers, and the other dealers who sold drugs on this block never even used these shotguns that seemed to have come with the drug territory, preferring to use handguns for whatever they may have needed to do. Naheem's account once again highlights the pervasive presence of guns in participants' environments—guns that were "just there," like the two that Tim found. Whether these "lost and found" guns were forgotten, inoperable, abandoned because they had been used in a crime and could have connected their owners to a shooting if found in their possession, or something else, they serve to punctuate their settings as places where gun violence is an everyday occurrence. Many of these guns were communal objects, or "group guns," shared by anyone connected to that drug corner. Although the particular weapon's origin may have been shrouded in the mists of time, its location was known to all connected with the enterprise, and it was available for their use. Part of the meaning of such guns was that only those "in the know," or "the people I was with," as Xavier put it, had access to them; such access therefore signified one's identity as part of the group. In the same way, obtaining a gun from a fellow gang member or member of the drug set also signified "insider status."

Other participants who sought to purchase guns, as Tim suggested in the opening quotation, would get themselves a "connect"—that is, an intermediary, be it a broker, a supplier, or simply a mutual acquaintance, and just buy their first guns. For example, Quinto described the purchase of his first gun, a slightly used .32 revolver: "I had bought me a .32 . . . From one of, somebody, somebody, I don't know. One of my buls, he had it. He had a .32; he had a connect . . . Yeah, it came in the box and everything . . . it had five shells, plus he gave me a box [of ammunition] . . . I bought it for two fifty. He used it before, but it wasn't damaged, like . . . He shot it a couple of times . . . It was basically new."

Ernie, too, a drug dealer and gang member, said, "I called one of the boys on my set, and he knows somebody that sells guns, like a connect. So he linked me to him. I met up with him, and I bought it." The many participants who purchased guns did not describe any difficulty in doing so. As Naheem put it, "If you was to try to get a gun, like buy one or somethin', see, in the hood, you, like, go places, you know everybody that sell a gun, like that. Everybody's sellin' 'em. Ask a person that you probably know. And just go ask them." Even Tony, who was not involved in street crime beyond smoking marijuana, simply asked around among the older men in the neighborhood, and readily found a gun to purchase for 50 dollars, although he never tested it for operability.

These men who provided guns were often just a few years older than the participants, sometimes involved in the participants' illegal activities, and sometimes not. In the absence of fathers in the lives of most of the young men, the "old heads" were regarded as older, wiser street veterans, even though they sometimes had a financial interest in the boys' activities as well. These men either had guns or knew where to get them, and regularly helped equip the adolescents for their lives in the street. Elijah Anderson (1999) had discussed the role of "old heads" in the inner city, explaining that the original "old heads" were traditional, positive African American male role models who lived in the neighborhood and could guide boys informally, particularly if a boy's father was not in the home.[16] However, as most middle-class and many stable working-class men left these neighborhoods during the latter part of the twentieth century, the traditional "old head" faded from these young men's life worlds.[17] The men who were left behind in these communities may be viewed as "new heads," who instead model the street life and its rewards.[18]

These men, still referred to as "old heads" by participants, served as ready sources for participants' first guns when the young men decided they were ready for them. The new "old heads" continued to mentor and guide the young men of the neighborhood, but instead of guiding them in traditional avenues, they helped them to navigate their lives in the street. They provided participants with what these young men considered to be valuable social capital in their communities, connecting them with what was viewed as a critical material asset in their shared milieu. All in all, participants reported that guns were easy to find and available in a wide range of prices.

As these young men entered the street fraternity, whether as gang members, workers in a drug set, or just starting to "hang," a gun often became a part of their lives. While some purchased them through well-known networks, others relied on "group guns" that were always available, or used guns that had been given to them. The constellation of guns, drugs, money, and violence was part of the fabric of their life worlds. As the old heads served to socialize younger adolescents into the life of the street, both the older men and the neophytes likely gained a sort of legitimacy from their social bond. Participants absorbed, and were absorbed into, a type of masculinity that seemed adaptive to their environments. In these worlds, money, guns, autonomy, and masculinity were often intertwined.

## Unpacking "Protection"

As discussed earlier, the boys in this study had typically traveled in dangerous circles prior to the time of their incarceration. They had originally acquired their guns for protection, and several described particular situations that either had occurred or they anticipated might occur when a gun could be used defensively.

Kilal, for example, was a drug dealer and adjudicated armed robber who, after being robbed at gunpoint, decided that he needed to carry his gun routinely. When another person, believed by Kilal to be an associate of the one who had recently robbed him, attempted to do the same, Kilal said he defended himself with his gun, although he declined to provide specific details. When I asked how he managed to avoid being robbed on this occasion, Kilal replied, "I had my gun on me, and stuff just got hectic . . . Nobody didn't get hurt, but . . . yeah." Whether he fired his gun, used it as a blunt weapon, or merely brandished it was unclear, but Kilal's point was that his gun had served to protect him from being robbed a second time.

Ernie, also a drug dealer and adjudicated armed robber, denied that a person would need a gun just because he sold drugs, but traced the usual connection for me: "It's just when people got money, the gun is what comes with the money, 'cause it really might prevent anything else." Thus in Ernie's mind, too, drugs, money, violence, and guns tended to cluster together, with a gun being viewed as "prevention" in the drug seller's environment.

He also viewed his high school as a place where he needed protection, saying, "That school was bad. I mean, I had a gun before I got locked up [referring to an earlier period of incarceration prior to beginning high school], but goin' up to that school MAKES you just want to bring the gun in school. Like, everything—everybody's fightin'." Ernie himself was among those fighting, often becoming, as he put it, "Dragged into" fights on behalf of one of his boys. He spoke of going to school one Monday: "I caught two of them, I beat both of them up, so while I'm beating them up, I look up, and there's more of 'em coming with machetes and stuff." Ernie complained that "nobody did nothin'" about the boys with the machetes in school. He said he "didn't wanna tell, so I didn't go to school for like a week after that. Then when I finally came back to school, I brought my gun with me. 'Cause, like, it was just gettin' deep now." Conflicts from the street were brought into the school by Ernie and, apparently, by others, with the result that Ernie felt the same need for a gun in school as he did on the street. Also as on the street, Ernie viewed himself as the protector of his boys and would not hesitate to take on their enemies within the school walls. He did not consider it appropriate to seek help from the school staff, and therefore believed he was left with the alternatives of absenting himself from school or arming himself when he attended. Thus for Ernie, the idea of protection included carrying a gun to school in order to defend himself against retaliation by those he had attacked there.

Another participant, Victor, had likewise been adjudicated for armed robbery, although it was his codefendant who had wielded Victor's gun. Prior to the armed robbery, he had served as a lookout during other robberies, and fought a lot. He reported that he had obtained his first and only gun by approaching an "old head" in his neighborhood because he felt he might need to protect himself from violence resulting from interpersonal conflicts. Victor said that while it used to be that you would fight someone and then the fight was over, things were no longer that way: "Growin' up now, there ain't no more fightin' . . . they're gonna wanna kill you . . . it's never over . . . Today, you can get in a fight in a moment, and they might decide to pull it out and shoot you." He concluded, "Nowadays, if you fight somebody, you might as well just shoot 'em," although he said he had never done so. Victor denied that he expected someone actually to come after him, "but if it ever happened, if it ever did, it just got to the point where I knew I needed to protect myself." Although Victor was not in a gang and did not sell drugs, between his fighting, stealing cars, and serving as a lookout for other robberies before participating in the one for which he was adjudicated, he was probably justified in sensing that his street activities had reached the point where he faced an increased risk of violent victimization. His belief that he now needed a gun to protect himself from these risks was understandable.

Someone like Victor might once have felt that he could successfully defend himself against foreseeable threats by fighting, but the widespread use of firearms had made him feel that he, too, now needed a gun. As several researchers using a public health model have suggested, contagion theory can be applied to the spread of guns in a community. Describing the same dynamic that Victor outlined, Alfred Blumstein, Frederick Rivara, and Richard Rosenfield (2000) argued that "the presence of an armed group in the population increases the likelihood that others will become armed to protect themselves."[19] Kjerstin Andersson's (2008) study of Swedish youths in detention, however, serves as a reminder that the American inner-city context, with its broad diffusion of guns taken for granted by both researchers and these participants, is not universal. Andersson's Swedish young men viewed carrying a weapon, by which they meant a knife, as unmanly. Andersson reported one of her participants declaring that "'over his dead body' would he ever walk around armed if he felt threatened. Carrying around a knife would implicate that you are not man enough to face the danger of a threat."[20] Andersson's research suggests that the meaning of manliness among violent youth can vary based on the type of weapons prevalent in their environment. Among her Swedish youth, carrying any weapon at all could be considered unmanly because, in an environment where a knife is the most lethal weapon one is likely to face, being a skilled fighter could see one through most violent encounters. In such a society, strong fists can garner more respect than carrying a weapon. In the American "gunfighter nation" it is normative to associate gun use with men[21] and, in some environments, with masculinity. As Victor suggested, the prevalence of guns in his neighborhood has rendered his skills as a fighter virtually obsolete. Later in this chapter, participants will discuss the place of guns in their own identity processes, sometimes problematizing the connection between guns and masculinity.

Guns also could protect participants from insults, or at least make them feel that they did not need to tolerate insults. Quinto said, "When I don't got a gun, I feel like I have to fall back more, like, anybody can say somethin' to me—'Oh, you bitch-ass nigger'—like that, and I won't do nuttin'." But with a gun, while he said he wouldn't shoot somebody, he would let him know that he had a gun and scare him, or smack him, as he claimed to have done in the past, "because I had that power. Let's put it like this: if I smacked them, if he know I have a gun on me, he's not gonna do nothin'."

Quinto obtained his first gun because of a group of boys who wanted to fight him as a result of something he had done on the street, and he was concerned that they might jump him. He said he didn't want to fight them and had told them so, but he worried that "they was just gonna let me stroll into somethin', and they was gonna end up jumpin' me or whatever." He had been selling drugs since he was 14, but it was not until this conflict occurred, when he was 15, that he felt the need for a gun. Some, but not all, drug-selling participants felt that a gun was necessary to protect themselves from the threats inherent in the drug trade. It is worth noting that Quinto was currently incarcerated for possessing a gun that he had just retrieved from his room because he anticipated trouble from interlopers on his drug territory that day. He later explained that one of the protective benefits of a gun was that its mere presence, made known to one's adversary, could be used to avoid or preempt a fight: "Because he know that once he lift his finger to try to punch me, I'm gonna shoot at him . . . All I gotta do is tuck it right here [indicating his waistband], tuck my sweater right here, under the gun." For him, a gun could be deployed variously to protect his business, his personal safety, and his honor. Moreover, the importance of "respect" on the street is not a matter of mere vanity, but goes to the issue of personal safety, as others may probe for weaknesses, both verbally and physically.[22]

As discussed earlier, the participants in the current study distinguished between their perceived need for a gun once they were "in the streets" and both their own perceptions before they were in the streets and the imputed perceptions of others who were not in the streets. Using a different methodological approach, Joseph Sheley and James Wright (1993) explored the question of motivations for gun possession quantitatively, surveying incarcerated juvenile offenders in four states, including New Jersey. Employing a self-administered questionnaire with primarily forced-choice items, Sheley and Wright demonstrated how broadly their respondents conceptualized the protective function of guns. For example, prominent among the reasons respondents felt it was important to carry a gun during an armed robbery was to protect themselves from possible violent resistance or retaliation by an armed victim.[23] Sheley and Wright's respondents, all serious juvenile offenders, also endorsed the more conventional protective functions of guns offered to them on the questionnaire. While Sheley and Wright concluded that the "perception that one's very survival depends on being armed makes a weapon a necessity at nearly any cost,"[24] I would suggest that it is important to emphasize that this perception is not universal among young men of color in the inner city. Sheley and Wright's self-administered questionnaire elicited a great deal of useful information from the serious juvenile offenders who responded to it. However, it was not designed to illuminate how these young men came to be gun users, or their changing perceptions of the risks they faced before and after they became involved in other types of offending. The participants in the current study, on the other hand, explained their feeling that neither they nor their neighbors needed a gun unless they were into the street "lifestyle." For this reason, placing the focus on the phenomenologically different life worlds that young men in the same neighborhood can experience, I would offer a qualification to Sheley and Wright's conclusion that "gun-related crime . . . will likely decrease only when juveniles are convinced that they do not have to carry guns for protection."[25] I would shift the emphasis to suggest that gun-related crime will likely decrease only when juveniles are convinced that they do not have to, or want to, embrace the street lifestyle with its attendant risks. Whether this is likely to occur under the conditions currently prevailing in the inner cities is the challenge facing policymakers and practitioners, as well as individual families.

## Guns as Consumer Objects and Symbols: "Everybody Likes a Glock"

Participants' feelings about guns ranged from aversion to self-proclaimed infatuation. Thomas praised the special qualities of the Glock .40 handgun: "The Glock .40? It's powerful. Um, it don't got no safety on it. The gun is made out of plastic, so it can be interpreted as a BB gun if you want to." He concluded, as though it were obvious, "But everybody likes a Glock."

In fact, participants often had differing gun preferences. While several maintained that functionality was their only criterion, others expressed distinct aesthetic concerns. When I asked Kevin whether there were particular things that made a gun attractive to him, he answered simply, "that it would take someone off the earth." Xavier, who had a number of different guns, said, "As long as it shot, I wanted it." Ernie said of his first gun, "It was ugly. I didn't care."

One utilitarian preference expressed by several participants was for revolvers because they do not leave potentially incriminating shell casings behind when fired as semiautomatics do. As Ernie explained, "When you shoot a revolver, the shells stay inside the gun." Conversely, Leon, while acknowledging this advantage of revolvers, maintained that he was more persuaded by aesthetic concerns, telling me, "What I don't like about revolvers is, because they look like Western guns. I really don't like the Western-like look." Victor, in turn, expressed an aesthetic preference for revolvers, saying he "likes how they look." He described his first gun, a revolver, as black and chrome, and expanded upon the appeal of guns: "I liked guns. I like how they look. I like the way they sound, and pop when they're shot."

Sam reported asking his cousin to pick up a small gun for him when he went to Virginia, telling his cousin he "wanted somethin' I could wear around my neck." Sam explained to me that such a gun is hung on a shoestring threaded through the gun's sight, so that when the wearer is stopped by the police and told to pull his shirt up, no gun will be visible around his waist. As Sam told me, "To wear your gun on a shoestring around your neck, that's real ghetto." He seemed to suggest that, beyond the practical advantage of avoiding arrest, this manner of wearing a gun was also an expression of insider street culture, marking the wearer as authentically "ghetto." Sam's cousin said he had paid only nine dollars for this small gun, and gave it to Sam as a gift.

Several participants considered themselves to be gun collectors and would purchase more than one gun at a time. Leon reported buying three guns on one occasion from the same seller, and Xavier also recalled having three guns at the same time. Ernie bought an unusual "handgun/rifle" because he had never seen or heard of anything like it.

These young men often displayed the nuanced knowledge of gun connoisseurs. Leon expressed regret that he had been locked up a month after getting a new gun, "so I couldn't really enjoy the gun as I wanted to." He explained that he liked to "go shootin'," saying, "You can go to a park, you can line up cans and stuff, and practice your aim," or "go on top of the railroads and shoot off the railroads." He enthusiastically compared the sounds made by various handguns and shotguns, describing how and where he tested each one. Expanding on the theme of gun enjoyment, Quinto went a step further when recalling a celebratory New Year's Eve session of shooting guns in the air in the company of his stepfather and other friends. He provided distinct sound effects for each of the different caliber guns used in the celebration, from "Bonk, bonk, bonk, bonk!" to "Donk, donk, donk!" and "Bah, bah, bah!" to a fast "Bop, bop, bop, bop, bop." Not surprisingly, Quinto declared that he liked guns, rhapsodizing, "The way that it's noise, like the noise, the spark, when it come out—all of that! I like all of them, the ones with clips, the revolvers, it's just special . . . There's just somethin' about 'em! I'm attracted to it!"

Quinto was not alone in his enthusiasm. Xavier exclaimed, "I'm infatuated with guns!" Sam, incarcerated for robbery, said that it was initially just his love for guns that prompted his desire for one:

**SAM:** I just WANTED a gun.
**DM:** Okay, so, 'cause you, now why would you say that you wanted a gun?
**SAM:** 'Cause I liked toy guns, cap guns—I just always liked to have them. I liked the pow!
**DM:** Did you say power?
**SAM:** Pow!
**DM:** Pow.
**SAM:** Like the kickback, all of that. I just love it.

Later, however, Sam continued to describe things that would make a gun attractive to him, saying, "Just the way it looked; if I could hold it in my hands." When I sought to clarify his response by asking if he was speaking of the gun's appearance, he responded, "The power." For Sam, the tactile attraction of the gun encompassed its association with power. To hold a gun in his hands meant to hold power.

Clearly, the various sensual pleasures of guns, especially their appearance and their sounds, contributed significantly to their appeal for many participants, but the subtext that underlay the materiality of gun possession seemed to be one of power—power to protect and, as will be discussed later, power to obtain money, respect, and a feeling of competence and self-worth. All the same, every participant who acknowledged possessing a gun was able to describe his first gun, no matter how many more had come after it, suggesting that the gun not only was a symbol in its generic form but had importance as an individuated material object as well. Moreover, many of these young men presented themselves as knowledgeable consumers, collectors, and even connoisseurs, of guns.

The least demanding or sentimental gun consumer was Tony, the relatively law-abiding participant who wanted a gun purely for protection as he walked around the streets of his city at night. He said he had no preferences whatsoever concerning the kind of gun he wanted to purchase, and never even test-fired his gun once he had it. For him, finding a gun he liked was not the problem; rather, because he did not have an independent source of income, he needed to save up money from little side jobs and his allowance before he could make his 50-dollar purchase. In truth, it seemed that Tony's gun served mainly as a talisman that made him feel safe simply by carrying it.

Finally, Vernon, although incarcerated for both selling drugs and possessing a gun, expressed his aversion to guns, saying that his codefendant was carrying a gun when they were arrested during a drug sale: "I wouldn't use 'em. I'd rather fight straight. But guns, that's lethal and serious . . . taking lives and all, I ain't into that. I'm more into makin' money."

This explicit aversion to guns was anomalous among the study participants, although several other adjudicated gun offenders said it was a codefendant or someone else who had the gun he was charged with possessing, and one participant suggested that the gun with which he was charged was an abandoned one or was planted by the police. As the sample was composed primarily of gun offenders, it was to be expected that most participants would have positive feelings about guns. Vernon also said he preferred not to carry a gun because "if you get arrested, I'd rather have possession of drugs, and not have possession of a weapon; then I'd have two cases." Nonetheless, because he and his friend were arrested together while "serving" a customer, as Vernon put it, he was viewed as having constructive possession of the gun even though it was not on his person. Having his colleague hold the gun as they worked together, which could still provide Vernon with the presumed protective benefits of the gun, did not insulate him from the gun charge as he had hoped.

### Ernie's Story: An Unreliable Product

Ernie, who had joined the Crips at age nine, became involved in many group-based fights while in junior high. As he put it, "I was always brawlin'." He began selling crack cocaine when he was in seventh grade, but did not feel the need for a gun while he was selling drugs, reasoning that if he were to be robbed he would not have an opportunity to reach for a gun, and the robbers might then take his gun as well. His description of how his perceived need for a gun evolved shows that, in addition to Victor's example of contagion as a motivation for gun acquisition, escalation also could operate to prompt a gun purchase. Ernie recalled that the fights between his "little gang" and another group began with less lethal weapons: "Like, one of my boys had fought with they boys at a park, playing basketball, and one of my boys got jumped 'cause he beat his boy up, and they called everybody else, and they jumped him. So that just started a big situation. So . . . ever since then, it's just been like a big little war." At first the fights were with fists, but then, "maybe bats, bricks . . . no guns." When I asked who escalated the fights from fists to bats and bricks, Ernie laughed and said, "I don't even know. I really don't know."

However, Ernie felt that his group was suffering unfairly because "every time we go to the area, we can never find them, and any time we walk around, they find us, like, they find us one by one." On top of this, Ernie regarded his adversaries as bigger and older, and after his "boys" had been repeatedly picked off one by one and beaten up by the rivals, he felt the best defense would be a good offense, with a gun as an equalizer. As Ernie put it, "You can't beat everybody, so I bought a gun." He seemed to view the planned attack within the rubric of protection, broadly speaking, and said the purchase of the gun was his friend's idea, as the friend knew somebody who had one to sell. Ernie, still in seventh grade, was selling drugs at the time, and therefore had the funds to finance the purchase. The gun seller met Ernie and his friend, and sold Ernie a .38 revolver. When a girl told Ernie's gang that the rivals were having a party, Ernie saw an opportunity "to catch all of them at this one spot." To Ernie's chagrin, "the gun ended up bein' broke," as they learned during the attack: "We went over there, and like, kicked in their windows and stuff . . . and they came out, knives and stuff, and my boy had the gun, he pulled it out, starts like trying to pull it, and wasn't nothin' happenin'. So then we started fightin', beatin' him with the gun, and I'm wonderin' why he started beatin' him instead of shootin' him. And when we ran, or whatever, then he told me what happened . . . The pin was missin'."

Other researchers have noted that gun quality can sometimes be an issue in underground gun markets,[26] but Ernie said he managed to obtain relief as a dissatisfied consumer:

**DM:** Did you go back to the seller or anything?
**ERNIE:** Yeah, I got my money back . . . and I kept his gun, too.
**DM:** Did he say he wanted the gun back?
**ERNIE:** Naw, he knew. He must've knew it was broke; he gave me my money back.

As Ernie related this episode of gang fighting, the line between having a gun for protection and having one for retribution blurred somewhat. Ernie claimed, "We didn't start the problems . . . They jumped one of ours, so we felt as though we gotta get even, we wasn't gonna let it ride like that." Ernie implied that permitting an attack to go unanswered would suggest to their rivals that his gang could be assaulted with impunity. In this way, a lack of "respect" could result in a lack of personal safety. As fists gave way to bats and bricks, and these in turn gave way to knives and guns, the escalating lethality of the weapons used increased the chances that someone would be killed or seriously injured. Ernie's efforts to protect his "boys" and establish his young gang's standing as formidable adversaries were typical of participants who were in gangs or otherwise engaged in street fighting. "The distinction between victim and perpetrator is often vague" from the perspective of juvenile gun offenders, as Sheley and Wright noted after analyzing the results of their surveys.[27]

Nonetheless, it is possible to view juvenile gun possession and use along a continuum ranging from pure protection to purely aggressive use, with the oscillating offensive/defensive dynamic of gang and street violence—or "beef," as participants called it—somewhere in the middle. The participants in the current study readily acknowledged the occasions when their gun use was motivated by factors other than protection, as will appear more clearly in the next chapter. The pattern that emerges from the data, however, is that their initial gun acquisition was driven by a desire for protection, albeit broadly conceived and contextualized within their "street" activities. Sheley and Wright likewise found that protection and the need to arm oneself against enemies were the primary reasons to obtain a gun.[28] It should be reemphasized that Sheley and Wright's respondents, all serious juvenile offenders, similarly defined protection quite broadly.

Ernie himself subsequently acquired other guns, and as will be explored later, expanded his use of them from gang hostilities to other activities motivated by profit and the quest for excitement. His first gun purchase, however, was made in the context of protecting his boys and establishing their reputation.

## Guns and Identity

Two young men, housed in different facilities, spoke of guns as making them feel like Superman. Victor described how he felt when he had a gun in this way: "I could say you feel a little more masculine. Kind of more cocky, better say. I don't know. I don't know. Kind of like Superman, more. In a way . . . you know you got like backup, like an army, like."

Xavier put it this way: "I felt as, I felt more protected. I felt protected. I just thought nothing could happen to me while I had the gun in my possession . . . When you got a gun in your pocket, you feel like you're Superman . . . It's like you're Superman, and the only thing that can stop you is kryptonite, and there ain't none, so there's nothing to stop you."

Xavier said he had ceased to believe that nothing could happen to a person with a gun in his possession, but his earlier sense of invincibility had enabled him to rob drug dealers and feel as if he "couldn't be touched."

Conversely, Leon, another armed robber, said, "When I don't have a gun on me, I felt naked and stuff. I felt I could be harmed; that I could be harmed." He contrasted this feeling with the way he felt when surrounded by his collection of guns: "Just having a different collection of guns just made me, it makes you feel like you got power. Just, I had power within myself. Like, if you want something, nine times out of ten you're gonna get it if you got a gun."

Thomas, too, drew on a discourse of a gun as bringing feelings of power:

THOMAS: With a gun in my hand, nothing was scary.
DM: How would you describe your state of mind at the time?
THOMAS: State of mind at the time, I'd describe it as, um, fearless, fearless. I felt powerful; I felt like nothin' could stop me.
DM: And where do you think the feeling of powerfulness came from?
THOMAS: Definitely my hand, because I had the gun in it.

His last response was quite literal, but at the same time illustrates how the sense of power from the gun becomes embodied in the person who holds it. Thomas's account demonstrates once again the phenomenological notion that the instrument is experientially incorporated into the bulk of the person's own body.[29] Leon, in the previous quotation, similarly referred to having power "within myself" when surrounded by his guns, evidently experiencing his own person as embodying the guns' power. For these young men, guns meant power and a particular kind of masculinity, or Supermasculinity, as Xavier and Victor said. They could feel "fearless," "protected," powerful, and as though they had "an army" backing them up when they had a gun.

Several other participants, however, seemed self-consciously aware that the idea of the gun as incorporated into their bodies, an extension of their bodies, or changing their embodied experience could raise problematic identity issues. Keith, in response to my asking whether he felt any differently about himself when he had a gun, replied, "No, not at all." When I pressed him on whether there was any kind of power dynamic going on, he repeated simply, "No." Keith emphasized that he just felt safer in case he should find himself in another situation similar to the one that had prompted his gun acquisition, when someone from another gang pulled a gun on him at a party. Perhaps significantly, Keith, although a drug dealer, had never been charged with using his gun in any way, instead being charged with possession of the gun following a car stop. His nonuse of his gun and denial that it was tied up with his self-image is consistent with his statement that he only carried it in case he was attacked again.

Yet Ernie, an armed robber, also responded in the negative when asked whether a gun made him feel a certain way: "No. Some people feel like they bigger with a gun, but you could die if you got a gun right in your hand. And so I don't think a gun should change a person . . . I think it was just something that had to be around." To provide a little context for his statement, however, Ernie had told me his cousin had been killed while holding two guns in his hands, so Ernie had good reason for contemplating the vulnerability of a person carrying a gun, or even two.

Finally, Nate, who said he had used guns to commit many armed robberies, rejected the idea that having a gun changed the way he felt about himself or his surroundings:

**NATE:** No. I don't feel different from when I have a gun in my hands or when I don't have a gun in my hands.
**DM:** No? Okay.
**NATE:** I'm a powerful man.

Although he certainly presented a powerful physical appearance, Nate's claim to power rang somewhat hollow with me in view of both his current lack of freedom and his harrowing early life experiences. In his book, *Asylums* (1961), Erving Goffman noted the particular need of the institutionalized person to insist upon, or call attention to, his personal dignity, since most of the usual accoutrements of one's "identity kit" have been stripped away for the duration of his period of confinement.[30] Toward the end of our interview, Nate's denial that he felt different when he had a gun in his hands also seemed somewhat unconvincing in view of his earlier statements. When I asked him what he liked about committing robberies, he said, "I used to like the feeling of having power, like." He said he also liked the money. Nate would sometimes rob people without using a gun, and at other times would use one. But when discussing guns specifically, he had explained, "That's why I had a gun. Just to know the power of a gun, to get what I want when I want it."

I felt that, perhaps, when he insisted, "I'm a powerful man," it was because I had backed him into a corner by asking forthrightly whether having a gun had changed how he felt "about yourself or your surroundings, or anything." Acknowledging that "the gun makes the man" was clearly a concession that Nate was unwilling to make, and I sensed that he pushed back when he saw that this was what I was suggesting. As Nate's bid for me to recognize him as a powerful man with or without a gun fell rather flat, I quickly shifted our discussion to a less threatening topic. Nevertheless, he had been adamant that his sense of himself as a powerful man did not depend on whether he had a gun. As he said this, I also wondered whether the institutional programming he was experiencing included efforts to separate young gun offenders' identities from their guns in the hope of instilling in them a strong sense of self that did not depend on having a weapon. In the same way that Nate insisted upon being recognized as a powerful man during our conversation, Connell (2005), Messerschmidt (1993), and Anderson (1999) argue that it is precisely because of their relatively powerless social positioning that low-income urban young men of color often feel so keenly the need to establish a strong masculine identity that both they and others can (and must) respect.[31] At the same time, such respect often translates to personal safety in daily interpersonal interactions.

For many of these young men, irrespective of how they reconciled the gun's place in their self-image, a gun meant the difference between extreme vulnerability (feeling naked, able to be harmed) and the extreme of feeling protected and powerful—unable to be touched, like Superman in a world where there is no kryptonite. The question of why some participants readily acknowledged the role of the gun in their identity processes while others did not is an intriguing one that merits exploration.

The embodiment that participants describe, however, is consistent with recent actor-network theory, which locates agency as often being distributed across the human and the nonhuman. Together the young man and the gun form a unit, or "cyborg," which is more capable than the young man alone.[32]

### "Why Wouldn't I Have a Gun?"

Participants' accounts of their pathways to gun acquisition illuminated the processes of mutual construction that gave form to their life worlds. As these young men described their gun acquisition and use, they both were shaped by and actively shaped their violent environments. The interactional dynamics of contagion and escalation that helped drive gun acquisition underscore this mutually constructive quality. Shepherded into the world of gun possession by older males as well as their peers, these boys were socialized by their childhood and adolescent experiences to view guns as sensible responses to the threats around them. Moreover, for young men who were socially powerless in many ways, the instant power conferred by gun possession often proved irresistible, particularly for those who had embraced the most perilous social contexts within their dangerous neighborhoods.

Many participants considered their gun possession to be transformative, whether simply as an effective tool or for their identity processes. They experienced having a gun as changing their feelings of vulnerability into feelings of agency. For Tony, who after moving from the suburbs never felt his urban environment to be "normal," having a gun made him feel able to walk around the streets at night, something he could not do without one. For most of the other participants, having a gun was experienced as protective against the risks they had assumed upon entering the street lifestyle. Being known as a drug dealer, for example, often made a young man a target for robbery, creating a powerful nexus among drugs, money, violence, and guns.

Likewise, having a gun could protect a participant from feeling that he had to suffer insults, and thereby change his experience from being one who had to "fall back" to one who could command the type of respect that is valuable on the street. For gang members or others engaged in street fighting, a gun could avert a fight, or be used either defensively or offensively if a fight occurred. Guns were also consumed as objects of "love," "infatuation," and "fascination" and used for fun and excitement in an environment that was otherwise often boring.

As Tim explained in the quotation at the beginning of this chapter, when the time was "right" in the participant's life world, a gun just came to him via any of a number of avenues as the participant got into the streets and began selling drugs, "gangbanging," or both. Acquiring a gun can be seen as another coping strategy clearly viewed by participants as an adaptive response to their circumstances at the time.

The guns possessed by participants, originally acquired for protection, often came to be used in other ways, as will be discussed in the next chapter. Whether as a symbol of power, a useful instrument, or a consumer item to be admired and enjoyed, a gun served many functions for these participants. As Nate summed it up, "Why wouldn't I have a gun? A gun is a key to anything you wanna do. A gun could be a souvenir, or you could use it to get what you want. That's why I had a gun. Just to know the power of a gun, to get what I want when I want it."

## Chapter Summary

This chapter explored gun acquisition, conceptualizing it as a coping strategy for the young man living "the street lifestyle" and exposed to that lifestyle's enhanced level of risk. Participants described the typical pathway to gun acquisition as leading through a period of pre-gun delinquency. They explained that, while law-abiding people in their neighborhoods—including themselves in their predelinquent days—did not need guns, a gun was a necessity for those "living the street lifestyle." This was because their street activities, such as selling drugs or engaging in street fights with a gang, exposed them to an increased likelihood of violent encounters. Most participants conceptualized their initial gun acquisition in terms of protection, albeit broadly defined. They reported no difficulty in acquiring guns, finding older men, or "old heads," in the neighborhood to be ready sources or guides in this regard. Participants found that their guns served many purposes for them, providing not only protection but also fun, excitement, bonding, and enjoyment as objects of desire. In addition, guns often figured in the young men's identity processes, making them feel "powerful" and sometimes "more masculine." Guns are more than weapons for these boys. As these young men struggle with their particular kind of adolescence and perform a particular masculinity characteristic of their circumstances, guns serve as metaphors for a host of meaning-making and belief system work. As the young men frame their worlds for us, patterns emerge, with guns filling many needs and representing many aspects of identity, some acknowledged and some not.

# CHAPTER 4

# Producing Violence
## "You Gotta Have a 'Don't Care' Attitude"

I always knew a gun was for protection; I knew that. But once I knew that you could use it for more than protection, that's when I started doin' this.

—Thomas

Thomas was referring to using a gun to commit robberies, and his statement was consistent with those of other participants who quickly began to appreciate the offensive, as well as defensive, potential of their guns. Participants explained that they had acquired their guns after they were already selling drugs, robbing people, or engaging in street fighting. With the exception of Tony, who had moved to the city from the suburbs at the age of ten, participants said their guns initially served as protection for their street lifestyles. Several young men whose street activities were drug related said they never expanded their gun use beyond its protective functions. As Thomas stated previously, however, if a young man was robbing people or engaging in street fighting—or was ready to do so—he would often realize how helpful a gun could be.

In this chapter, I explore participants' experience of producing violence, usually with guns. Having become immersed in the lifestyle of the streets and acquired guns for protection in this milieu, many participants began to use their guns in other ways. Just as participants had viewed their gun acquisition as part of a pathway out of material deprivation, powerlessness, and vulnerability, some now saw that they could use their guns in more aggressive ways. The process of moving from protective to aggressive uses of guns did not take place for all participants; those who did use guns aggressively against others described their feelings about the violence they produced in a variety of ways. If a participant found that gun use was helpful in solving his problems, he tended to incorporate it into his repertoire of responses to his life world and began to acquire an identity as a gun carrier.

This chapter also unpacks several violent events in order to comprehend the actor's perspective. None of the participants in this study had been adjudicated delinquent for shooting or killing anyone, although three had been adjudicated delinquent for attempted murder with a knife. However, to the extent that they felt comfortable doing so, participants discussed various types of shootings, at persons or property, for which they had not been adjudicated. Where possible, I attempted to investigate with participants the unfolding of a violent event as an example of situated interaction, as Deanna Wilkinson and Jeffrey Fagan (2001) suggested, in order to show the microinteractions that brought about what were often highly contingent outcomes, such as shootings.[1] In the same spirit, I also invited participants to consider what might have facilitated a different, nonviolent outcome. David Farrington and Brandon Welsh (2007) observed that the point at which the risk or potentiality for crime becomes an actuality in a given situation has been an understudied event.[2]

With a few notable exceptions, researchers are generally not privy to the unfolding of the violent event itself, and even when they are, the actor may not provide a narrative of his own thoughts and feelings that precipitated the violent outcome, leaving the researcher to make inferences from observed actions. However, several of the participants in this study provided detailed recollections of occasions on which they produced violence, explaining as well how they remembered feeling at the time. As Wilkinson and Fagan proposed, an interactionist approach from the perspective of the young gun offender can help us to deconstruct various dynamics of the event, illuminating the multiple choices and decisions that led to the final outcome. I also discuss in this chapter participants' accounts of several episodes of violence without guns, both because their dynamics are similar in many ways to gun crimes and because just as guns fulfill many roles for these young men, violence itself, with or without guns, also serves many functions for them.

I begin with two accounts of episodes of gun violence provided by participants in order to illustrate the ways in which shootings erupted among some of these young men. These accounts exemplify several of this chapter's primary themes, which are how violence was produced by adolescents, how participants felt about the violence they produced, and how carrying a loaded gun made it all too easy for a young man to respond to provocation with lethal violence. Seven participants said they had shot at people, while another four preferred not to say.

In the first example, Quinto explains how his gun was able to assist him in performing what Arlie Hochschild and Barrie Thorne would call his shame work;[3] he both expressed his anger and restored his own sense of pride through an act of gun violence. While no one was injured in this incident and Quinto was never arrested or charged in connection with it, the episode illustrates how a gun carried ostensibly for protection can become an offensive weapon in the street battle for respect.

## How Quinto Got His Dignity Back

Quinto, a drug dealer, set the scene for what eventually happened by explaining that he had previously told a younger boy of about 14—who was just starting to sell drugs after having served as a runner (running drugs back and forth for other dealers on the street)—that if anyone bothered him, he could come to Quinto for help because Quinto carried a gun. Quinto said he had then shown his gun to the young boy to illustrate his point. One day shortly thereafter when Quinto was walking to the corner store to buy a cigar, this young boy, now flush with cash, came by in a car. As Quinto emphasized, the reason he was walking to the store was "'cause I didn't have no car." The boy approached Quinto and showed him a lot of money, asking where he might be able to get a gun. Once again Quinto emphasized to me his feeling that this boy had quickly eclipsed his own success, saying, "He knew how to get that money better than I could." The boy continued to press Quinto, now inquiring about the .32 that Quinto had previously shown him. Quinto said he told the boy he had sold it, and "he looked at me weird." The boy then said something to Quinto that Quinto interpreted as disrespectful and walked away from him. (It is notable that although he related this story in minute detail, Quinto did not tell me what the boy had said that was so offensive, although presumably it was something suggesting that Quinto was so insignificant an actor that he did not need a gun. Just as Quinto had been evasive about confessing himself to be a "rice-eater" in

Chapter 2, the actual insulting remark was probably too injurious to his pride for him to repeat it to me.) As Quinto reprised his overall impression of the encounter, "Would you come up and talk to me, then when you ask me for a certain object, and then when I say, 'Nah, I need it,' you're just gonna turn your back on me, and you're all . . . some bullshit, and walk to one of your boys and start talkin'?"

Quinto evidently believed that this younger boy had made him feel, in front of others, less of a person than the young and successful up-and-coming drug dealer, who drove up in a car while Quinto was on foot, flashed a lot of money, and implied (or said) that he had more need of Quinto's gun than Quinto did. When Quinto declined to accommodate him, the boy turned his back on him dismissively and walked off to talk to one of his boys, presumably about Quinto. Quinto was made to feel that, in short order, he had declined in status from the respected elder (or "old head," young though he was) to the unimportant person who had less need for a gun than this young boy with the car, the money, and the "boys."

Finding this situation unbearable, Quinto continued on his way to the store and bought his cigar, fuming all the while. He then pulled his hoodie up over his head and entered an alley where he had a view of the boy's car. As he hid behind a protruding board, he saw the boy and one of his associates sitting in the car and shot the car full of holes with the .25 he was then carrying. When the police arrived upon hearing the gunshots, the younger boy had to abandon the car and flee, as he was clearly unlicensed and did not own the vehicle. Quinto's gratification at dispossessing the boy of the car was complete when the boy and his friend ran past Quinto as he was walking home and Quinto was able to smile at him and ask blandly, "What happened, bro?" Quinto laughed as he delivered this punch line, clearly satisfied that he had restored his honor through the act of retaliation.

As Wilkinson and Fagan (2001) suggest, studying the unfolding of this violent event as narrated by Quinto permits us to enter into his interpretive frame of the interactions between him and the boy that brought about the shooting. In so doing, we observers and analysts can garner something of his definition of the situation. What Farrington and Welsh (2007) call "the moment when the potentiality for offending becomes the actuality of offending"[4] is seen as dependent upon a multitude of factors, including the "weird look" the boy gave Quinto before he turned his back on him and walked away and the presence of a bystander, in this case the young boy's associate, that may have converted a private conversation into a public humiliation.

We could also analyze this interaction in terms of mutually unsuccessful bids for recognition,[5] with Quinto's bid to be recognized as a successful man of the street and capable protector being rejected by the boy, and the boy's bid to be recognized by Quinto as the new big man in the neighborhood being rejected in turn by Quinto in front of the boy's associate, prompting the boy to walk off in a huff. The incident reveals how perceived vulnerability, fragile masculine identity, loss of public respect, anger, and the agency conferred by a loaded gun combine to form a violent outcome in the form of a triumphant narrative.

In addition, this example suggests how such socially meaningful interactions have the potential to spawn a pattern of escalating retaliation. An affront that results in the shooting of one's car could in turn lead to the perceived need for violent retaliation against the assailant. Quinto felt protective toward the younger boy one week, shot up his car the next week, and could have been shot by the same young man or one of his partisans the following week. An exchange that some might view as trivial could easily have had fatal consequences. While Quinto did not raise this issue, other participants did, as will be discussed in the next chapter. Also, as Quinto was careful to explain, in order to understand the violent event it was important to appreciate its context. From Quinto's perspective, the interaction that led to the shooting had its genesis days earlier when Quinto offered his protection to the younger boy and showed him his gun.

What seemed remarkable about Quinto's account was the "you are there" quality of his narrative, which included an interior perspective that permitted me, as his audience, to hear not only what happened but also how Quinto reacted to each segment of the interaction and why he found the boy's comments and conduct so offensive. This advantaged view rendered both his anger and his reaction comprehensible to me, clearly an outsider to this social world. Quinto's self-image suffered grievous damage on this occasion and, perhaps, was partially repaired by relating the incident to me. His mortification at the time, however, was such that he could not restrain his impulse to strike back, especially in a way that attacked the symbol of the other's superior status, his car.

Quinto also related the bodily experience of preparing for the shooting and—just as he had earlier described how he breathed immediately prior to firing at the rat in his kitchen when he was much younger—spoke now of taking three breaths before firing at the car, forming his lips into an *O* shape to demonstrate inhaling, then making a breathing noise and exhaling, repeating this process three times before describing the shooting itself. Quinto's ability to recall and communicate both his emotional and physical experiences so vividly helped me understand an event that I might otherwise have found opaque.

In retrospect, even Quinto conceded that the slight he suffered may not have been deliberate and that his own perception of the boy's words and actions may not have been what the boy had in mind. As Quinto put it, "What motivated me to, uh, shoot at him was that, uh, he had played me. Actually he didn't, but in my mind, he did. Like he didn't play me, but in my mind he did play me." Intended or not, the actions that resulted in Quinto's sense that he had been "played" produced a rich store of memories and feelings, and his decision to volunteer such a detailed account permitted me to comprehend what he had experienced and why he reacted as he did. In return, as Americo Paredes (1977) suggested,[6] I expressed my appreciation of the performative aspect of Quinto's rendering of this story, with its satisfying (for him) denouement. While I have no way of being certain, it was entirely possible that the narrative he had shared with me was among Quinto's cherished anecdotes, despite the fact that, in the version I heard, Quinto presented himself as an insecure young man who could not even impress a younger boy in the neighborhood with his drug-dealer persona.

## A Gang Shooting Ernie "Didn't Want to Get Into"

Ernie also described a shooting that may have been precipitated by the presence of other young men. As Ernie recalled the event, it too seemed to follow a highly contingent interactive script. Unlike the confrontation Ernie described in the previous chapter, which he sought out by crashing the party of a rival gang, Ernie said of this episode, "I didn't even want to get into it with them." Although Ernie was currently incarcerated on a gun possession charge, he had never been arrested for the shooting he described here. As background for this narrative, Ernie said he had originally joined the Crips at age nine because he thought their deportment was much more appealing than that of the Bloods. He said they never acted crazy and would not permit anyone else to act crazy on the block where he lived. According to Ernie, these Crips "kept that block straight," and "wouldn't let nobody come over and rob, break windows," or do anything that would "bring cops to that area. You weren't even allowed to argue with your own mother." Ernie said, "They wouldn't let nothing happen to the kids" on the block, although he conceded that these Crips, like "everybody on that block," sold drugs.

On the day of the shooting, Ernie and three of his friends were on Ernie's block when two members of the Bloods confronted them. In keeping with the tradition of not doing anything that would attract police, Ernie explained his attitude: "I didn't want to bring no trouble to my block." He reported that he was walking away but the two Bloods "just kept comin' at me . . . sayin' stuff, calling us all types of things," and when he still continued to ignore them, the Bloods began "throwing rocks and everything. Just kept comin' and comin'." Ernie, carrying a gun, said he did not feel threatened and maintained that he was determined to let it go because he lived there. Although it is unclear from Ernie's account what caused the Crips finally to rise to the bait, Ernie said the Bloods "kept throwing stuff," and "so we made a U-turn, we went towards them, now they finally walkin' away, right, they like nothing just happened. And then, my boys like called out to 'em, and they turned around, said a few things, he threw a bottle at me, so I start shootin'." Ernie emptied the entire clip and then ran seven or eight blocks before discarding the gun in some bushes. As for the outcome of the shooting, when I ventured to ask Ernie whether he had hit anybody, he dropped his voice very low and said, unconvincingly, "I don't know." In response to my question, he did say that he never heard anything about the episode afterward and never saw either of the two boys again.

The outcome of the incident as recounted by Ernie seemed to turn on the decision of Ernie and his friends to "make a U-turn" and begin following the Bloods once they had begun to walk away, coupled with the conduct of Ernie's boys in calling out to the Bloods, prompting the retreating Bloods to turn, make some more remarks, and throw a bottle at Ernie.

This episode illustrates how an adolescent with a gun, even though unwilling to become involved in a shooting on his own block, can be goaded into doing something clearly against his better judgment. I believed Ernie was sincere in his initial reluctance to engage in this fight, but he seemed to have been overtaken by events, and this ultimately caused him to fail to live up to his ideal of not bringing trouble to the block. Apparently both the persistent taunting by his rivals and the evident desire of his peers to engage them overcame Ernie's reserve. Carrying a loaded gun made it all too easy to respond with lethal violence.

After this interview, which was the second one in the project, I learned to clarify responses that seemed evasive or unconvincing by suggesting to participants that it would be helpful for me to know whether, for example, Ernie really didn't know whether his shots had hit anybody or whether he would prefer not to discuss it. This proved to be a useful approach in subsequent interviews, and several participants revised their responses to acknowledge that they did not feel comfortable giving a straightforward answer. Such responses usually signaled that a particular discussion topic had reached the point where the participant had become concerned about incriminating himself, and I would then move on to something else. Although participants had been cautioned both in writing and at the beginning of the interview not to discuss, for example, any unsolved homicides, or to provide any specific information such as dates, places, or names related to any offenses for which they had not already been adjudicated, participants understandably had varying comfort levels for discussing, even in nonspecific terms, offenses for which they feared they might still be charged.

As the previous two examples suggest, some participants offered narratives that were so thorough in describing both their past actions and their mental processes leading up to a violent event that their involvement in the events became easy to understand.

### Framing Juvenile Gun Violence from an Etic Perspective

Many law-abiding adults are at ease with the idea of having and using guns for protection, sport, and—as in the case of gun collectors and sportsmen—enjoyment as material objects. Even using a gun, or as in Quinto's case, a BB gun, for pest control may be seen as having its conventional analog in shooting rodents or other small game. These more or less socially approved uses of guns are now more widely accepted for women as well, as Lindsay McCrum's 2011 photo book *Chicks with Guns* illustrates.[7]

Yet while the participants in this study belong to the gender category that we most frequently associate with guns, their gun possession seems problematic for a number of reasons. Among the most important is that we do not like to associate children with violence for social and moral reasons, finding such an association antithetical to our customary concept of childhood.[8] In addition, the age of the participants is not typically associated with responsible gun use—that is, most people view children and adolescents as too immature to handle firearms without adult supervision. Laws concerning gun possession and use are generally congruent with this view, and current research on adolescent brain development can be interpreted as supporting it as well.[9] Compounding the concern about age is the urban setting in which participants typically possessed their guns. The traditional image of the rural young person with a gun, in contrast, seems less threatening, the wide open spaces suggesting more socially acceptable uses of guns. While participants in this study, like rural youth, used their guns for target shooting and exuberant New Year's Eve celebrations, engaging in these activities in an urban setting seems inherently more life threatening. Still, as with participants' desire for protection, their enjoyment of guns is not difficult to understand. Guns are an iconic part of American history and culture, and American popular culture, including film, has contributed for more than a hundred years to guns being viewed not simply as useful tools but to their being fetishized and the men who used them portrayed as strong protagonists, whether hero, villain, or antihero.[10] Finally, however, considerations of race and class also complicate the etic perspective on juvenile gun possession and use, as low-income urban young men of color, even without guns, signal danger to many observers. These participants' age, race, class, gender, and urban location, none of which they have chosen, combine to marginalize them in the minds of many, and often in their own minds.[11] Not coincidentally, the high rates of gun violence in many low-income urban neighborhoods of color cast juvenile gun possession in a menacing light. All these factors combine to shape our view of gun possession by the participants in this study.

As this exploration moves beyond the more familiar territory of socially accepted ways of using guns, however, understanding the young person's perspective proves more challenging. In the contemporary Western world, the use of guns to settle personal disputes, including matters of honor or

respect, is generally viewed as outdated at best. The eras of both the duel and
the righteous Wild West shootout have faded, although, as Anderson points
out, the ancient code that requires men to fight for their honor persists
in some communities. Anderson names working-class Scotch-Irish, Italian,
and Hispanic communities—in addition to the inner-city African American communities whose violence he was seeking to explicate—as among
those pockets where the operation of the code can be still observed.[12] While
participants did not explicitly reference such ethnic or racial mandates,
much of their gun violence arising from disputes over individual respect or
family honor can be viewed within this traditional frame. Yet as Anderson
argues, urban poverty, the often ruthless nature of the underground drug
economy, and the abundance of guns intensify the likelihood that disputes
will culminate in gun violence.

In other types of violent gun offending, such as armed robbery, the actor's
perspective and the decision-making process that his perspective produces
may be even more difficult to grasp. Perhaps here more than anywhere else
in this study, Maurice Merleau-Ponty's admonition that we are "necessarily
destined never to experience the presence of another person to himself"[13] is
fitting. While addressing how and why participants said they acquired and
used guns, what they used them for, and how guns made them feel, this
project cannot answer the question of why some of these boys—the armed
robbers in particular—were able to suppress or deny feelings of empathy for
their victims. Philippe Bourgois (1995), in his ethnography of Latino crack
dealers in East Harlem, argued that suffering "is a solvent of human integ-
rity."[14] If true in the case of these young men, it would probably require
more than one 60- to 90-minute interview to understand fully how this
process evolved for each of them. In the present study, I have attempted
to heed Howard Stevenson's recommendation that research with minority
urban youth be approached with "a curious appreciation of their world."[15]
After all, each of these incarcerated participants has already been judged;
my goal is to achieve a better comprehension of the life worlds that brought
them to this place.

Analysis of the dynamics of these young men's gun violence is further
complicated by the fact that participants used guns for both instrumental and expressive reasons, often during the same event. The instrumental
roles included protection as well as use as a tool for committing crimes,

while the expressive roles encompassed identity-related elements such as the demonstration of power or anger.[16] In addition to its instrumental functions, because a gun can serve as a symbol, a marker, or a badge of belonging, it was important for participants to provide sufficient context in their descriptions of the violence in which they engaged for this complexity to be appreciated. The process of meaning-making for such objects and actions grows out of social interaction, and the multiple meanings of the gun and gun violence for participants may therefore be best understood by entering the interpretive frame of the actor so we can understand what meanings he attributes to them. The two previous accounts of violent offending were described at some length in order that the multiple functions of gun violence, and other kinds of violence as well, could be seen both among and within the various interactions.

## Framing Gun Violence from Participants' Perspectives

Participants positioned themselves and their actions variously in relation to both other offenders and victims. In the quotation at the beginning of this chapter, Thomas was referring to committing armed robbery, for which he was currently incarcerated. He was among nine participants who reported that they both committed robberies and sold drugs. Like one other participant, he maintained that he only robbed drug dealers, believing this was not as bad as robbing innocent people. Yet he conceded, "robbin' is robbin'." He recalled one occasion when he watched his friend rob an "old lady" and said he was thinking, "That's really messed up." Thomas distinguished himself from his friend who had robbed the elderly woman, while at the same time explaining why the friend would do so:

> In my head I was thinking, that's really messed up. But then again I knew what type of life he was living; he didn't have nowhere to live, I mean, he couldn't make the moves like I was makin'; he wasn't in the social area that I was in. I'm thinkin' to myself that that's messed up, but then again I'm thinkin', like, at least he gonna be all right for the night. So yeah, I do feel sympathy. But that's just me. There's some people out there that's ruthless, like, they don't care about nobody; they don't care about nothin'; they rob their mom if their mom had the right amount of money.

Thomas positioned himself as less desperate than his friend and therefore able to select what he considered to be more appropriate targets for his robberies. He considered himself to be better situated socially—at least having a place to live—and thus able to make more well-considered "moves." At the same time, he denounced some robbers as "ruthless" for failing to show any sympathy or to discriminate between suitable and unsuitable victims. In the hierarchy of robbers, he held himself above the "ruthless" ones who didn't care about anybody and the homeless ones who could not afford to make such distinctions.

For Thomas, robbery was not about anger or anything personal: "It's got nothing to do with them," meaning the victims. It was simply a way to get money quickly. Thomas maintained that he didn't like robbing people or stealing but said sometimes he had to do it. In the case of his last armed robbery, for example, he had recently been released from detention and said he needed money and a supply of drugs in order to get back into the drug-selling business, so he robbed some drug dealers in their home. He recounted the story of this robbery, for which he was now incarcerated, as a chaotic episode wherein several gunshots had been fired inside a confined and crowded space. He and two armed associates had entered a home where men, children, and a dog were present. As Thomas noted, the robbery had not gone according to plan. While he wanted the two male drug dealers to be present to show him where the money and drugs were hidden, he had not counted on the children or the effect of the dog. The barking pit bull alarmed his two codefendants. Adding to the disorder of the event, the clip fell out of Thomas's gun when he tried to fire it at the dog. He then had to struggle to regain control over his victims and the scene. He eventually succeeded in obtaining a large amount of money and drugs from the house and said he was able to sell a lot of the drugs and hide the money before he was arrested. Although Thomas said he sometimes had to rob people in order to get money, he also said he could have lived in his parent's home but did not wish to abide by the rules there, preferring to live with his girlfriend. His mother, by whom he had been raised, lived with a drug dealer that Thomas described as abusive toward him. Thomas had been sent to live with his biological father but said this living arrangement did not work out because he could not tolerate being ordered around by a man he had just met. In addition, Thomas believed he should have been free to come and go as he pleased, spending time with his girlfriend and staying out late. Thomas said his father had "kicked him out" because he was getting in too much trouble, but his father still brought him some soup when Thomas had the flu. His account highlights a number of issues, including one of the familiar practices used by adolescents to explain why their violent offending is not as bad as it might seem.

## Sidestepping Guilty Feelings

One way the armed robbers avoided feelings of remorse was to distinguish "between appropriate and inappropriate targets." While Thomas and another participant, Xavier, said they only robbed drug dealers, others, such as Nate and Leon, said they did not rob women or the elderly. One participant claimed his victims could run or defend themselves if they wanted to, and another, describing a robbery for which he had previously been incarcerated, said the victim was "flossin'"—that is, "lookin' like you got money . . . chains and everything." Leon, too, said he looked for a person in an expensive car or with nice jewelry, saying, "I see what I can see on them; so, like, if you're flashing, you're gonna be robbed." Leon and Ernie both intimated that such ostentation was almost tantamount to an invitation to be robbed. As Gresham Sykes and David Matza (1957) argued, such "neutralization techniques" permit adolescents to minimize the crime by suggesting that the victim, because of who he is or how he is acting, is not really that much of a victim.[17] At the same time, robberies such as those described by Thomas, Xavier, Nate, and Leon prompted other participants, especially those involved in selling drugs, to feel the need to carry a gun. Being known as a drug dealer could be enough to invite robberies, but if the young man also used the income to adorn himself with jewelry or to drive a nice car, he would stand out even more readily to other young men who were looking for someone to rob.

Leon also cited the ubiquity of armed robbery as a justification to continue doing it: "Well, it just make you feel like if you stop, then somebody else still gonna be doin' it, so, what's the need for you to stop?" Leon sought to normalize his robbing by making reference to its prevalence in his environment. When I asked the question that elicited this response, I had been attempting to prick his social conscience by pointing out that he had been robbed by people just like him, and that he in turn was robbing people just like him, but my appeal to solidarity did not resonate. His racial, class, age, and gender similarity to his victims was not seen as a reason to refrain from robbing them. On the contrary, by pointing out that women and the elderly were inappropriate victims, Leon reinforced his understanding that young men were the proper demographic group to target as victims. In this regard, he underscores Antony Whitehead's (2005) argument that men demonstrate manhood in relation to other men.[18] According to Whitehead's thesis, a young man cannot prove his masculinity by attacking a woman or an aged man. That the young men Leon would victimize were likely to be of the same race and class as he was presumably resulted from the preponderance of persons of color in his world rather than from an intentional choice to target them. The other participants in this study also victimized young men of color, in keeping with the pattern documented elsewhere that most crime is intraracial.[19] The prevailing explanation for this pattern is based on access in that offenders tend to exploit the easiest opportunities. As people who live, work, and socialize near one another tend to have the same social demographics, this makes them the most convenient victims. In effect, the combination of ready access, a tendency to exclude other age and gender groups from the target pool, and a preference for demonstrating manhood in relation to other men leaves young men of color as the target of choice. Community members and outside researchers alike have noted the intraracial and intraclass nature of juvenile violence. The impact of gun violence by young men of color in particular upon other young men of color is one of its most troubling features.

## Emotion and "Feeling Rules"

Participants' responses to questions about how they felt before, during, and after violent events raised another issue: the more general question of what types of feelings, if any, a person "should" have about his violent offending. Unlike Quinto, who had freely acknowledged that the reason he was burning the front of his neighbor's house was that he was bored, some participants were hesitant to say that crime could serve as entertainment.

Ernie, describing the commission of numerous armed robberies even though he said he was making plenty of money selling drugs, maintained that he didn't really need the money and that he started doing armed robberies to accompany his friend. If true, this reason for offending would be consistent with Messerschmidt's idea that this type of group behavior is a sort of bonding activity, a way of constructing a tough and productive masculinity.[20] Ernie said that he sometimes would use a gun and sometimes a knife for these robberies. He reported that he soon discovered that robbing people was such an easy way to obtain money that it was hard to resist. In response to a question about whether it was fun, he replied, "Naw, it can't be fun robbin' people." But a follow-up question asking whether it was scary prompted this response: "Yeah, it was scary; it was like . . . a rush. It was like, it's just kinda like when you're in it, it's like you're in a movie. And when you're getting away, when you got away, like you got this joy, like, it's like a roller coaster sometimes." He agreed that robbery was a thrilling kind of crime. His choice of words—describing committing robbery as a rush, like being in a movie, like a roller coaster, and as producing joy— made it clear that he was getting more than just money from committing these offenses.

Yet when he was first asked whether these robberies were fun, Ernie rejected the possibility out of hand, saying robbing people can't be fun. His initial reaction suggested that he was calibrating his reported emotions against a yardstick of socially appropriate "feeling rules." Hochschild (1979) introduced the concept of feeling rules, which she defined as "social guidelines that direct how we want to try to feel."[21] She pointed out that "feeling rules reflect patterns of social membership. Some rules may be nearly universal, such as the rule that one should not enjoy killing or witnessing the killing of a human being, including oneself. Other rules are unique to particular social groups."[22] She suggests that the ways we are "supposed" to feel in different situations are socially constructed and that people in social groups are aware of the feeling rules for various occasions that apply to members of that group.

While Ernie clearly experienced these robberies as thrilling and fun, like being in a movie, as he put it, he demonstrated his awareness of the feeling rule that robbery was not supposed to be fun for the perpetrator. While he may have seen it as acceptable to disregard this mainstream feeling rule when among his peers, where other rules may have applied, his reaction to my question was almost one of shock that I should suggest that robbing people could be fun. Yet his vivid description of his remembered feelings during the experience itself belied his original conventional reaction. Another participant, Earl, likewise seemed to be aghast when I asked whether fun might have been part of his motivation for being a lookout in the armed robbery for which he was incarcerated: "What? Robbery? Fun?" Hochschild explains that feeling rules go beyond the usual conception of impression management, as they involve the type of "deep acting" where a person seeks to actually feel the appropriate emotion rather than simply display it. The fact that Ernie's protestation was so swiftly followed by a recollection of the joy he felt suggests that he had not quite succeeded in convincing himself that robbing people cannot be fun.

At the same time, by using such vivid and widely understood images as riding on a roller coaster or feeling as though one is in a movie to describe his feelings during a robbery, Ernie sought to communicate his experience of the events in such a way that I too could sense something of what he experienced. Paredes (1977) suggests that the absence of shared understandings can be a barrier in cross-cultural interviewing, and he offers ways for researchers to be aware of and overcome these barriers.[23] When the research participants, however, extend themselves to enable a shared understanding on the part of a researcher from another culture by bridging the gap through references to common experiences, genuine communication can occur. Several participants went to great lengths to "put me in their shoes" in their attempts to have me understand their feelings or their actions.

From another perspective, Ernie's initial assertion that robbery can't be fun may also be an example of what Heith Copes and Andy Hochstetler (2010) call a "penitent reconstruction," which they define as a form of retrospective account provided by a prisoner after he has experienced the consequences of his criminal activity.[24] As the authors suggest, the penitent reconstruction may reflect "a more thoughtful and potentially more regretful interpretation" of the offender's acts than that which prevailed at the time of the offense. Both concepts, those of feeling rules and penitent reconstructions, illustrate aspects of the socially constructed nature of feelings in retrospective accounts. The penitent reconstruction may also reflect the possibly temporary influence of the institutional environment, which is designed to encourage reflection with the goal of instilling a more socially approved cognitive view of one's antisocial behavior. While the purpose of both feeling rules and the juvenile institutional ethos is to bring the person's feelings into line with those accepted by a given social group, Ernie's positive memories of his feelings during the commission of robberies seemed almost to override any regrets that he had developed in the interim. Rather than attempt to persuade young men that delinquent activity cannot be fun and exciting, institutional staff may often aim more modestly to convince residents that the rewards of such excitement are not worth its possible costs.

## Mixed Motivations and the Subjective Experience of Robbery

Several other participants said the fun and the money were both important reasons robbery was attractive to them. Luke said he had committed numerous armed robberies with guns before being arrested for the one for which he was incarcerated. During that robbery, Luke's friend wielded the gun while Luke took the male victim's earrings, chain, and money. He said he felt "excited" during the robbery but felt disappointed after this one only because he didn't get away with it. He denied feeling bad after his previous successful robberies and maintained that both the money and the excitement drew him to this type of crime. Luke described himself as consumed by the desire to do an armed robbery the way a "cokehead" needed his drug:

> **LUKE:** But sometimes it wouldn't be a gun, though. Like, I could have had a knife on me. Whatever I had on me, I'd use it . . . Before it, uh, I'd feel needy, just anxious to get a person.
> **DM:** When you say needy, needing what?
> **LUKE:** I need it. It's like when you're taking drugs. Say a cokehead, and he stop usin' for a couple days, usually he gonna wanna come back, 'cause he need it. It was sick . . . So that's how it was with me, it just making me sick, not like "sick" sick, but wanting to have to do something so that I could get more money . . . and that's it, I just go get one more person.
> **DM:** That's a good question that you talked about before; were you needy of the money or the excitement, or equally, or what?
> **LUKE:** I would say equally.

In addition to feeling excited during the robbery, Luke said that afterward, "I just feel proud of myself." When I asked what he was proud of, Luke said, "That I got the job done. I coulda been caught." What Jack Katz called the "seductions of crime" were described by participants as many and varied, including excitement, power, a sense of accomplishment, and of course, in the case of armed robbery, money.[25]

Kenneth likewise enjoyed the transgressive aspect of robbery, saying it was "exciting": "it's like when you know you're gettin' ready to be doin' somethin' you know you're not supposed to be doin', it just feel different; you feel good." Kenneth was carrying a switchblade knife rather than a gun during the robbery for which he was incarcerated but said he didn't use it. Instead, he hit the victim in the face and later learned that he had broken the bone around the victim's eye. He took the victim's cell phone, house keys, and more than a hundred dollars. He said he did not make a demand or announce that it was a robbery but simply hit the victim immediately and took his stuff. Kenneth was a member of the Crips and recalled that when he did carry a gun, "It makes you feel like can't nobody touch you." Katz includes the idea of "being mean" among the seductions of crimes where others are overpowered, as well as among the seductions of the weapons that can be used to do so. He contrasts "being mean" with simply showing power: "In contrast to 'power,' 'being mean' captures the project at stake: to assume a tough, alien posture beyond all danger of mockery and metaphysical doubt that ensures that one will be taken seriously. These things excite by attesting to a purpose that transcends the material utility of power."[26]

While participants did not frame the excitement that attracted them to armed robbery in Katz's terms, his description does capture the alienation seemingly necessary for the project of overpowering another person and taking his property. As Katz argues, the same excitement is engendered by possessing weapons that can be used to compel others to take seriously the intentions of those who wield them. This perspective provides an additional gloss, not explicitly articulated by participants but helpful in explaining their actions, on the power of the gun, the attraction of armed robbery, and by extension, on producing violence in general. When Kenneth described the excitement he felt as he approached a stranger and, without preamble, punched him in the face hard enough to fracture a bone, his feelings seemed to arise from more than simply the utilitarian ability to acquire the man's phone, keys, and cash. In our single interviews, the young men who chose to speak with me did not explicitly voice their alienation or what Katz referred to in the previous quotation as their metaphysical doubts about whether they would be taken seriously, but their alienation often seemed implicit in the actions they described. Likewise, their gratification at being taken seriously and recognized as someone who must be obeyed was clearly important to them.

Other participants maintained that they robbed people only for the money, denying that fun or excitement played any part. Leon, for example, said there was nothing besides the money that made him feel good about committing an armed robbery: "No, there's nothin' else that makes me feel good, 'cause givin' fear to somebody else really don't make me feel good."

Instead, he described a combination of a racing heart and a "rage" that he said was not anger but nerves accompanying his armed robberies and suggested that these feelings helped keep him safe, but at the same time drove him to continue robbing:

> LEON: At my first robbery . . . goin' towards the robbery, I was really, you know, heart beatin' fast . . . but after I seen how fast they give it up, it's so much easier [with a gun] than strong-arm robbery . . . Even after, until I'm stayed put, until I'm in a safe place, my heart beats fast. But it's just a rage, though.
>
> DM: Now what do you mean by rage?
>
> LEON: Like, your heart beats fast, you're gonna be a little scared, so when you're scared you're gonna do the right thing, you're gonna make it to a safe place so you won't be in danger, won't be in harm's way. By the cops, or by the victim comin' back for retaliation, anything like that, because things like that can happen, too.
>
> DM: . . . What do you mean when you say rage?
>
> LEON: Well, with the rage, you do not wanna stop. One robbery not gonna be enough. Like, when I did this robbery I'm locked up for now. . . . It wasn't gonna be the only one. I was actually gonna go and do two, do like two more . . .
>
> DM: But what does the rage mean? Do you mean like anger, or in a different way?
>
> LEON: Well it like, not even like the rage of anger, like the rage of nerves. It's the nerves be raging, it be screamin' like you wanna do somethin', you wanna get away, you know what I'm sayin'?
>
> DM: Okay, but what, so you say, is it, how does it, now this is the kind of rage that makes you do another robbery right after you just got done doing one, right?
>
> LEON: Yeah . . . You go out to a different town, and do it all over again.
>
> DM: And so what is that feeling inside you? What does it feel like?
>
> LEON: It feel good! 'Cause I know I could be sittin' for a while with a little money, I know I don't be havin' to worry 'cause I'm not gonna rob every day. So if I can get a good amount of money to last me a week, or two weeks, or

> maybe even longer than that, I'll get that amount of money and I'll just live with it. Then when I need it again, I'll just go out and do it again.

Leon described raging, screaming nerves that drove him to do armed robbery after armed robbery until he felt he had enough money to stop for a while. His description suggests the complex meanings of—and relationships among—money, power, and autonomy in motivating his behavior.

Nate seemed equally driven, but emphasized how his "love" for robbery developed. At first, he said, he admired people who sold drugs and robbed people: "I see them doin' it so I'm gonna do it; it was more like follow the leader game. But after I started doin' it, I started gettin' a love for it, like. It was more like, when I was doin' the robberies, I used to like the feeling of havin' power, like. And the money."

He said he would sometimes "do ten armed robberies in a night and not get caught." At around age 14, he and his friends would order Chinese food or pizza delivery and then rob the delivery person. He said he would get an adrenaline rush right before the robbery. As time went on, however, Nate seemed to become emotionally dependent upon the rush: "And it got to where it was what I needed to do and I had to do. It's just what I needed, what I needed for myself, to keep goin'. It got to where, like, if I don't smoke, I don't feel right. So with me, robbing people was the same thing. Early in the morning I'd be lookin' to get somebody, to rob 'em."

Nate, by his own description, seemed to embody the title theme of Jack Katz's book, *Seductions of Crime* (1988). As he recalled his subjective experience, he had been initially drawn in by his admiration for other robbers and then held by the magnetic attractions of robbery, including both its psychic and monetary rewards. Nate's description of the phenomenology of being a robber in some ways parallels that of Howard Becker's subjects in "Becoming a Marihuana User" (1953) in that the meaning of robbing, or at least its effect on him, seemed to change over time until he became psychologically addicted to it.[27] Katz, in *Seductions of Crime,* argued that the widespread belief that crime is motivated by material concerns has blinded researchers to the subjective experience of the offender, in which not only noneconomic but also nonrational motivations are critical.[28]

In this regard, Nate reported that he did not need the money at all as he had lived in a comfortable neighborhood with an aunt who gave him plenty of spending money since age ten. Perhaps, like guns, robbery has multiple ways of seducing participants. Those who committed robberies cited fun, money, excitement, "feeling good," exercising power, and just plain love of robbery as among its lures. How much it really is about the money likely depends on the individual actor's circumstances. In addition, neurobiologists have discovered that changes in reward sensitivity occur during the adolescent years. Researchers in adolescent brain development note that reward-seeking behavior is intensified during this period, accounting for food-, sex-, and drug-related behaviors that make young people so susceptible to eating disorders and addiction.[29] As the participants in the previous sections describe the "rush," the emotional "need," and the intensely gratifying "feelings" that make them "go get" another robbery victim, the parallels they themselves draw to addiction seem particularly apt. Anne Kelley, Terri Schochet, and Charles Landry (2004) argue that the very same drives that impel both human and animal adolescents toward risk-taking as they move from the dependence of childhood toward the independence of adulthood expose young people to increased morbidity and mortality during these years.

This argument dovetails with that of David Oswell (2013) in which he draws upon Jacques Lacan to propose that agency is distributed across the unconscious and the conscious in such a way that "what is said and known by the subject can never be transparent, the basis of reflexive knowledge and the means of control."[30] When one combines Katz's discussion of nonrational motivations for crime with participants' own descriptions and the aforementioned research on reward-seeking and risk-taking behaviors, Oswell's vivid image appears more realistic than fantastic: "Children, as it were, are given the driving seat of a car with no controls, but with the illusion of a steering wheel that works, and a whole lot of baggage that keeps popping up from the back seat, distracting the driving."[31] While it is undoubtedly true that juvenile gun offenders rob people because they want their money, there seems to be a lot more going on.

### Power to Purchase

Once we direct our attention to the relevance of both material and noneconomic motivations for robbery, we can begin to question the emotional and symbolic meaning not only of robbery but of its nominal object—money.

The excitement and power dynamics that complicate the seemingly straight-forward project of robbery also attach themselves to the money obtained thereby, as the title of Elizabeth Chin's 2001 book *Purchasing Power* implies. The converse of purchasing power, the powerlessness to purchase, pervaded the life worlds of many of the participants and its effects demonstrate that "consumption is a fundamentally social process."[32] Chin offers a wide-ranging critique of the sensationalistic media trope of the "combat consumer," her term for "the 'inner city' youthful consumer," who commits violent crimes in order to obtain "sneakers, a flashy gold chain, or a car."[33] She argues that not only has this image been used to mischaracterize consumption by "black kids" in general, but it strips consumption by African Americans of its historical and social context. The result of this decontextualization has been a "complex, twisted skein of ideas" that tends to pathologize black consumption as morally corrupt and to contrast it—especially that of the poor—to the "norm" of mainstream, or white, consumption.[34]

But the "combat consumer" trope also decontextualizes the adolescent's consumption of clothing or luxury items from the life world of the individual child, ignoring the broad range of things children need that cost money but are outside the scope of the "combat consuming" image. Children need food, shelter, and many other material things, but the combat consumer trope does not encompass the image of Quinto going from his father's home to his mother's home in search of food and coming up empty at both places. Nor does it account for such practices as participants Xavier, Naheem, Kevin, and others described in Chapter 2 contributing to the payment of household bills. It obscures the provider role that their purchasing power permitted young offenders to perform, such as 13-year-old Kenneth's taking his mother and sister to the annual carnival in his town or taking them out to eat with the proceeds from his robberies. In other words, the "combat consumer" trope selectively presents only the most visible and sensationalistic tip of the consuming iceberg, which is congruent with the representation of consumption by inner-city youth as pathological. Participants in this study also spent the money they obtained on a host of more basic needs; in addition to buying food and clothing for themselves, many provided both essential and symbolic caregiving for family members. Thirteen participants said they spent the proceeds of their drug sales or robberies on clothes, seven named food, seven cited giving money to their mothers or contributing to bills or family needs, and four others were not more specific than to say they spent it on stuff they needed, spending money, or simply not having to ask their mothers for money. Not only the getting of the money but also the spending of it could be exciting and empowering social experiences. Money, power, fun, excitement, guns, and violence were often knitted closely together in complex ways that blended the material and the symbolic, the physical and the emotional.

## Managing, Suppressing, or Embracing Bad Feelings about Violent Offending

The young men who described committing robberies reported similar physiological responses accompanying the offenses, but little in the way of empathy for their robbery victims. Sam, though denying any feelings of compassion for his victims, did express relief that he still experienced the physical symptoms of an adrenaline rush and rapid heartbeat prior to committing an armed robbery. He opined that being able to commit such an offense without having a physical reaction would mean that he had passed some dangerous threshold that he did not wish to cross. He thus acknowledged his own "feeling rule" in that he expected his body to "signal" him that he was doing something out of the ordinary prior to an armed robbery, shooting, or even a fight:

> I don't know if you know, but every time we all about to fight my heart start beatin' real fast . . . And before I robbed 'em, my heart started beatin' real fast . . . My adrenaline get pumpin'. If my adrenaline not pumpin', that's a BAD thing, 'cause that means I LIKE it. If I do somethin' and my adrenaline not pumpin', my heart not beatin' fast, that means I'm too used to it and I need to stop. I'm serious. If I can do it, if I can shoot somebody and feel no, nothing, and my heart not beating, I'm not nervous, that mean I'm, there's somethin' wrong with me, I need some help.

After prefacing his explanation with an acknowledgment that I might not have personal experience with the phenomenon he was about to describe, Sam gave me his interpretation of his physiological response to impending violence. To him, the "rush" seemed to mean that he was not a sociopath. While he did not feel guilt, he was relieved to feel something.

Other participants took a utilitarian approach to their feelings, which tended to involve deliberately suppressing any qualms they might have. When I asked Leon what kind of mental process he went through to tell himself that it was OK to commit an armed robbery, he explained, "Ah, you really don't think about is it OK to do it . . . sometimes [you feel bad]; you can't let it get to you, though . . . Because then you might feel that you shouldn't do it." In response to my follow-up question whether he meant that if he felt bad, he "would kind of push those feelings out of his head." Leon responded in the affirmative, repeating my words. In describing the emotion work that attended his robbing, Leon acknowledged that he might feel bad for a victim, for example, upon seeing "the way they cry for their stuff back," but it was at these times that he said he couldn't let it get to him. Any humane feelings that intruded needed to be suppressed so that the armed robber could feel the way he knew he was supposed to feel. Focusing on the task of armed robbery seemed to require that he dehumanize the victim, at least to some extent, as well as himself.

Victor gave a similar account of his mental preparation for the armed robbery for which he had been adjudicated. The background for that offense was that he and two codefendants had decided to find a drug dealer to rob because, as Victor explained, they had been to the movies, had then started drinking, and saw that their "money was gettin' a little low." During the robbery, his male codefendant carried the gun and Victor went through the victim's pockets while their female codefendant stayed in the car. He said that before the robbery "you wanna feel more dominant." As Victor described it, "I guess your testosterone's buildin' up."

By describing his mental preparation for the robbery with phrases such as wanting to feel more dominant and building up his testosterone, Victor seemed to be connecting his violence with key aspects of traditional masculinity. When I asked if he felt anything for the armed robbery victims, either the previous times when he was just a lookout or this time when he was an active participant, Victor explained, "No. You can't. You're not supposed to," because that would just "make you feel bad." He said, "You gotta have a 'don't care' attitude. That's how you have to go about it." When I asked whether that attitude became natural or whether he had to make himself have it, Victor said, "For me, I just don't care." After hearing that both he and the victim were young African American boys from the same city, I asked Victor whether he ever thought, "That could be me." His response was "No. You just don't care. You don't put that thought in your mind . . . At that time, you're not worried about that. You don't wanna even try to think about it. It doesn't even come into your brain."

Of course, as Leon candidly stated, it would not be useful to recognize feelings of empathy for one's victims since to do so would interfere with the project of robbing them. The only practical feeling rule for armed robbers is not to have any feelings about the victim. Yet Leon complicated his account by claiming that putting people in fear did not give him pleasure while at the same time acknowledging, "if I pull the gun and put them in fear, then I ain't gotta do nothin' with the gun. It does make me feel good to know that they gotta fear me now," but this is because "only a stupid person fights me then." According to Leon, the power of the gun to make the victim turn over his possessions without a fight was gratifying, although putting victims in fear was not pleasurable for its own sake. If Leon's account can be taken at face value, he describes a somewhat more nuanced emotional experience of armed robbery than does Nate, who simply says he "loves" committing robberies for the power as well as the money and doesn't feel right if he's not doing it. Combining Leon's account of the feelings that impelled him to commit robberies with the feelings that he, Sam, and Victor described toward victims, it appears that having a gun enabled Leon to accomplish the robbery with a minimum of effort—that is, he did not have to beat the person up in order to take his money as he said he needed to do before using a gun. For him, the power of the gun was that by showing it during a robbery he did not have to use additional force. From his point of view, it reduced the amount of interaction he needed to have with the victim.

In their retrospective accounts, participants seemed able to call up and reflect upon their remembered emotional states while at the same time reporting a minimal concern for what their victims experienced. Victor drew connections between his own conception of masculinity and the dominant physicality of armed robbery when he explained both that he feels "a little more masculine" when he has a gun and that, in preparing for a robbery, "you wanna feel more dominant; I guess your testosterone's buildin' up." He seemed to view the violence he was about to commit as an expression of his masculinity. Some other participants explicitly rejected any connection between masculinity and either guns or violence. Anderson argues that the concept of "manhood" for those on the street implies precisely such physicality and ruthlessness,[35] and that the armed robbery in particular provides a rich site for the playing out of issues of power, respect, and alienation.[36] Hecht found the same dynamic to be present among the street children of Brazil when "a young adolescent explained to [him] with a certain tone of pleasure, 'We ask people for money and they say "I don't have anything." You point a .38 at them and then you see how fast they come up with some.'"[37] For an alienated adolescent in the United States or Brazil, a gun can provide the power to compel at least compliance with a demand for money, if not respect. Without a gun, the same person may feel that he has no power, no respect, and no way to get money.

## Doing Violence, Doing Gender, and Doing Emotion

Participants' expressed absence of compassionate feelings for their victims raises several issues, including the gendered nature of emotion. Emotion, of course, has long been viewed as highly gendered, at least in Western cultures, and emotional gendering is viewed as suiting men for violence and women for nurturing. As Stephanie Shields (2002) has pointed out, gendering of emotion was first described as biological in origin.[38] As the fields of psychology and sociology emerged in the nineteenth century, an evolutionary basis was ascribed to men's more violent, less sympathetic emotional constitutions: "In the course of the struggles for existence among wild tribes those tribes survived in which the men were not only powerful and courageous, but aggressive, unscrupulous, intensely egoistic. Necessarily, then, the men of the conquering races which gave origin to the civilized races, were men in whom the brutal characteristics were dominant."[39]

Brutality and unscrupulousness were thus associated in early sociological literature with masculine survival through the evolutionary course. While these characteristics are not overtly approved for men who live in contemporary Western societies, they remain associated with masculinity rather than femininity. Today, however, many theorists view both gender identities and emotional identities as socially constructed rather than biologically given.[40] Children are seen as being socialized into their gender identities as well as their racial, ethnic, and class identities. As Herbert Spencer argued more than a century ago, an emotional identity is still associated with one's gender and may be associated with one's race and class as well, although Shields suggests that this has not been as well researched.[41] Today, race, place, and class may combine to forge a particular emotional identity among both male and female adolescents, with the result that violence is now considered to be more common or normative even among young women in these same underresourced inner-city communities of color.[42]

Young men have many models to draw upon when learning to "do emotion." For the young men who participated in this study, those models are likely to be men of color who live in low-income urban neighborhoods and media representations of men in similar environments. Mothers, too, as well as peers, teach boys what emotions are appropriate.[43] Messerschmidt cites bell hooks's description of how her brother was socialized into masculine behavior and emotion: "In our southern black patriarchal home, being a boy meant learning to be tough, to mask one's feelings, to stand one's ground and fight."[44] Perhaps it would be appropriate to say that some young men are socialized out of certain emotions, and the question remains whether they simply mask these emotions, deny them, or eradicate them.

One participant recalled that when he was 11 or 12 years old he began to play a game his group called "knock-out." In this game, the group of boys would select a victim of approximately their own age, hit him, and take whatever he had in his pockets. If the first assailant's punch did not knock the boy out, the other members of the group would take turns hitting him until the boy lost consciousness. Often the victims would have no money at all, but getting money was not necessarily the point because, as Sam said, "that was fun to us." From this game the boys progressed to beating up homeless men who were sleeping on the street as well as other "crackheads" and "fiends." Next for Sam came armed robberies with borrowed guns, and finally robberies with his own gun. In this way, Sam was socialized into a particular form of violent masculinity whose performance left little room for empathizing with victims. The same participant, who said he had shot at a lot of people, responded this way when I asked whether he thought his shots had ever hit anybody: "I think I had a couple people's mothers crying in the hospital a couple of days."

Significantly, he reserved his compassion for the boys' mothers rather than for the victims themselves. (This compassion for women is congruent with some participants saying categorically that they never robbed women, and none admitting to doing so, probably because robbing women was also disfavored as "unmasculine.")[45] Discussing the armed robbery for which he was currently incarcerated, Sam first told me that he did not feel anything for the victim because it was not his intention to hurt him "as long as he give it up." He initially volunteered that he probably would not have fired his gun even if the victim had resisted, but reconsidering, he amended his response to say, "I ain't gonna lie to you, I probably would have shot him." Far from resisting, the black male victim, who was texting on his cell phone as he exited the train station, began to cry when Sam pointed a gun at him and asked him, "Do you want to die?" He turned his entire wallet over to Sam, who did not then realize that the victim could identify him even in a ski mask because they had a mutual friend.

Staying true to his "street guy" persona throughout our interview, Sam maintained that if he were ever robbed he would decline to identify his assailant to the police and take his "revenge" upon the robber himself. Shields considers the social meaning of emotion to be about telling the boys from the girls.[46] She argues that as boys perform their gender and emotion identities they learn through their social interactions that the "tender emotions" of sympathy and pity are associated with women. Moreover, as Candace West and Don Zimmerman argue (2009), the interactional perspective on the ways in which people "do gender" can be expanded to help us understand how gender, race, and class can all be viewed as a "social doing" that structures how we "do difference."[47] Particularly in the case of young men of color who are forging their masculine identities in the streets, it appears that they are socialized into violence partly by being schooled in how they should feel about violence. Participants' positive feelings about violent activities showed that, for them, violence could be described as fun as well as instrumental. Like guns and armed robbery, violence in general could fulfill many roles for these young men.

## Violence with, and on Behalf of, Others

Producing violence, for example, was something participants did for the benefit of family members as well as for themselves, often in their role as protectors. Xavier was currently incarcerated for an offense committed with a sawed-off shotgun. He said the episode began as an attempt to intimidate an older man of around 19 or 20 who was bothering his "little cousin." Xavier's cousin, with whom Xavier lived, had complained to him that a local drug dealer kept approaching her with sexual overtures while she was on her way to school. Xavier, also a drug dealer, recalled, "I was supposed to scare him with the shotgun," but the attempt was unsuccessful. After Xavier displayed the unloaded shotgun and told the man to leave his cousin alone, the man simply called Xavier some names and then, when Xavier pointed the gun at him, "smacked it down to hit me." The incident evolved first into a fistfight, and then the older man produced a small bat. The man was knocked down and, in the scuffle, his chain and cell phone fell to the ground. The event ended as an armed robbery because Xavier and his friend took the chain and phone before they left. Although Xavier volunteered that he did in fact engage in the practice of robbing drug dealers, he was emphatic that on this occasion "it wasn't supposed to be a robbery, though, and that was the whole thing!"

From Xavier's perspective, this violent event was composed of several elements but did not seem to him like an armed robbery because he did not enter the interaction with the intention of taking the man's property by force. It was important to Xavier to emphasize to me that robbery was not what this incident was about. The completed event demonstrates, however, the many different functions that violence can serve even in one interaction.

Xavier had armed himself with a sawed-off shotgun before approaching the older man in an effort to look formidable when he warned the man to stay away from his cousin. He wished to be taken seriously and expected the shotgun to help in this presentation. Xavier's bid to be recognized as a powerful protector through a threat of violence, however, was rejected by the man and Xavier then felt obligated to fight him in order to gain or retain some respect. Certainly, the alternative of retreating would have left not only his cousin but also Xavier in a worse position than when he started. Before the fight ended, the other man had produced a bat and Xavier evidently enlisted his friend, whom he had brought along as backup, to assist him in subduing his adversary. As Xavier told the story, the man's chain was broken when Xavier grabbed him by the neck to throw him to the ground, and the cell phone fell out during the same struggle. Having been insulted by the man he had hoped to intimidate, Xavier could not resist punctuating the interaction by seizing the man's chain and phone as he departed. While, in the context of the entire interaction, this parting gesture may have been seen by Xavier as equivalent to kicking sand in the man's face, the power dynamic became the same as that in any robbery. Xavier had ultimately overpowered the man by force and taken his property, and even he later recognized that, as the event unfolded, it had eventually acquired all the legal elements of an armed robbery. Yet violence to protect another, violence to retaliate for an insult, violence to overpower someone who had attempted to hit him with a bat, and finally to prove that he had done so by taking his property are all implicated in this episode.

A parallel account of violence on behalf of a female family member was provided by Kevin, who was incarcerated for beating another young man about the head with a gun. However, he also described an earlier offense, without a gun, for which he had not been arrested. Kevin explained how, on that occasion, he had had to settle for assaulting a female proxy when the man he wanted to assault was not readily available: "Well, he had hit my sister, and I went to his baby mom house, but he wasn't there, and that was when I beat his baby mom up." Kevin was the oldest male in his household at the time and felt it was incumbent upon him to avenge a wrong done to a female member of his family, a norm Adrian Nicole LeBlanc had described in *Random Family* (2003).[48] Despite his inability to locate his intended target, Kevin had successfully demonstrated that no one could hit his sister with impunity.

Likewise, Mark described the attempted murder for which he was adjudicated as a preemptive strike on his younger brother's behalf. Mark said he had stabbed a boy of about his own age, 17, because the boy said he wanted to fight Mark's brother, a middle school student. Although that offense had been committed with a knife, Mark said he had purchased his first gun when he was 15 and would often carry a gun if he anticipated trouble. He spoke—without directly implicating himself—of gang fights where his gang would use every kind of weapon from fists to bats, bottles, chains, knives, and guns to injure their opponents. He had suffered a broken ankle during one fight after being kicked while he was already on the ground. Mark said he did not believe in displaying a gun simply in an attempt to scare somebody off: "As far as takin' a gun out . . . If you're gonna take somethin' out, you're gonna use it. Otherwise, what's the point?" Mark denied feeling any remorse on occasions when he did use a gun, although he declined to go into specifics about particular shootings. Asked what he felt after using a gun, he answered, "Nuttin', really. I didn't feel nuttin'."

He said he had become involved with his gang first by socializing with them and going to parties and then they started fighting together. Mark, who had come to New Jersey from Mexico with his family, placed a high value on the mutual ties of loyalty and trust he experienced within his largely Latino gang and said his gang would sometimes initiate fights "because other people thought they were tough, and we'd, like, put 'em in their place, I guess."

## Gang Violence

Ten out of 25 participants considered themselves to be gang members while an additional young man viewed himself as merely "affiliated" but not technically a member of a gang. Each one said he had joined his gang while on the street and not while in custody. This study was not focused on gang violence as such, and much of the violence that may have taken place within a gang context is discussed in other sections that deal more directly with my research questions, such as how and why guns were acquired, how they were used, and how they made participants feel. Moreover, many participants who identified as gang members declined to discuss their gang activities because of group norms that discouraged such discussion. Nonetheless, several participants spoke of matters that seemed to emanate from the gang ethos, and I discuss them separately here. Not surprisingly, their remarks allude to violence by one group against another group as well as group norms that encouraged violence toward outsiders and loyalty to fellow gang members.

Sam belonged to a gang called Mob Piru but declined to say why he had joined or to discuss its activities. He said he had shot at a lot of people but never got caught for it. He was currently incarcerated for an armed robbery with a gun. Sam preferred not to provide details of his gang-related shootings, asking rhetorically, "What can somebody do to me for something they don't know about?" He nevertheless obliged me by providing the example of an occasion when he and his friends left a party and "somebody start shootin' at us! . . . When we came outside and people started shootin', we just started shootin', too . . . Kill or be killed."

Upon seeing my reaction to this statement, Sam emphatically assured me that I would have done the same thing under the circumstances: "No! I'm telling you, if you were out on the streets, and you were chillin' in the hood, and you got a gun in your hand, I'm telling you. You might say that now, but if somebody start shooting at you, you'll shoot back." I had no doubt that I was listening to the voice of experience and recognized that Sam had attempted to normalize some of his own previous instances of producing gun violence for me, albeit with the use of several big "ifs" required to put me in exactly the same context.

On the other hand, Thomas, a member of the Bloods, had decided after reflection while in custody that many of the times he had shot at people were merely attempts to impress others or, even worse in his eyes, to prove to himself that he was tough enough: "I was always tryin' to prove myself. If I wasn't tryin' to prove myself to somebody else, I was tryin' to prove myself to myself . . . that I was a gangster."

While the views Thomas expressed to me could well have been characterized as penitent reconstructions, he indeed provided one example of a time when he had shot at people that seemed frivolous at best. He said the first time he had fired at someone without provocation he was in the company of his cousin and others who were discussing a gang-related "beef" and everybody was showing off their guns. Thomas, unimpressed by the guns the others had, said he was displaying his Glock .40 "for everybody to look at, and see how big it is," when one of his companions pointed out a group of people across the street standing in front of a store. These people were "the opposite group of people that we didn't like," and Thomas, feeling that he had been put on the spot, "started shootin', the crowd started runnin', and they start shootin' back." This episode provides an example of guys bonding over guns and competing for status in a friendly (among each other) way, but as Thomas acknowledged, it culminated in his feeling the need, whether to impress himself or others, to shoot at the "opposite group."

Thomas next shot at somebody because of his gang's involvement in the drug trade. As Thomas described his position in the gang at that time, "I was holdin' a little bit of power with the gang . . . I was high up; I could tell people what to do." One of the subordinate members that he was paying to sell drugs for him failed to turn over the proceeds from the drug sales, and Thomas said he shot at this person but did not hit him.

Finally, Thomas said he had shot at a member of the Crips with whom he also had a dispute over money. Thomas claimed that his shots were intended as warning shots: "Yeah, I wasn't, I wasn't really shootin' at him to hit him or kill him; at the time I didn't really know the rules of the game. The rules of the game is, if you draw on somebody, you gotta kill 'im. Because if you don't, they're gonna come after you, and that could be YOUR life. I was shootin' to let him know that I was there, like, that it could happen, any time you think I'm not around, I'm around."

Thomas's naiveté on this issue ended when the other person did in fact come after him, and the outcome of that encounter will be described in the next chapter. Evidently, Thomas later internalized what he had called "the rules of the game," because when I asked whether he had ever hit anyone when he shot at them, he availed himself of his option not to talk about it.

Loyalty ties, of course, are another important part of gang violence, as Mark pointed out when he said he knew his fellow members of the gang would be right there for him if he called upon them, and that they in turn could count on him. Tim, a member of the Bloods, alluded to similar ties of loyalty when he explained that the difference between a friend and an associate is that a friend is loyal to you, cares about you, and would be by you whether you were right or wrong.

## Many Roles of Violence

Philippe Bourgois (2012) described how, during the course of his research in an inner-city Latino community, he witnessed violence among boys and adult men together serving as a kind of glue to bind members of the community to each other. In what Bourgois called "the moral economy of violence," community violence, sometimes in the form of group fights, functioned as a form of social capital that was both instrumental and expressive, permitting men and boys alike to draw upon their ready reserves of anger to enforce community norms and to defend themselves, their families, and their friends from insults or injury.[49] His findings suggest that the boys and young men he studied were socialized into public, or communal, forms of violence in an organic way, absorbing this form of violence and being absorbed by it as they observed and interacted with the men of their neighborhood. This dynamic is similar to the ways in which participants often acquired guns through neighborhood "old heads" and shows how an environment suffused with both gun violence and other forms of violence becomes normalized for young men. While the mechanism of acquiring these street values is consistent with traditional social learning theory,[50] the process Bourgois describes, of boys being socialized into a form of community violence that is viewed as adaptive by much of the neighborhood, helps to illuminate why young men find such violence to be so captivating. Similarly, when "old heads" both modeled gun violence and groomed young men of the neighborhood by helping them to acquire guns, participants found it both natural and easy to be inducted into a street lifestyle where gun violence was pervasive.

It is clear from participants' accounts that engaging in violence served many functions in their life worlds. Among these were fun and excitement, bonding, making money through robberies or employing violence to enforce financial obligations, enforcing respect from others and shoring up one's self-image, and protection, both in a conventionally defensive way and also broadly conceived as in the context of gang fighting. This violence could occur with or without guns, but guns added a symbolic or mythic gloss to violent activities, in addition to rendering them more lethal. On the basis of participants' accounts, both gun use in particular and violence in general can be viewed as pathways utilized by participants to make their way out of some of the constraints they experienced. Violence, like guns, could convey masculine power, status, agency, and control in a world where these qualities were otherwise in short supply.

As participants often emphasized, however, the outcomes of these processes are not determined purely by structural constraints. While the street lifestyle may often be the most visible path before them, these young people emphasized that they have agency and can choose different lines of action, including whether to participate in or avoid the life of the street. As an adolescent girl in Nikki Jones's *Between Good and Ghetto* (2012) put it, "It's not where you live, it's how you live."[51] Yet one participant, while acknowledging that there were "good things" he could have done instead of engaging in delinquent behavior, summarized his experience of his neighborhood by saying, "you gotta search with a fine magnifying glass to find something good to do." For at least these participants, the "good things" they could have been doing were either less visible, less attractive, or both.

### *Anger and Alienation: Present but Not Accounted For*

Anger, alienation, and racism were not among the subjects that these young men cared to discuss in explicit terms. While several participants offered to recount specific violent incidents prompted by anger, the anger they described was of the sort that arose out of situated interpersonal interactions. Participants rarely discussed the more generalized anger and alienation often described in the literature. Occasionally, however, glimpses of alienation appeared, as when Ernie described returning to selling drugs after being fired from his job because he felt that, at that time, selling drugs was what he was good at. A similar feeling may have been present during the robbery for which he had been previously incarcerated and the many other robberies in which he said he had participated. In Ernie's description of his "demoralized" state after losing his job, one can hear echoes of the strain created by the discrepancy between his goals and his socially structured opportunities.[52]

The ways in which socially structured opportunities were related to race and class was a topic that few participants discussed, yet it seems likely that many, if not all, were well aware of such processes. While Quinto simply compared his own situation unfavorably with that of people who lived in the suburbs and had money for things like vacations, Tim had done a great deal of reading in the three years that he had been incarcerated and was well versed in the politicized discourse of race and class inequalities. The extent to which Tim's preincarceration thoughts about social inequalities might have influenced his self-described "gangbanging" is unclear, but Howard Stevenson has pointed out that "the idea that urban African American youth may be angry (e.g., pissed) should not be a surprise given their social experiences."[53] They "often feel misinterpreted, disrespected, and angry about their life possibilities," or "Missed, Dissed, and Pissed," as he called his 1997 article. In the study on which that article was based, Stevenson discovered that his sample of low-income African American youth, who were students in an urban community social skills development program, did in fact score higher than a nationally standardized sample of adolescents in self-reported anger experience and expression.[54]

Pedro Noguera (2003) found it difficult to discern whether race or class was the more salient feature for African American boys' anger. In "The Trouble with Black Boys," he argued that structure, culture, and individual choice and agency are all important in adolescent development.[55] Noguera believed that black males, evidently without regard to class, learned at an early age that by presenting a tough exterior it was easier to avoid threats or attacks.[56] Based on a good deal of experience, he also speculated that the treatment to which black males are subjected in school or on the streets may, as he put it, "Elicit postures of aggression and ferocity toward the world." Noguera and Stevenson thus concur that the negative reception that young African American males receive from the world at large may contribute to their negative outlook and response to the world.

Participants, on the other hand, tended to place the origins of such feelings squarely in the intimately interpersonal realm, rather than in the macrosystems of broad social attitudes or forces. Kevin believed his angry feelings stemmed from being beaten by his mother's former boyfriend as well as from seeing his mother beaten by the same man. Norman, who used to get into lots of fights, said he "was always a happy boy, playing around, playful person," and could not explain why he had grown into an adolescent who would fight at the slightest verbal provocation: "And I just got older and I had anger problems; I don't know where that come from." While he felt he had benefited from techniques he had learned in anger-management programs, he could not offer any insight into the source of his violent behavior.

Thomas, rather than connecting his robbing of drug dealers to any angry feelings, made a point of saying he cultivated a calm mental state in preparation for a robbery: "That's why I like to go in and do things calm, with no problems. 'Cause if I go to rob somebody and I'm angry . . . I'm gonna end up doin' somethin' to that person. And so, believe it or not, I really don't like violence. Sometimes you just gotta send out somebody a lesson to learn. It's more of a physical thing, 'cause once I feel my body gettin' hot, and once I feel my heart start beatin' fast, it's just, there's no thinkin' after that. There's no stoppin' me."

Thomas's point was that the calm and deliberate state of mind he needed for his robberies was incompatible with the "no thinkin'" state he experienced when he was angry. He spoke in general terms of times when he had shot at people in anger, failing to stop and think before doing so. When asked to recall one of those occasions and consider what it would have taken for him to have walked away instead of shooting, Thomas answered, "It had

crimes such as armed robbery facilitated the execution of these projects. Some participants had been socialized into violence as young boys and guns simply expanded their repertoire. Others found that they became emotionally addicted to the thrill of robbing people and likened the feeling to a drug addiction. Several participants described the unfolding of conflict-based violent gun events in detail, emphasizing the interactional and contingent aspects of each step leading to the ultimate violent outcome. Not only gun violence but violence in general proved to be rewarding for participants in many ways. It was often a means to an economic end but it also served as a way to defend or restore personal, family, or peer-group honor, a source of fun and excitement, or a way for young men to bond. In an environment where participants often felt powerless, violence in general and gun violence in particular produced gratifying feelings of power.

# CHAPTER 5

# Consumed by Violence
## Negative Outcomes, Uncertain Outlooks

Like, people that I robbed in the past, they still look for me, so I never walk around without a gun, and I never walk around without a vest.

—Leon

I have dreams all the time that when I go out, I'm gonna get killed . . . I always have to watch my back . . . There's times when I've left my gun in the house, I've left my vest in the house, and just went outside to play basketball with my friends . . . It felt so good, just to be laughin' and playin' . . . That every car that go by, I don't have to look, or every time somebody walk by, I have to look. I mean it felt good. I just wish I could have chose the other life. Gettin' money the easy way, it's really not easy. To have to be on point 24–7. I'd rather just sit at a desk and not have to worry about nothin', and just type all day, and know I can go home, and know I'm gonna be all right . . . I lost so many people, just livin' this life.

—Thomas

The participants in this study described many negative outcomes of their interactions and activities in the streets. Of course, one experience they all shared was the loss of their freedom during the term of their incarceration. As several participants expressed, they had missed out on important teenage experiences that could never be replaced, such as proms and graduations with their childhood friends.

But as Leon and Thomas explained, another outcome of their violent offending was that even when they had been free, they felt trapped. They lived in fear, during their waking and sleeping hours, of enemies they had made on the street. This chapter will explore various negative outcomes described by participants as attending their lifestyles. As young men of the street, gun carriers, and violent offenders, participants found themselves incarcerated and facing uncertain futures. Their experiences and perspectives show the lived processes underlying previous research findings. Gun carrying, gang involvement, engaging in delinquency, and adhering to the code of the street all helped young men in the streets to feel less fearful (at least initially) while increasing their actual risk of harm. These young men took control of their circumstances and environments in ways that they thought would improve their life worlds. While they did not tend to narrate themselves as victims, the actions they took often resulted in their becoming victims in a variety of ways. As most participants would be returning to the same environments from which they came, they and the Juvenile Justice Commission staff were aware that redefining themselves in a more positive way would likely prove challenging.

## Shot for a Reason

One of the consequences of producing violence for these young men was suffering actual or anticipated retaliation. As Victor said in an earlier chapter, once you make an enemy on the street, "It's never over," "they're gonna wanna kill you," and "you're gonna end up shootin' somebody." Participants often learned that the aggrieved party might retaliate in kind, or by escalating the level of violence. The three participants who had suffered gunshot wounds all reported being "shot for a reason" in the accounts that follow.

Thomas was shot as he returned home one night, despite wearing a bulletproof vest and watching his back, as he described in the opening quotation. One bullet's impact was blunted by his vest, but the other one wounded him in the leg. He had previously fired at his assailant because of a dispute over money, although Thomas maintained that he had not intended to hit the other man on that occasion. As Thomas learned, the victim did not take being fired at lightly, and waited for an opportunity to catch Thomas as he was walking home: "So when I look up, I hear bullets goin'. I hear a gun goin' off, and I just see a blue light comin' out the gun. I got hit in the back once, but I had the vest on, so I was all right . . . He hit me in my leg, so I was gonna get to the house, but my whole, my jeans was just full of blood . . . I called my girlfriend, her sister's a nurse, so she came over, she took it out . . . and she stitched me up herself. I had a bruised back for like a week."

Kevin likewise framed the gunshot wounds he received in terms of previous exchanges in his social world. He sustained injuries to both his leg and his jaw during the shooting he described, and pointed out the small scar on his jaw. He explained what led up to the shooting:

> **DM:** So uh, what was that about?
> **KEVIN:** Well, he had hit my sister, and I went to his baby mom house, but he wasn't there, and that was when I beat his baby mom up.
> **DM:** Okay, so he had hit your sister, you went to his baby mom house lookin' for him, he wasn't there, so you beat her up.
> **KEVIN:** Yeah.
> **DM:** So then he came back and, did he ambush you when he shot you?
> **KEVIN:** No, I was sitting out on my steps, and I seen somebody walking up . . . and he came from the side, I seen him, and I went to go get up, I felt something hard pop against me, and against my leg, and I fell.

Kevin suffered "a little fracture" of his jaw and did not seem surprised that he had had to pay a price for beating up the mother of his assailant's child. Rather, it was all part and parcel of the protective masculinity he had assumed, in his incarcerated father's absence, by punishing (via proxy) the man who had hit his sister. When subpoenaed to court, Kevin declined to identify his assailant and the case was accordingly dismissed. Kevin believed that it would not have been right for "a person like me, a gangbanger, a gangster" to "snitch," "so I just left it like that." He evidently viewed this matter as a purely personal dispute. Identifying his assailant in court would not have been in keeping with the spirit of the entire social exchange. Kevin knew that he had been shot "for a reason."

Nick, the other participant who showed me his gunshot wounds, had been shot in the chest and upper arms. He said he sold drugs, primarily crack cocaine, and while he did not care to discuss the details of his own gun victimization, said it happened because of what he was doing at the time. He offered that "what goes around comes around," and said he had brought the shooting upon himself. He was incarcerated for possession of a gun that had been found in a car in which he was one of several passengers, but he did not acknowledge his culpability for that offense.

All three of these shooting victims were drug dealers, and they were all incarcerated for gun offenses. Thomas was arrested following an armed robbery of some drug dealers in their home, where several shots were fired; Kevin had hit another man over the head with a gun during a dispute over drug territory; and Nick was charged with possession of a gun in a car. Their accounts put flesh and bone on the quantitative studies, discussed in the next section, that document the high rates of violent victimization among young drug dealers and gun carriers.

While there are many victims of random gun violence, each of these young men believed he had been shot for reasons arising out of his interactions and activities in the street. This often gave rise to a belief on the part of participants that these matters were not appropriate for police or court intervention. As Nate put it, "I don't want nobody to tell on me, and I'm not going to tell on nobody else. One rule that everybody—whether anyone came from the hood or not—tellin' is not the way to go . . . If I'm out there committin' crimes and stealin' cars, anything that I'm not supposed to be doin' that's wrong; breakin' the law—if I'm breaking the law, obviously doin' something to harm other people, I'd certainly deserve it if I got shot."

Participants named at least four reasons for not "snitching," which Xavier stated carries an "ugly" connotation. Two were alienation from police or the criminal justice system and fear of violent retaliation by the criminals or their partisans. The other reasons were fear of social disapproval because providing information to the police is not viewed as acceptable by many of those in their community, and a related belief in street justice—that is, people are generally "shot for a reason," as Nate said.

Based on the participants' accounts as a whole, there seem to be at least three levels of exposure to violent victimization in the neighborhoods where these young men reside. First, there is what participants referred to as the "normal" exposure to random violence, including gun violence, to which young men who grew up in these neighborhoods seemed to become acclimated, and that did not prompt them to acquire guns. Next is the increased exposure of the young men who are "in the streets" and who may be targeted in an impersonal way, such as the drug dealer who may be targeted for robbery because he is viewed as likely to have money or drugs. I argue that this type of exposure did prompt participants to acquire guns. Finally, there is the exposure of the person who is known to produce violence, whether by robbing people, shooting at people, or hurting people's family members. These young men are likely already to have guns, and are targeted for violence in a more personal way, often in retaliation for violent offenses they have committed in the past. Others are literally "gunning" for them.

Tim explained to me how this type of gun violence feeds on itself: "You shot at me, so now we're shootin' at each other . . . I just know that you tried to kill me, and it's not even now . . . Next time I see you, it's on." Wilkinson (2003) found that, among violent events she categorized as "with guns," "with other weapons," or "with no weapons," her respondents considered retaliation to be most likely following violent events that involved guns.[1] It is not surprising that young men in the street lifestyle who have been shot, shot at, or threatened with a gun are the most likely to consider retaliation necessary or appropriate.

## Victimization in Offending Populations

It is notable that 3 of the 25 participants in this study were shot before turning 18, but this number merely invites further inquiry into the rates at which offenders experience violent victimization. In a similar "snapshot" study published in 1995, John May, a physician, discovered that 26 percent of adult men admitted to the Cook County Correctional Facility in Chicago had experienced prior gunshot wounds.[2] Of the sample studied by May, 70.8 percent were African American and another 10 percent were either Mexican American or Puerto Rican.[3] Dr. May also noted that in addition to those wounded offenders who survived to be arrested again, in large urban areas anywhere from 44 to 67 percent of homicide victims had prior criminal records. May added that most of those victims were young men, and most were killed with guns.

Other researchers have studied violent victimization among juvenile offenders. A longitudinal study of Pittsburgh youth found an even more pronounced impact on young African American men. Rolf Loeber, Mary DeLamatre, George Tita, and colleagues (1999) found that 100 percent of the young men killed by guns during the course of their study, and 90.5 percent of those wounded by guns, were African American.[4] The family backgrounds and offense histories of the victimized Pittsburgh youth are in many ways similar to those of the young men depicted in the previous chapters, and the authors' findings suggest not only that offending leads to victimization but, more specifically, that gun carrying leads to gun victimization. The young men from Pittsburgh who were shot or killed were most likely to have mothers who were single (88 percent versus 66 percent), unemployed (43 percent versus 24 percent), poorer, and receiving public assistance than those children who were not victimized.[5] Likewise, 84 percent of participants in the current study were raised in female-headed households. While I did not determine how many of these women were unemployed or receiving public assistance, the pathway described by many participants was that, with a poor single mother or mother figure, employed or not, the young men felt pressure to get into the street and make money, which led to their acquisition of a gun. The typical participant was raised by a mother who was struggling financially, as were the victims in the Pittsburgh study. (As discussed in Chapter 2, the participants in the current study tended to be ill at ease when discussing family finances and, since they had signed on for a study about guns and not poverty, I considered it an unfair intrusion to question them too directly about their mother's sources of income. If a participant opened that door, I would go through it, but I did not ask each participant where the family's money came from.) The Pittsburgh victims tended to be drug sellers and to carry guns. Of the New Jersey participants, at least 68 percent reported selling drugs, and all participants except one either admitted having a gun, was adjudicated delinquent for having a gun, or was adjudicated delinquent for an armed robbery where his codefendant carried a gun, although this summary includes one participant who committed an armed robbery with a BB gun. The Pittsburgh victims were killed in gang-related or drug-related disputes, or as the result of the escalation of a previous conflict. Four of the nine deceased Pittsburgh victims for whom there were police records were armed at the time of their deaths. As the authors concluded from these results, "The data suggest that these delinquent activities led to victimization . . . In short, the proximal events leading to death tended to be serious delinquent activities."[6]

Among the most disturbing aspects of the above findings is that the children raised in the most economically stressed homes were the ones most likely to be killed by gunfire. These young men were all African American. The nexus among race, poverty, drug-selling, guns, and the death of young men leaps starkly from these data. The Pittsburgh findings—which I believe are relevant for the New Jersey youth, including the Latino participants—make it easy to understand why Thomas said, "I lost so many people, just livin' this life." At least 14 of the New Jersey participants had friends or family members who had been shot. At one of the transitional programs I visited, the superintendent mentioned that two of the program's graduates had been shot and killed a few days earlier in two separate incidents on the same day. The events were believed to have been gang related in a city where gangs were organized around the drug trade.

Several months later, a participant who was confined in another area of the state for an armed robbery reflected on his philosophy, shared by many participants, that "everything happens for a reason." When he said he believed he had been locked up for a reason, I asked what he thought the reason was, and he replied, "A lot of things been happening. You never know. One of them bodies out there could have been mine." As he himself had declared, if he were the victim of a robbery, he would not leave the matter in the hands of the police but would take his own revenge on the robber. He seemed worried that one of his victims might likewise prefer violent retaliation to legal recourse. This participant, Sam, was well aware that his violent offending could result in his own death and considered his incarceration as a sort of reprieve from that risk, at least for a time.

Participants sometimes described their time incarcerated as "time out," and it seemed that they too perceived that, at the least, their dangerous trajectories had been temporarily interrupted, if not changed. While weapon carrying, especially gun carrying, made many of the participants in the current study feel less vulnerable and more agentive, the evidence is persuasive that these young men, at least those who engaged in aggressive behaviors, greatly increased their risk of violent victimization by carrying guns.[7]

## Feeling Less Fearful, Being Less Safe

Participants said they joined gangs for social reasons rather than for protection, but they likely increased their chances of being injured or killed by doing so, just as they did by carrying guns. Previous research findings concerning gang participation and victimization parallel those regarding gun carrying and victimization. Dana Peterson, Terrance Taylor, and Finn-Aage Esbensen (2004) discovered that, even though a large proportion of the young men they studied who joined a gang said they did so for protection, their actual rate of victimization increased during their period of affiliation with the gang.[8] As the authors suggest, this is likely because youth who engage in offending behavior, such as gang-related activities, are often in situations where violence is likely to occur. Yet Chris Melde, Taylor, and Esbensen (2009) have also found that—just as with gun carrying—youth felt less fearful, while in fact they were more likely to suffer violent victimization after joining gangs.[9] It appears, as the authors suggest with regard to gang membership, that both having a gun and being in a gang provide more emotional than physical protection for young men in the street, making them feel either safer or less fearful, while at the same time making them more likely to be harmed.

Eight of the ten participants in the current study who identified themselves as gang members said they joined for social reasons, stating that they were already friends or family members of the people in their gangs so it seemed like the thing to do, or looked up to members of that gang because "they were the coolest ones," and so on. One said he joined for "the love, the money, the drugs, the love." This participant was among several who said their gangs were organized around drug sales, which added an economic as well as a social reason for joining. None said they joined for protection. Nevertheless, many participants experienced their life worlds as significantly improved both by gun carrying and by gang involvement, and this perception tended to persist at the time of our interviews. Several participants stated that while they hoped to stay out of trouble upon their release, they would maintain their gang ties and membership, which they considered to be central to their identities. Keith, for example, said, "I am what I am as far as the gang, so I can't just say that I'm going to stop completely all my contact with them, 'cause I know that would be a lie." Thomas likewise maintained, "I mean, I'm ready to live life like I'm supposed to, it's just that, inside my head, I know I'm always gonna be Blood, and even if I tell people I'm not, in my head I'ma think, like, in reality, I know I am."

Gun carrying and gang membership aside, continuing delinquency itself has been found to decrease a young person's fears while increasing his risks. Chris Melde (2009) examined victimization perception and risk with delinquents in general, rather than gang members specifically. He found that "in the end, involvement in a delinquent lifestyle actually serves to decrease fear of victimization while increasing the actual likelihood of experiencing such an incident."[10] This finding is consistent with participant Kenneth's report that when he first started stealing cars and robbing people he had some hesitation, but the more he did it, the less he thought about the possible consequences to himself. When I asked whether he ever worried about his robbery victims attacking him with a weapon, he said he did not because "I was just livin' the life." When, despite their known dangers, a course of delinquency, gang membership, and gun carrying makes young men feel less rather than more fearful—at least in the short term—it becomes even more apparent why the lures of the street lifestyle are so strong. These young men "feel" powerful and protected when they are "livin' the life," even though they may be cognitively aware that they are increasing their risks. The tough presentations adopted by many of these young men also invite challenges by others similarly situated and similarly armed, which in turn leads to both more victimization and more violent offending.[11]

### Participants' Views on Their Dangerous Life Worlds

Although participants rarely talked about being fearful, their dangerous life worlds often left them in an uneasy place between hypervigilance and fatalism. The participant most literally in an uneasy place was Kilal, affiliated with the Crips but living in a neighborhood dominated by Bloods. He said, "I just watched my back, if they would see me going in and out the house . . . The projects was right across the street . . . so if I was on my way to the house, you could see me go in and out the house, though, so I would have certain times when I would come in and out of the house that I know there won't be anybody around that would see me coming."

Kilal's belief that he needed to sneak in and out of his own house in order to avoid harm from a rival gang was an extreme example, as most participants felt relatively safe within a limited area surrounding their homes. Kilal described his apartment as surrounded by members of a gang that would be likely to attack him, so he attempted to keep a low profile when entering and exiting his home. Other young men, however, while avoiding admissions of fear, spoke of some abiding concerns.

Tim and Mark mentioned the importance of loyalty and of having friends whom they could trust. Simultaneously, Tim seemed concerned that there might be no safe haven even among those he held close. He had differentiated between the terms *friends* and *associates*, saying friends would be with you whether you were right or wrong. Yet he also declared that "it can be your own friends are the ones that shoot you, kill you. Like the ones that know you the best are the one that get you, I'm sayin', and I was always told that, so that's what I used to go by." The fact that Tim's beloved stepfather had been shot and killed, as Tim presumed, by his associates in the drug trade, probably reinforced this lesson for him. Leon, too, while concerned about retaliation from people he had robbed, claimed he was also concerned about being shot by everyone else as well:

> LEON: From strangers, it could be ev—nowadays, it could be your friends that'll kill you. You never know. It could be a family member—I know somebody whose brother killed him, and friends kill friends all the time. So like the ones you keep close to you be the ones that do you in, so you gotta even watch out for them.
> DM: So you kind of feel that at any given time you could be shot by almost anybody?
> LEON: Anybody.

As expressed by Tim and Leon, this fear of violent injury even from friends suggests a complication to the process of social bonding, at least for these two participants. Norman, another participant, may have been alluding to something similar when he said he limited his circle of friends to two or three close ones in order to avoid "beef and drama." Similarly, Quinto, explaining the reason he bought his first gun, said, "I started to see, like, that people—you can't trust everybody you chill with." As Tim was in a gang while Leon, Norman, and Quinto were not, gang membership did not seem to eliminate the concern entirely.

## Anticipated Early Death

I explored the idea of present concerns versus future plans a little further with Tim, who had always done well in school and loved school sports, but had drifted away from school into the drug trade and "gangbanging." I wanted to know why he had not found the "stay-in-school" success narrative persuasive:

> DM: So I'm sure that people would say to you, like, "Stay in school, you'll get money down the road," but you didn't want it down the road.
> TIM: No. I couldn't wait 'til down the road. And down the road ain't promised, to tell you the truth. You know how people say, "Here today, gone

tomorrow"—you could be here today, gone today. You know what I'm say-ing? We could die at any minute, and that's the only thing we are promised in this lifetime—death. So uh.

**DM:** Did you really have that feeling that anything could happen to you at any time?

**Tim:** Yeah! Really, that's true! That's reality to anybody, rather it's from violence, murder, homicide, or heart attack or a stroke or somethin'. Anybody can die at any time. So I was always livin' with that state of mind. Like tomorrow is not promised.

Tim went on to describe how risky life was in his neighborhood, even for someone who was simply out walking his dog, and maintained that his view that he could die at any time affected his actions. His remarks raised the issue of whether his view that he could die at any time affected his offending, or if his offending colored his view of his chances of dying. The question of how the idea of anticipated early death affects young people's decision making has been the subject of considerable research. In their article "Might Not Be a Tomorrow," Timothy Brezina, Erdal Tekin, and Volkan Topalli (2009)[12] used both national survey data and interviews with active street offenders to study the relationship between this sense of "futurelessness" and youth crime. While the authors found both a strong and positive association between the two, they believed the causal order-ing is still somewhat unclear. While on the one hand it appears plausible that anticipated early death could result in what the authors call "a lack of investment in conventional pursuits, namely, those associated with delayed benefits, such as school or legitimate work," they point out that it is also possible that the increased risks to one's own personal safety inherent in offending may result in an increased belief in one's anticipated early death.[13] Tim's remarks about not being able to "wait until down the road" would seem to suggest the former view, while Thomas's statement that "livin' this life" (the life of an armed robber) had prompted constant nightmares about being killed, would support the latter view. Also, as Brezina, Tekin, and Topalli point out, anticipated early death may serve as another rationaliza-tion, or neutralization technique, to justify offending. Finally, both offend-ing and a belief in one's anticipated early death may mutually reinforce each other, resulting in a feedback loop.

The authors also suggested that a young person's acceptance of the pos-sibility of early death may enhance his fearlessness during risky criminal pursuits.[14] In this way, the knowledge of vulnerability can, paradoxically, lead to fearlessness, which provides a sense of freedom and (often criminal) agency. Brezina, Tekin, and Topalli likened the attitudes of their study participants to coping responses that arise during wartime, quoting war correspondent Robert Cox on "facing the daily threat of violent death": "Courage, I discovered while covering the 'dirty war' in Argentina, is a relatively simple matter of overcoming fear. I realized one day that I could deal with the idea that I would be killed, simply by accepting it as fact. The knot in my stomach loosened considerably after that. There was no reason to fear being killed once that reality had been accepted. It is fear itself that makes one afraid . . . Some Iraqi reporters explain that their ability to function is because they accept their inevitable date with death."[15]

A similar acceptance of the real possibility of violent death may be the best explanation for the fearlessness with which the New Jersey participants embraced their street activities. While it could be argued that they did not discuss their fear because it would have been incompatible with their masculine street presentations to do so, it seems more likely that, had they not found an acceptable way of dealing with the high risk of death inherent in their lifestyle, they would have abandoned their street pursuits in favor of something less fraught with danger. Even while participants spoke of a gun as making them feel that nobody could touch them, they articulated a cognitive awareness that this was not the case, occasionally pointing out that one can be killed when carrying a gun, or even two guns, as in the case of one participant's cousin. A gun seemed to provide more of an emotional "feeling" of invincibility than an actual belief that one could not be harmed and, combined with an acceptance of the knowledge that death was a possible outcome, gave many participants the fearlessness or "nerve" to engage in high-risk activities.

It is not difficult to understand how the belief that one is likely to die soon, whether accurate or not, can influence one's actions. To the extent that such a belief allows young men to embrace a violent lifestyle that often kills them, it can be compared to the concept of the self-fulfilling prophecy, prediction, or belief. Strictly speaking, while the self-fulfilling belief is defined as "producing the very circumstances erroneously assumed to exist,"[16] in this case the belief in anticipated early death may serve to exacerbate a genuine risk of early death by leading young men to disregard such risks due to a fatalistic belief that they are likely to die early anyway. Their perceptions may thus lead them into interacting with their environment in such a way that their belief becomes a fact. As Robert Merton explained, "If men define situations as real, they are real in their consequences."[17] Merton distinguished between the self-fulfilling prophecy as a sociological dynamic and as an individual psychological dynamic, but I would suggest that for young men like the participants in the current study the two dynamics may blend to create a disastrous outcome that exists at both the individual and sociological level, with each dynamic reinforcing the other. The relationship between individual vulnerability and agency parallels the relationship between social structure and agency, as the structural elements that result in the child's vulnerability—such as poverty, dangerous neighborhoods, a hostile world, racial or ethnic discrimination, and a lack of opportunity—may lead the youth into both offending and a belief in his early death. His actions thus make his dangerous environment even more dangerous for him.

Tim explained how he now viewed his encapsulation, to borrow a term from John Ogbu (2004),[18] in the world in which he grew up:

> Like, this is my own little theory. Like, what you know is what you're taught. We all come into this world as little babies, and we don't know anything but what our parents teach us and what we see . . . If you're born, and you're taught somethin', and that is all you know, which means you're BLIND to everything else—that is what you know. And that, eventually, is what you're gonna do. I'm sayin', if you was born, and your father or mother was to tell you strictly, "Sports, sports, sports," it's a good chance that you're gonna grow up and play some sports . . .'Cause that's really what you were taught, and that's all you know, and you just blind to everything else—that's what you eventually gonna do. Like, probably like 90 percent of the time, that's what you're gonna do.

Tim believed that growing up in his neighborhood had left him "blind" to other ways of living. He said he was now able to see that he had sold drugs and joined a gang because that was the life he saw all around him, including at home, with a stepfather who sold drugs.

The related idea of fatalism, which has been noted by Brezina, Tekin, and Topalli (2009), among others, seems to both reflect and shape participants' limited sense of agency to influence their life worlds. At one point, Luke explained his attraction to the street life by saying, "Some people like the good life, some people like the bad life." He was incarcerated for an armed robbery with a gun, saying he had committed many. He also sold drugs and was a member of the Bloods. When I invited him to consider whether any other kind of excitement might have satisfied him, he said he used to play football, "but I dropped out." He continued, "You can't do much about it" because "not many people like me make it." I tried to clarify whether he meant that there was something specific to him that led him to believe he wouldn't "make it" in football or whether he was speaking in more general terms:

> LUKE: I'm just sayin', like, people in gangs, doin' the things that I'm doin' out there, usually don't make it too far. Some of us don't even live past 25, like. Some do, some don't.
> DM: Well, does the idea of not living past 25 bother you?
> LUKE: I don't really know. I WANNA live past 25, but if I can't, I can't. If I don't, there's nuttin' I can do. The fact is, I didn't choose this life. This life chose me.
> DM: Do you really think that? That's a good way of putting it. Why do you think the life chose you?
> LUKE: Because, I don't know. Everything happens for a reason. You know.

Luke seemed to view his life as tightly circumscribed in terms of both longevity and opportunity. When I asked whether he believed there was anything that might have made things different, Luke echoed many of his fellow participants by saying, "If I had a father figure, then maybe," before trailing off. By declaring that "This life chose me," Luke seemed to suggest that fate had selected his path for him, and that he was powerless to change it: "There's nuttin' I can do."

Luke's remarks illuminate one reason communicating victimization risk to young gang members and armed robbers can be such a hard sell. As Melde suggested,[19] these young men must first be convinced that they have the power to influence their probability of being victims of violence, and that their fate has not already been fully determined by outside forces. The four participants who maintained that "everything happens for a reason" seemed prepared, in some respects at least, to accept whatever fate held in store for them. While this stoic outlook may have been adaptive for coping with some of their difficult life circumstances, it could not do much for them as an empowerment philosophy. In other words, it is important for these young men to believe that they are capable and competent social actors who can create safer social spaces for themselves by making decisions about their hours, locations, associates, and activities that will keep them more distant from violence, despite the structure and street culture that surround them. When many aspects of their lives conspire to convince them that they are powerless—except to commit crimes—this belief in itself may be difficult to attain.

Beyond the challenge of convincing young men that they can reduce their probability of violent victimization by turning away from the street lifestyle, there is another obstacle. The many boys who embrace the street life must also find or be persuaded that the law-abiding life is worth living, as the myriad rewards and gratifications of the street continue to seem more appealing than the alternatives available to them. As discussed in previous chapters, the "stickiness" of the street is difficult to overcome, and several armed robbers described being emotionally addicted to armed robbery. For many young men, the prospect of an early death while enjoying the street life's rewards is more palatable than the alternatives of having no income and little excitement, or a boring, low-paying job and no status.

## What Could Have Made a Difference?

Participants most frequently named two things they believed could have made a difference in their lives: growing up in a better neighborhood, and having a positive father figure. Although I did not ask all participants to consider what might have changed things, nine said that growing up in a different neighborhood would have helped, five cited having a dependable father or father figure, and four named both of these things. Having a job or having more money, staying in school and involved with school sports, and staying away from "that group" also were mentioned. Tim, who was being raised by a working mother who, by his description, seemed very caring, also believed being able to talk at length with an adult who was not exhausted or preoccupied would have been helpful:

> TIM: And another thing, though. See, when you grow up, they're, some people just need that counsel, like, somebody to talk to, because people don't got that, you know what I'm sayin'? People don't got—the truth is, people work, people got a life, people got bills to pay, come home from work tired, 'cause there's a lot of things people do in their lifetime, and they don't have a lot of time to actually sit there with their child and talk to 'em, see what I'm sayin'?

**DM:** Yep. Long, heavy talks.

**TIM:** Yeah. Long, heavy talks—emotional talks, you know what I mean? Because some people may be havin' thoughts and feelin' some type of way, but another person to express their feelings to, and sometimes that may be all that people need! I'm saying, they don't take that time, so that could be another thing wrong.

I asked Tim whether he believed a mother could fulfill this role:

**TIM:** I think, naw, I'm not gonna say that it would take a man. It could take a female, too, but I think a man, it would be better. Because only a man can teach a boy how to be a man. A female can't teach you how to be a man because she's not a man. All she can teach you is what she know about a man and what she was taught. But to teach you, ain't nobody can teach you how to be a man but a man. You know what I'm sayin'?

Tim's career goal was to counsel kids who had been in trouble. He said he had never robbed anyone, but had sold drugs, carried a gun, and engaged in "gangbanging." He had read a great deal, and spoke about race and class dynamics, diplomatically eliding the two by saying that lower- and middle-class whites as well as blacks were suffering from current economic policies. He did not have any children, but spoke of the plight of men who did:

When you think about it, though, when you're in the hood, or you're in the streets, let's say, or—and you try, you try to get a job, and you know right now, the employment rate is, like, goin' down. And you're tryin' to work. But you can't. You can't get a job. You can't get hired. But you got kids, and you got a family. And you still have to support your family. And if you can't get a job, and let's say that you even tried programs and things that'll help you, and like nothin' is comin' through for you, but you still have to be that man and provide for your family, and if they're not givin' you no jobs, and they're not lettin' you work, or whatever, make a steady income, but they throw drugs at you, more than likely, you're gonna sell 'em.

Tim concluded, "So it was basically that for a lot of people, like all of them from where I'm from. That's what they know. They's father probably was gangbangin', their grandfather was probably in the streets, you know what I'm sayin'? It's like a cycle. Everybody goes through it." Tim's "little theory" combined social learning theory; a structural, opportunity-based argument; and a gender-based "man must provide" piece. In addition to his earlier remark that once a young man gets into the streets, "a gun just comes" to him, Tim provided a cradle-to-early-grave schema for the life of many young men in his city. Unfortunately, his little theory seemed all too accurate, with the possible qualification that for the participants in this study, the "man must provide" part seemed to begin while they were still boys under their mother's roof, either providing for themselves or contributing to the household at large precisely because their fathers did not provide for them.

Tim would soon be at a crossroads, reentering the world as an adult looking for a legitimate and satisfying job, possibly helping youth in a community program as many other ex–juvenile offenders have done. It was clear, however, that if he hit a dead end, particularly once he had children, he could easily return to the drug trade, where he believed his stepfather had been killed. It seemed that, for him, a job would make all the difference between a safe and productive life and the risk of being consumed by gun violence as his stepfather had been.

The staff in the juvenile institutions I visited recognized the impact of environmental influences and were well aware that most of the residents came from similarly criminogenic environments. Moreover, they knew only too well that most of the young men would be returning not to a changed world, but to the same world from which they came. This would be true even if vocational, educational, and other resources were provided as part of the programming leading up to reentry into the community.

The incarcerated young men were encouraged to reframe their perceptions of themselves as actors in the world who, within the constraints of their environments, can choose not to engage in gun violence. Accordingly Ernie—having consumed more than a year of institutional programming—after citing his violent neighborhood as the source of his offending, made a point of adding, "Yeah, but it's also my choice. I could have stayed out of it. I controlled what I did . . . if I just chose the right things." Most said they planned to do this by focusing on family, school, and work. Soon to be released, Ernie had a one-year-old daughter that he had never seen and an uncertain relationship with the baby's mother. When I wished him the best of luck at the conclusion of our interview, he replied, "Well, I think that might be a little tough."

In fact, the good intentions of many young men did not long survive their return to the community. At one recruiting session for participants in this study, the assistant superintendent recognized a resident who had been released a few months earlier, following the successful completion of a transitional program. When the young man lingered after the session to ask the superintendent a question, the superintendent asked him, "What happened? You were doing so good!" The resident replied that he had been arrested on a new gun charge. They both seemed distressed as the young man explained that he got into something on the street. Evidently whatever the problem was that the boy had encountered, a gun still seemed like the answer as the street absorbed him once again.

## From Dreams to Plans

Thomas told me, "I wanted to be a basketball player, but that dream wasn't strong enough. Me wantin' money was for me stronger than wanting to be a basketball player." His observation echoed that of Luke, cited earlier. Luke loved the excitement of playing football but said, "Not too many people like me make it." Both turned to armed robbery, Thomas specializing in robbing drug dealers, and Luke just seeking good targets on the street.

In fact, sports were the only youthful aspiration mentioned by any of the participants, although I did not question them about their early goals. At least seven participants had been athletes during their student days, and clearly valued their fit and strong bodies as a "personal resource," to use the words of Alford Young (2004).[20] Whether on the football field, the basketball court, street fighting, or pulling off a robbery, they likely regarded the human capital represented by their bodies as "one of their best assets," as Young said of the marginalized black men he studied.[21] Perhaps this was another reason so many participants claimed to eschew the use of hard drugs. As he admired his athletic physique reflected in a nearby window, Nick said proudly, "Do you know anybody who uses crack that looks like me?"

With so few other resources at their disposal, it is hardly surprising that participants would look to their athletic abilities as their hope for the future. A career as a professional athlete, however, is not a practical objective for more than a very few young men. Moreover, the dream of becoming a professional athlete slipped away as the more pressing concerns of daily life drew participants away from school and into the street. In addition, their sharp minds, much in evidence during our interviews, ceased to be trained for the types of jobs or careers that might provide them with a good income in today's job market.

Jay MacLeod (1995) explored the idea of leveled aspirations among white boys living in a housing project.[22] As MacLeod's research demonstrated, the environments in which some young men grow up tend to limit their dreams, as they see those around them constrained by their circumstances and anticipate similar outcomes for themselves. The participants in the current study seemed to come from environments that not only limited their dreams to unrealistic ones but drew them into contexts that could prevent them from achieving those or any other dreams.

During participants' "time out" from the streets, the adults around them sought to replace their old dreams—including those of being successful criminals—with new dreams suited to the world of work. For some young men, the focus was on academics; for others, vocational training. Many participants had earned, or were earning, their high school diplomas at the institution, and these diplomas would bear the name of their home district high schools rather than that of the institution. This practice was in keeping with other traditional features of the juvenile justice system, such as the confidentiality of juvenile records, designed to facilitate the young men's access to future opportunities unimpeded by the stigma of a public record of offending or incarceration. Others had earned their high school equivalency certificate, and several participants in the transitional programs were earning college credits at local county colleges. Some attended off-site vocational programs, such as culinary training, that could lead to jobs at those programs or elsewhere.

Norman had transferred from one transitional facility to another specifically to take advantage of the culinary program available there. Vernon was due to be released in two weeks and planned to live with relatives in Georgia, where he hoped to be an electrocardiogram technician. He had recently completed an electrocardiogram course and obtained certification at a nearby county college. Tim hoped for employment, ideally in a sports-related program, where he could work with kids who had been in trouble. Kenneth, as discussed in Chapter 2, had received a job offer from his father to work in his construction business. Several residents were hoping their working mothers could help them secure jobs with their current employers. Another thought he might work in sanitation and sell some marijuana on the side.

These dreams were not as glamorous as the lives of professional athletes, nor as exciting as those of the characters they admired in films such as *Scarface* or *New Jack City*. Whether participants could embrace these less exciting lives depended partly on whether they could succeed in finding jobs in the legal economy and partly on whether they were genuinely ready to leave the street life behind. Thomas sounded sincere when he said—in the quotation that opens this chapter—that he was tired of always looking over his shoulder, and was ready to abandon the perils of the street in favor of a more humdrum life. He already had been shot, and now had a child to think about. Like the six other participants who were already fathers or about to be fathers, he probably wondered whether he would manage to be a better father to his daughter than his own father had been to him. On the subject of his daughter, he offered, somewhat tentatively, "So maybe, I'm hopin' that she is gonna keep me honest when I get home." But I thought he sounded rather dubious about even this aspiration, perhaps because he and the baby's mother were no longer together.

## Significance of the Gun

In an environment where violence is acceptable, even encouraged, and guns are plentiful, these young men found that—in the short term at least—their needs for money, respect, protection, power, fun, and excitement could be met by guns. Guns, which could serve so many purposes, seemed to offer a ready pathway out of many of the participants' wide-ranging troubles. As these young men framed their worlds, they told me how they attempted to take control of their circumstances as competent actors in a realm where money, guns, violence, and drugs were closely intertwined.

These young men attempted to exchange their vulnerability for agency, their shame for dignity, and their dependence for independence. Even when discussing their violent offending, they often narrated themselves as protectors or providers, constructing themselves as capable men who met their many challenges head on. In many of these projects, a gun—whether as a tool or a symbol—was key. The contexts that shaped participants' identities, and the emerging identities that in turn shaped their contexts, created an important place for the gun in their lives.

This chapter explored some of the negative outcomes, such as incarceration, being shot, and living in fear of retaliation or other violent victimization that participants faced in the course of—and as a result of—their street lifestyles. It also examined participants' reflections upon what might have made a difference in their lives before they began offending, and considered their plans for the future upon their release. Participants most frequently offered that growing up in a better neighborhood and having a father might have kept them away from delinquency. It seemed that even if some had tired of the risks inherent in the street lifestyle and had benefited from the institutional programming and mentoring at the Juvenile Justice Commission, their futures remained quite uncertain. One important factor in determining whether these young men could remain law abiding and free for the rest of their lives would likely be their ability to find legal jobs with which to support themselves. Nineteen participants explicitly cited money as a motivation for their offending, whether committing robberies or selling drugs. An additional three participants reported selling drugs but did not explicitly cite money as the reason, although an economic motive would seem to be a strong possibility. If they could acquire a meaningful stake in the legal economy, participants might conclude that the attractions of the street lifestyle and the rewards of illegal gun use were no longer worth their attendant risks.

## Chapter Summary

This chapter discusses ways in which gun possession and use, while appearing to participants as an adaptive response in the short term, resulted in various negative outcomes. Some participants found that their violent offending had serious repercussions aside from their current status as incarcerated persons. The three participants who had been shot all related their injuries to their own activities, two of them specifying that the shootings were in retaliation for their own violence, and the third saying more vaguely that "what goes around comes around." Two participants, including one who had been shot, wore bulletproof vests and reported that they were rarely free of the fear of violent retaliation. Earlier quantitative studies support their fears, with findings that gun-carrying youth, gang-involved youth, and delinquent youth are all more likely to suffer violent victimization—including death—than others not involved in similar activities. Participants reflected on what might have prevented them from offending, with growing up in a better neighborhood and having a positive and supportive father figure the most frequent responses. They shared their plans for the future, hoping for legal work that would help to keep them from being reincarcerated. As 19 out of 25 participants cited money as a motivation for at least some of their offending, and an additional 3 participants reported selling drugs, their belief that a legal source of income could help to keep them safe and free from further arrest appears warranted. For this group of participants, the street lifestyle, with its attendant gun possession and use, provided only a short-term solution to their many challenges, and presented multiple hazards of its own. Despite their use of guns in attempting to construct a capable and agentive masculinity, many young men seemed to feel, while still on the street, trapped in lives that that were tightly circumscribed in terms of both opportunity and longevity. In short, they seemed to experience their life worlds in terms of marginalized masculinity.

# CHAPTER 6

# Conclusion

## "A Gun Is a Key to Anything You Wanna Do"

Why does a boy get a gun? In the world of the street, a boy gets a gun so that he can be a man. The accounts of these incarcerated young men show us what they believe it means to be a man in their world. For these boys, the idea of masculinity means being fearless, powerful, and able to take care of themselves and others, both in material terms and by protecting themselves and those they care about. They may perform this particular type of masculinity through violence; by having guns, using guns, and knowing about guns. The project of being a fearless, powerful, capable man in their environment sometimes means suppressing emotions that could interfere with its performance, such as shame that comes from material vulnerability, or compassion for those they harm.

Many of the questions that this study sought to address appear very concrete and straightforward: How did participants acquire guns? Why did they acquire them? What did they do with them? As participants discussed these matters, it became apparent that they and I drew upon dissimilar discourses to frame their worlds. For me, as researcher, the discourse of childhood vulnerability and agency, or "child in danger" and "dangerous child"[1] was initially salient and consequently framed my approach to the question and my view of the question itself. For the incarcerated young men with whom I spoke, a different discourse and framework seemed to be operative. This was the discourse of the agency and hence power conferred by the gun. As a generally law-abiding—and indeed once law-enforcing—middle-class professional, a firearm from my perspective indicated and perhaps invited trouble. For these youth who oriented themselves to a particular notion of the "street," guns offered protection and a measure of status. The two perspectives coalesced in this study to suggest that for the adolescent participants, guns were often conceptually situated at the place where vulnerability meets, and is transformed into, agency—that is, "A gun is a key to anything you wanna do."

The current incarnation of the young, male gunman that is the subject of this study is often viewed by those outside of his community as something of a new or alien development, perhaps because he is likely to be a young man of color. Yet the contemporary gun-wielding male arguably represents the latest manifestation of a long American tradition of guns and gun violence, with roots in the mythology of the American West, and even earlier. Slotkin (1992) conceptualized his *Gunfighter Nation* study in terms of the American frontier as myth, metaphor, and reality.[2] He noted that upon the closing of the frontier just before the turn of the twentieth century, there was widespread concern about how and where the young men of America would find opportunity—that is, how they would be able to create a social and economic space for themselves.

Both the urban gangsters of the early twentieth century and the modern juvenile "gangstas" seem to have turned their sights inward toward the home fronts of their own cities, making a frontier of illegal opportunity in their own communities. But unlike the historical and literary "social bandits" of the nineteenth century, they take aim, not at the moneyed classes or their institutions, but at their own neighbors, who are unlikely to be much better off than they are. Viewed within this tradition, the youth toting a firearm can be regarded as addressing his socially and economically powerless position by using a gun to get what he wants and thereby fitting into, rather than challenging, one American cultural script for characteristically male action. Guns allow him to get things done.

This same figure can also be seen through the lens of mid-nineteenth-century English formulations of delinquency as an outgrowth of the traditional social problem of the urban child who takes care of himself through illegal means.[3] As Sampson and Laub (1993) demonstrated, race and drugs are but the most recent factors to appear salient in connection with juvenile delinquency.[4] Yet today's combination of delinquency, guns, and (often) the drug trade has resulted in many urban youth of color finding not the freedom they seek but injury, death, and confinement. Communities, too, suffer. Although the illegal drug trade may provide a significant portion of the income in many neighborhoods, it ultimately becomes, as Bourgois (1995) noted, "an active agent in personal degradation and community ruin."[5] The young participants in the current study searched for a social and economic place for themselves, taking what many described as the obvious path in front of them. Often armed with guns, they attempted to construct a capable masculinity but became consumed by their surroundings even as they seemed, in the short term, to master them.

It is unclear from this study the extent to which any of these men understood themselves through these perspectives. What is clear is that the current combination of economic hardship, structural racism, and geographical concentration has proved especially deadly for many young men, and that guns serve as a way through—a vehicle for—their life worlds as they see them.

## Ecologies That Nurture Gun Possession and Use

Throughout this study, participants explained how the risks and challenges presented by their environments created stress for them, to which they responded in various ways. Tony, who had moved to the city from the suburbs when he was ten, was the only participant who felt so frightened by the ambient level of violence in his relatively new neighborhood that he believed he needed a gun for protection even though he was not involved in street crime. Most of the other participants found gun possession and use to be a helpful coping strategy for their lives in the street. The perceived positive outcomes from having a gun encouraged their further gun use. For example, Quinto's gratification at being able to retaliate for an insult by shooting the other person's car helped reinforce his belief that with a gun, he didn't have to tolerate slights to his dignity.

Many participants coped with money pressures by selling drugs, and this activity provided sufficient rewards that they continued doing it. Kevin said, "When I saw how fast the money come, I stopped askin' my mom for a dollar—I had dollars in my pocket." Many spoke with pleasure of the "fast money" and how much they enjoyed it, even to the point where this fast money disincentivized lawful employment. Naheem came to feel that his legal job was a waste of his time, as he could have been selling drugs during those hours instead. Ernie and Xavier coped with disappointments in the legal job market by turning (or returning) to drug sales and robbery. As Ernie described his feelings after losing his job, he thought, "Screw it . . . I couldn't do nothin'. I just felt like the best thing that I was good at was sellin' drugs." Xavier described a similar thought process when his job applications netted no results and his father repeatedly let him down. He said his view was "That's all right—I'll get it myself," and he did.

But these coping strategies in turn gave rise to the perceived need for a gun, as the risks inherent in the drug trade or other street activities prompted a desire for protection. Participants endorsed the effectiveness of being armed, with two of them saying they felt like Superman when they had a gun, as though nobody could harm them. Others expressed similar sentiments, saying they felt protected. As these strategies proved effective, many participants embraced identities as gun-carrying adolescents. Nate's observation, "Why wouldn't I have a gun?" may have summed it up best.

For these young men, the risks and challenges they encounter upon their release may be the same ones they faced before their incarceration. Even if they have embraced new ways of thinking and have developed strategies for remaining offense-free while in custody, these strategies may not withstand the pressures of their familiar environments. One young man did well in his transitional program, but was back with the Juvenile Justice Commission on a new gun charge after he got into something on the street, evidently much to his own disappointment as well as that of the Juvenile Justice Commission staff. I encountered another young man while observing a focus group at a detention center. He was returning to the custody of the Juvenile Justice Commission for a second term with a recently acquired bullet in his leg. His view was that, in order for adolescents like him to make a change, they would need to be able to find jobs when they came home; otherwise, the same economic pressures that attracted them to illegal activities in the first place would do so again, as they had with him.

## Many Meanings of Guns

The overarching theme emerging from the interviews was the multiplicity of meanings that guns held for these young men. Guns meant protection for both the participant and others, in fantasy as well as reality. One youth described how he had wished for a gun as a little boy so that he might protect his mother from her abusive boyfriend. Another used a gun in an attempt to make someone stop harassing his younger female cousin. A third participant was shot because he had beaten up his assailant's girlfriend. Among the valuable functions of guns were not only protection or defense but also getting and holding onto money, enforcing respect, feeling powerful, or simply enjoyment. Street fighting, sometimes in gangs, was also an arena for gun use in which issues of respect, power, fun, and excitement were again implicated. Many participants admired and even fetishized guns as consumer objects, saying they "loved" guns, or were "fascinated" or "infatuated" with them. Guns sometimes figured prominently in participants' identity processes, making them feel "more masculine" or "powerful." Such descriptions highlighted the ways in which gun possession could include an element of embodiment, as the young men incorporated the gun's perceived strength. By appropriating the power of the gun, participants ceased to feel "naked" or as though they could be harmed.

Even those young men who did not explicitly connect their gun possession with feelings of masculinity described a gun as key for their masculine projects of providing and protecting, as well as for making a powerful presentation. In the meaning-making of these young men, the gun often resided both symbolically and practically at the place where vulnerability meets agency—that is, a gun was key to constructing the capable masculinity they believed was required to successfully navigate their worlds.

Guns also symbolized the negative aspects of participants' life worlds. One youth explicitly identified early gun exposure as a marker of a less-than-ideal childhood, saying, "If you don't see a gun between [ages] eight and twelve, you've had a good life." A young drug dealer who preferred not to carry a gun (although his partner carried one) called guns "lethal" and "serious," saying, "Takin' lives and all, I ain't into that."

### "Man of the House": The Juvenile Offender as Provider

Their pathways to gun acquisition and use show how participants both were shaped by and shaped their ecologies. The typical participant was pushed and pulled to the streets by economic and social forces. Many responded to the economic pressures on their families, usually headed by their mothers, by seeking income to provide for their own needs or to contribute to the household at large. Even those participants who made forays into the world of legal work ultimately found themselves participating in the illegal economy. These processes occurred as participants began to construct a masculine identity that precluded their financial dependence on their struggling mothers. The young man may often have served as the de facto man of the house. The dynamic of the child provider with an illegal source of income proved troublesome for many participants and parents, who negotiated this terrain between parent and child in a variety of ways. Participants sometimes conveyed both their own and their parents' squeamishness regarding this topic when discussing it with me. Relations of dependence and independence, responsibility and irresponsibility, and parental authority and adolescent autonomy were clearly implicated, while pride and shame seemed to commingle as participants described their roles as providers.

We may wonder why the juvenile offender's frequent provider role is so often unseen. I would suggest three ways in which the provider role of these young men is rendered invisible. First, it is hidden because of its illicit nature, deliberately kept in the shadows in an effort to remain out of sight of the authorities. It is likewise difficult to quantify, as the extent of this type of support does not lend itself to official documentation. Second, the child's role in supporting either himself or the family at large through illegal activity may be obfuscated by both the child and the parent, who— viewing this inversion of the traditional parent-child dependency relation as somehow shameful—may conspire to shroud the child's provider role, and the parent's inability to support the child, in a web of denial or disavowal. Finally, we may have a discursively created blind spot on the subject of these particular young providers that leads us to overlook this function. Assumptions about race, class, and age may coalesce to obscure our perception of this role. Our customary view of children as dependent upon their parents, and provided for by them, is inconsistent with seeing them as providers, even though we may not actually think of inner-city children of color as always within the traditional category of protected and provided-for children. As well, a more insidious image of these children as what Elizabeth Chin called "pathological" consumers[6] may blind us to their use of illicit street income for more basic needs. Between these two powerful images there may remain little room in the imaginary for the juvenile offender as provider. Yet the young man's emerging construction of his masculine identity, in this case mediated by his stressed economic circumstances, subverts the parent-child dependency relationship, particularly when the young man is living in a female-headed household. Or as Tim put it, "You have to be that man and provide."

## Living the Street Lifestyle

The streets were also a powerful source of social attractions, and the combination of social and economic inducements often defeated the school ambitions of even good students. Ten participants reported that they were gang members and an eleventh was "affiliated," but each said his gang involvement predated his incarceration.

Participants who had grown up in the neighborhoods where they were arrested viewed their surroundings as "normal" or "regular." The surrounding violence became normalized for them, and they said they did not feel the need for a gun for protection until they were "in the street lifestyle." The pathway to gun acquisition, then, led through a period of pre-gun offending, such as selling drugs, group fights, or committing strong-arm robberies. At some point most participants perceived that their new "street" ecologies exposed them to a level of risk of violent victimization that exceeded what they were accustomed to. This was when they usually became interested in acquiring a gun, and they reported no difficulty in doing so. Guns could be found, borrowed, received as gifts, or purchased, often with the aid of "old heads" in the neighborhood. These "old heads," sometimes just a few years older than the participants, were men who had street knowledge that they were pleased to share with participants, sometimes gratuitously in the manner of mentors, and sometimes with an eye toward recruiting them into their own enterprises.

Some participants expanded their gun use from defensive to aggressive uses, committing armed robberies, engaging in gun battles in the street, or using a gun to avenge slights to their individual or family honor. As they described the eruption of several violent conflicts in detail, it was clear that having a gun made it too easy for participants to resort to lethal violence. In addition, several described how they suppressed any feelings of empathy for armed robbery victims, noting that acknowledging such feelings would interfere with the project of robbing them. Others said they had become emotionally addicted to committing armed robberies in the same way that a drug addict needed his drugs. Both gun violence and violence in general could produce gratification beyond simple monetary rewards, although some participants maintained that it was all about the money. Certainly money, guns, autonomy, and conceptions of masculinity were intertwined in participants' discussions of their violent offending.

Participants suffered other repercussions as a result of their street activities in addition to the loss of liberty that they all shared. Three had been shot, each attributing the shooting to his own actions, and two—including one of those who had suffered gunshot injuries—routinely wore bullet-proof vests to protect themselves from retaliation by former victims. Many reported that friends and family members had been killed as a result of "living this life."

The juveniles who were attracted to the street lifestyle by its economic and social rewards often discovered that they needed guns to feel protected there. The guns themselves also held multiple attractions for these youth, as well as facilitating the escalation of conflicts to lethal levels. Juveniles in the streets were well aware that they could become targets for retaliation by others. This knowledge led some participants to believe that their incarceration had happened "for a reason," with one participant saying, "One of those bodies out there could have been mine."

## Policy and Interventions

The incarcerated young men shared several ideas about what might have changed their previous course. Their thoughts not only centered on being raised in better neighborhoods and having a positive father figure but also touched on broad political and economic policies that would provide for more good jobs, and such personal issues as making better choices. The range of the participants' thinking reflects the scope of the factors affecting their trajectories, and points to the need for policies and interventions directed at multiple fronts in order to reduce juvenile gun violence. One of the strengths of Bronfenbrenner's Ecological Systems Theory,[7] especially as applied in intervention frameworks such as J. David Hawkins and Richard F. Catalano's (1992) "Communities That Care" model,[8] is its ability to illustrate that interventions and policies intended to address public health problems such as youth gun violence must take place at multiple levels. Interventions at the level of individual young people are critical, but the spheres of family, neighborhood, and school must also be addressed. Moreover, the broader cultural and economic structures that produce and maintain the environments in which youth gun violence thrives are likely to continue generating juvenile gun offenders as long as they remain unchanged.

At the individual level, a myriad of interventions throughout the private, nonprofit, and public sectors proliferate, often including collaborations among multiple sectors and agencies. Individual young people can be self-referred or court-referred or can connect with interventions and services in a number of other ways. The important point for this discussion is that it is sometimes apparent that an individual child or adolescent can benefit from some type of intervention, and people may be able to mobilize and address the issues of an individual young person, with varying degrees of success. As both private and public funders now tend to demand an evaluation piece for programs and projects, the complementary trends toward evidence-based practice in program design and evaluation of outcomes should promote both new and established efforts that show the most promise in address-ing the needs of individual adolescents. Current initiatives directed toward young offenders, and those considered to be at risk of offending, span the continuum from prevention to reentry, and feature programming specific to young people's needs at all points in between.

As this study has shown, some boys join gangs as early as age nine, and handle guns even earlier. Recent initiatives in some locales have included programs for children prior to the third grade level intended to divert them from involvement with gangs and guns. For adolescents, jobs are of para-mount importance as alternatives to the street economy. Both the money itself and the pride of being a provider and accomplishing something are clearly central to their survival as well as their identities. This study dem-onstrates that many young men are determined to obtain money, and will do so in whatever way they can. Moreover, many of those who are making money in the streets are likely to feel that they need a gun for protection or for other reasons. Jobs or careers that provide economic security as well as a sense of dignity and accomplishment can therefore be viewed as a cru-cial form of crime prevention, and worth the investment they may require. This investment is likely to include job training and placement programs. While some young men may choose the "fast money" of the street over a legal job—at least for a time—it is critical that legal employment be a real option.

When such job programs are already established, it is important for program directors to be attentive to the needs of their clients and be prepared to adjust their programming to respond to those needs. For example, interventions that begin as job training programs may, of necessity, grow into more holistic ones addressing broader issues. One program in Camden, New Jersey, called Hopeworks 'N Camden, recently expanded its focus beyond training in computer skills in order to better accomplish its original mission. After exploring why some of its young clients who had received job training and been placed with employers did not succeed, Hopeworks 'N Camden began to address issues of trauma and loss similar to those described by participants in the current study. Program staff believed these unaddressed issues were interfering with the ability of their clients to maintain the types of work relationships and habits necessary to sustain their employment. Incorporating promising approaches such as trauma-informed care may prove to be important when readying youth with similar experiences for the world of work. The same program has also expanded to address a need of some of its clients who are starting college, by providing housing in a supportive environment where residents can not only live and study but also continue to access the support staff of the program. By identifying and addressing multiple barriers to success, this program can strengthen its clients for both work and higher education. Funders therefore should be open to the potential of flexible and iterative program designs that respond to the needs of young clients as they become apparent.

The domain of the family, too, is often the focus of intervention efforts. In fact, "the parents" are often blamed for all the problems of an offending adolescent. Many times the parents themselves are crying out to the family court for help, as they see their parenting relationship with their adolescent child spinning out of control. The experiences of the participants in the current study suggest that one area of family dynamics relevant to gun offending may be the pressure many young men feel to take on a provider role. The assumption of such a role may have unintended consequences within the family, such as subversion of parental authority, or inversion of power relations between parent and child. These problems may often remain unresolved for an extended period of time, only to surface when the power struggle results in a crisis that brings the family into court. Multisystemic therapy is one approach to problem solving that provides intensive family therapy in the home setting. It is designed to build upon the existing strengths within the family across a number of domains. By helping families to understand some of the processes that lead to shifts in power dynamics and roles, such interventions may assist family members in addressing some of the relational issues that are occurring within the home. The importance of strengthening families at multiple points, including during the period when a juvenile offender is incarcerated and upon his reentry into the community, has become the focus of increased attention in recent years. Still, there remain many gaps in supportive services for families of court-involved youth that need to be addressed in order to reduce the adolescent's risk of reoffending. Among the participants in the current study, one came out of detention and did not feel that he could go home, one couldn't find enough food to eat at either of his parents' residences, and one said he "don't really got no family."

Much violence among young men plays out in neighborhood and school contexts, and participants in this study described how violent events that erupted among adolescents in the streets often spilled over into school. At times, these events were the result of such longstanding "beefs" that participants could not even remember what had started the hostilities. The group dynamics that spark violence among young men present themselves as inviting points of intervention for community initiatives, nowadays often in partnership with academia. Several promising models have been identified to intervene either before or after violent events occur in an effort to prevent further bloodshed in the neighborhood. David Kennedy's 2011 book *Don't Shoot*[9] describes one such model, which mobilizes various community resources, including street workers and mothers, to interrupt patterns of escalating retaliation. Another model takes advantage of the hospitalization period following shootings as the point of intervention with adolescent victims, exploiting both the patient's temporary status as a captive audience and his acute awareness, at that point, of his vulnerability to injury. Schools, too, have initiated programs designed to interrupt violence among students. Among the strengths of creative approaches such as these, which capitalize on relationships built between adolescents and caring adults in the community, is that they can present young people with palatable alternatives to "shooting it out."

As important as efforts in all the previous spheres are, it is the supply of and the demand for guns that enable and generate juvenile gun violence. Not surprisingly, these have been the most intractable challenges to address. Whether we believe that "guns kill people" or that "people with guns kill people," it is the combination of the two that has created the serious problem of gun fatalities and injuries. One line of macrolevel reform initiatives seeks to reduce the number of gunshot injuries and fatalities by influencing the availability of guns. Philip Cook and colleagues (1995, 2000, and 2007) have investigated both legal and underground gun markets, seeking to identify the points at which it might be feasible to reduce the supply of guns that reach the hands of gun offenders.[10] Supply side approaches could be a significant part of the solution, although they are beyond the scope of this book.

The demand, moreover, for guns among juvenile offenders is robust, and participants in the current study have abundantly demonstrated that they have no difficulty in acquiring them. In view of this reality, macrolevel approaches that address the demand side of juvenile gun acquisition are critical if anything is to change. This study has confirmed, using data from participants with documented gun possession, what Peter Ash and colleagues (1996)[11] found in their study of detained youth—that juveniles with guns will often use them for more than protection, even if protection was the original reason for acquiring them. Taken together with the findings of other researchers[12] that the juveniles who acquire guns and other weapons tend to be those who engage in assaultive behavior, it is plain why juvenile gun possession is so deadly. Macrolevel changes, of course, are not likely to be quick fixes. Nonetheless, approaches that confine their efforts at reducing juvenile gun violence to those that focus on individuals, families, and even neighborhoods or schools, vital as these efforts are, have limits in the sense that they do not get to the root of the bigger problem.

To the extent that media and cultural representations of gun violence have encouraged young people to acquire and use guns, efforts to change the image of gun violence could be worthwhile. Joy Osofsky (1997) argued that deglamorizing the violence that is currently so prevalent in media representations could be one way to reduce violence and victimization.[13] As she points out, media campaigns have been effective in changing public perceptions of such public health issues as seatbelt usage and cigarette smoking. In fact, public service announcements have recently begun to appear on television showing a person holding a handgun, along with the message, delivered by an African American male on camera, that violence is "uncool." If the association of guns with masculinity and power, so long fortified in American culture, could be subverted, perhaps the allure of guns for powerless young men could be weakened. This is a tall order, however, as the experience of these young men, according to the participants in this study, has largely confirmed them in the belief that a gun confers power, at least in the short term.

Yet even changing the image of guns and gun violence seems easier than changing the conditions that make guns so attractive to these participants. Middle-class young men soon outgrow their boyish desire to play with toy guns. They generally leave their interest in guns behind, except perhaps for sporting uses and home protection, as they turn to more adult pursuits that lead them toward their life goals. The participants in this study, however, found guns more, not less, relevant to their lives as they entered adolescence. The grown-up pursuits to which they turned, such as making money in the streets, exposed them to levels of danger that made having a gun seem sensible.

As Carter (2005) demonstrated in her study of African American and Latino adolescents, the more socially isolated her subjects and their parents were, the less likely the youth were to feel connected to conventional routes to success, such as school achievement.[14] Yet these isolated and alienated youth embrace mainstream American values, including consumerism, in a "whole-hearted" and "desperate" way, as Oswell (2013) points out. This combination of disconnectedness from the means to prosperity and connection to its material objectives leaves these young men in the position of being "microconsumers," simultaneously pursuing mass-produced goods and excluded from real wealth.[15] The money that participants acquired through their drug sales and robberies bought them clothing and jewelry, but could not lift them or their families out of their poverty. On the contrary, as Loeber and colleagues (1999) found, the gun-carrying young drug dealers from the poorest families in their study were the most likely to be killed in the course of their delinquent activities.[16] The severe social and economic instability in the neighborhoods where the participants reside both shapes and reflects this dynamic.[17] In many cases, genuine privation was present, which participants sought to remedy by using the same means that the adult men around them employed.

The effects of social structures, such as the connections among race, place, and privilege, and between poverty and family structure, often left participants feeling that having a gun was the best way to attain control over their life worlds. These conditions are likely to continue generating juvenile gun offenders unless and until they are addressed.

## Limitations and Directions for Future Research

As this book is based on a phenomenological study, its foundation is the young men's interpretation of their own experiences and how these interpretations affected their actions. The important developments in areas such as epigenetic and neurobiological effects of various forms of trauma and toxicity are not explored here, although the recent research is intriguing and has clear relevance to boys growing up in circumstances similar to those of the study participants.

These boys had no adjudications or convictions for homicide or shootings, nor had any of them been waived up to adult court. For this reason, my opportunity to explore either the antecedents or the embodied experiences of committing such acts[18] was limited to discussions, often in nonspecific terms, of shootings that were not the subject of arrests. Therefore, among the questions that remain for me are the extent to which juvenile gun offenders who have been adjudicated—or convicted in adult courts— for the gravest offenses had different early life experiences, adolescent activities, world views, and identities than the participants in the current study.

Another limitation is that only 3 participants in this study were still under 18 years of age at the time of their interviews. It is unclear whether a younger group of participants would paint a different picture. While a number of incarcerated boys under the age of 18 expressed their willingness to participate, I was unable to overcome the hurdle of parents who did not return consent forms. The adolescent's right to participate and have his voice heard in interview studies is an important one that is sometimes not accommodated, and that needs to be considered and balanced alongside other important concerns.

This study leaves many other questions to be answered by future research. For example, I did not examine why some participants embraced the gun's importance to their identities while others explicitly rejected such a discourse, insisting that the gun was nothing more to them than a tool. In addition, I was left to infer many things about parental attitudes from their sons' accounts. A research project exploring issues raised in this study from the parents' perspectives could be enlightening.

## Looking Back, Looking Ahead

It would be a mistake to view contemporary gun violence by these young men of color as something outside of our homegrown American culture. These boys may be alienated in many ways, but they are not alien. Rather, as on the earlier frontier, young men today use guns to defend against threats, to provide for self and family, to dominate territory by displacing others, and more. They are determined to show that they are capable actors, men who can handle their environments. The illegal means they use to construct a social and economic space for themselves make gun use seem sensible to them, if not to us.

The participants shared with me their belief that guns were useful to them in many ways: for protection, fun, money, respect, and power. The conventional view is that illegal guns are dangerous for juveniles, and likely to result in their injury, death, or incarceration. In the participants' worlds, there is ample evidence to support both perspectives. What is missing in the public conversation about gun violence in poverty-stricken areas is any extensive attempt to delve into how guns and gun use can "make sense" to those delivered to these situations. In order to move beyond viewing the violence as inevitable, we must attend to the factors that drive young actors' demand for illegal guns. The challenge for those who envision a future without epidemic gun violence by and against young people is to create an environment where young men will not believe a gun is the key to anything they want to do.

# APPENDIX A

# Interview Protocol

Where are you from?
How long have you been here?
What are you here (incarcerated) for?
Can you tell me about how that happened? Walk me through it?

Is this your first time at Juvenile Justice Commission?
If not, how many times before have you been committed?
Where were you (housed) during your previous commitments?
How old are you now?

When was the first time you remember seeing a gun?
Where was it?
How did you feel about it?

Could you tell me about the first time you had a gun (if had one)?
What kind was it?
Where did it come from?
When did it happen?
How did it happen?
Why did you have it?
(If a prompt is necessary, ask was it for work [i.e., drug dealing], to commit
    some other crime, for general protection, to be part of group, or to
    feel a certain way?)

What did you think about it?
Did it change how you felt?
About yourself? How?
About your surroundings? How?

Who were you living with when you were arrested?

What was your neighborhood like?

Did you feel safe inside your house?

Did you feel safe once you stepped outside of your house?

What was school like for you?

What was happening for you at school (at the time of your acquisition of a gun)?

What else was happening with your life then? (In addition to asking about school, ask about work, any community groups, family, social life, etc.)

How did your school experiences, community groups, child welfare involvement, etc., affect you?

Were you in a gang?

Have you ever been shot? Shot at?

Have friends of yours been shot?

Have you ever been robbed?

Could you tell me about the first time you used a gun?

How did you use it? (To threaten, shoot, or show off? Something else?)

What kind was it?

Where did it come from?

When did it happen?

How did it happen?

What did you think about it?

Did it change how you felt?

About yourself? How?

About your surroundings? How?

Have you ever shot at anybody?

(If he made money from his offending) What did you spend your money on?

Did your family know where your money came from?

Did you ever have another gun charge (or offense) before this one?

(If yes) Did that experience change the way you felt about having/using a gun? If so, how?

Does your current charge/incarceration change the way you feel about having/using a gun? If so, how? What about the experience made you see things differently?

What kinds of things about a gun make it more attractive to you?

Do you think there was a time when something could have been done to keep you from wanting/needing a gun, or using one?

(If yes) When would that time have been?
What do you think might have made a difference?

(If used a gun) What would it have taken for you to have walked away at that
    point (before using the gun)?
What do you think could keep you from coming back here? (Being rein-
    carcerated? Reoffending?)
Is there anything I left out that you would like to tell me about?
Thank you, and so on.

# APPENDIX B

# Demographic and Data Snapshot of Participants

*Caveat:* Some categories are indicated by minimums due to incomplete data.

**Current offense:** Unlawful possession of a gun—9
  Armed robbery with a gun—7
  Armed robbery with a gun, but he was the lookout—1
  Armed robbery with a BB gun—1
  Aggravated assault with a gun (beating, not shooting)—1
  Attempted murder with a knife—2
  Armed robbery with a knife—1
  Strong-arm robbery (robbery without a weapon)—1
  Aggravated assault with a car (boy denies the assault)—1
  Drug distribution (previous adjudication for robbery)—1
**Age**: Mode: 18; mean: 18
**Race**: 22 African American, 2 Latino, and 1 self-described as half African American, half Latino
**Family composition**: 17 lived with mothers, 3 with aunts, 1 with grandmother, 3 with mother and father, and 1 with father
**Had a gun**: 19 participants said they had guns, 1 had a BB gun, and 5 said they did not have guns even though some had been adjudicated delinquent for gun possession
**Money motive**: 19 participants said at least some of their offending was motivated by the desire to obtain money and an additional 3 said they sold drugs without explicitly citing money as a motive
**Previous juvenile court history**: At least 18 participants had previous charges

**Sold drugs**: At least 17 participants sold drugs

**Robberies**: 13 participants said they had committed robberies

**Shot a gun**: 10 participants said they had used a gun to shoot and 4 preferred not to say

**Shot at a person**: 7 participants said they had shot at a person and 4 preferred not to say

**Gangs**: 10 participants said they were gang members and 1 said he was "affiliated." All said their gang involvement predated their incarceration

**Robbery victim**: At least 6 participants had been robbed

**Family/friends shot**: At least 14 participants had family members or friends who had been shot

**Been shot at**: At least 12 participants had been shot at

**Gunshot wound**: 3 participants had been shot

**Bad neighborhood**: At least 18 participants characterized their neighborhoods as bad but only 1 participant said he obtained a gun because of his neighborhood

**Had children:** At least 5 participants already had children and 2 more were expectant fathers

**Work history:** At least 6 participants had earned money legally at some point

**Sports**: At least 7 participants had played on school sports teams and 1 of these also played in a traveling league. An additional participant played at the Boys and Girls Club

# APPENDIX C

# Background Information on Individual Participants

**David Quinn**—18-year-old African American currently incarcerated for gun possession, a .38 caliber revolver. He said that as he entered his teens, he began to feel that he was too old to ask his mother for money "to live his life with" and went to the streets to make money for himself. He said he didn't feel a pressing need for money, "but everybody has wants, so that's about it." He said he was speaking of clothes, shoes, even a car, if he had the money. He has been shot at, but not hit, in connection with his street activities, which he declined to describe in detail, but he said it involved doing things he shouldn't have been doing. He has had a number of guns, some of which he paid cash for, and some of which were just handed to him. He didn't always carry his gun, and he didn't carry it when he went to parties or even walking around in the city, just when he was doing those certain things. He also declined to say whether he ever felt the need to shoot his gun. He actually lived in a quiet town, but went to the nearby city where he had relatives to engage in his illegal money-making activities. From around ages 7 through 16, he played football as a linebacker and basketball. Once his street activities became a priority, he stopped going to school and stopped playing sports. He was not in a gang, and lived with his mother, his grandfather, and one sibling.

**Earl Quaid**—19-year-old African American incarcerated for armed robbery, for which he was a lookout. He said he did not enter the house with his two adult codefendants, one of whom had the gun. He had previously been incarcerated for distribution of cocaine. He was not in a gang. He lived with his mother and younger sister. His father lived elsewhere, but was involved in his life. Earl said he did not have or use guns, but said those around him who sold drugs did have them. He would use his money from selling cocaine to buy clothes and sneakers and to "enjoy himself," and he would also save his money to buy more drugs to sell. He said he still has some of the money "stashed." He did well in school, and said he would go to school and then go out and sell drugs. He said he feels badly about embarrassing his father, who runs a basketball league "trying to help troubled kids stay off the street, and he can't help his own kid." He also feels badly about embarrassing his mother, who would have gotten him anything he wanted. He just graduated from a program at the local county college and says he's going to culinary school upon his release.

**Ernie Madison**—19-year-old African American, a member of Crips gang since he was 9 years old. At the time of his arrest, he lived with his mother and her fiancé. He is currently incarcerated for gun possession, and said he has previous adjudications for armed robbery with a knife, burglary, criminal trespass, and drug distribution. He has a child. He grew up in a rough part of the city, full of gangs, drugs, and guns. He started selling crack in seventh grade but says he liked school and did well in middle school and high school. However, he said his high school was a dangerous place that would make you want to bring a gun to school. He said, "Everybody want money . . . If you get it when you're home, if you get a lot of it, ain't nothing to run away from." He used the money he obtained for "anything I wanted. Like clothes, food, whatever. I ain't gotta ask my mother for nothin'." He has shot at people and has had many friends and relatives who have been shot. He has had a number of guns, but only purchased two of them. He talked about different kinds of guns that he likes. He had a legal job at a women's clothing store, but when he lost that job, he became "demoralized" and resumed selling drugs. On gun acquisition, "Almost all of us were dealing. You got a lot of money, and with the money comes guns, so . . . when you have money, people aren't going to like it; people are going to come after you for certain reasons." He laughed and emphatically said no when I asked whether he or his group used crack, but when I asked what he thought of those who bought it from him, he simply answered, "That was their business." He believed that growing up in a different type of area, without so many gangs, drugs, and guns, might have made things different for him.

**Keith Samuels**—18-year-old African American currently incarcerated for gun possession, who said he had previous adjudications for receiving stolen property and joyriding. He is a member of a gang, and lived with his mother and two younger siblings. He described his neighborhood as full of drugs, gangs, and "crackheads." He said school was easy for him, and he played varsity football his freshman year in high school, but he lost interest in school and dropped out of football, preferring to hang out with friends and "females." He didn't feel the need for a gun when he "wasn't really into the streets," but once he was in the streets and joined a gang, he felt he needed one. He was also selling drugs. He said he never used his gun, not even to threaten somebody, but he felt that it ensured his safety. He said the only gun he ever had was the one with which he was arrested. He worked for a while at a university food court. He plans to attend his local county college.

**Kenneth Urban**—15-year-old African American incarcerated at 13 for robbery and possession of a switchblade knife. He lived with his mother and sister. His relationship with his father was strained and intermittent. He was a member of the Crips, and said he had committed robberies since he was ten, but did not sell drugs. He had guns, but didn't commit crimes with guns. Guns made him feel like "can't nobody touch you." He was stabbed in retaliation for robbing someone's younger brother and has been shot at but not shot. He would use robbery proceeds to buy "clothes and stuff," would sometimes take his mother and sister out to eat, and once took them to a carnival. He also gave a lot of money to his sister. He liked school and did well, but got into lots of fights that resulted in suspensions. He had an earlier arrest for arson, which he described as an accident, plus car theft, burglary, and other weapons charges. He liked revolvers, and his first gun was a Smith and Wesson .38 caliber revolver. Before being locked up at age 13, he was looking for a job, and he says he might have stayed out of trouble if he'd had one.

**Kevin Jesus**—18-year-old with a Latino name who described himself as half Puerto Rican and half African American, incarcerated for beating someone over the head with a gun. He did this because the victim was selling beat [fake drugs] in front of Kevin's house, which was Kevin's drug-selling territory. He was a member of the Bloods. He lived with his mother and five younger siblings, and his father was incarcerated. He had two children of his own and was previously shot in retaliation for avenging a wrong against his sister. He did not consider it appropriate to identify his assailant in court, and declined to do so. He said a drug dealer needs a gun because people envy you and will try to take what you have. He liked selling drugs because he didn't have to keep asking his mother for money, and instead could help her out. He said he had anger, and believed this may have come from being beaten up for no reason by his mother's ex-boyfriend, who also beat her up. He felt that the anger-management program at Juvenile Justice Commission may help him when he gets out.

**Kilal Carson**—18-year-old African American who was incarcerated for armed robbery of a convenience store and gun possession for the same incident. He said he had done other robberies before getting caught for this one. He was not technically in a gang, but considered himself "affiliated" with the Crips. He lived with his mother. His first gun exposure was at age ten, when his father showed him one when they were in a car. He thought it was cool. He got his first gun for protection in the streets, and since then has bought some and received others from friends. He sold heroin and crack. He would spend his money on himself for clothes, partying, and drugs and would give his mother money if she needed it. He said his mother had money problems and knew where his money was coming from. He said school was wild and violent, and he was involved in the fights. He declined to discuss his other gun involvement besides armed robberies. He said he felt more powerful and safer when he had a gun. He has been shot at but not shot. He believed his tough neighborhood "had everything to do with" why he got in trouble.

**Kyle Cameron**—18-year-old African American who seemed quite out of place, with a very pleasant and preppy demeanor. He was incarcerated for allegedly hitting a police car, which he denied, and then leading the police on a long car chase, which he admitted. The charge was aggravated assault with a deadly weapon, the car. He came from a tiny town right down the road from the institution, in a semirural area. He was previously on probation for minor offenses such as disorderly conduct and criminal mischief. He had no personal gun involvement, although a half-brother with whom he lived briefly was in a gang and had guns. He lived with his great-aunt, who had adopted him, but lived for a while with his mother and brother in a bad neighborhood. While living there, he lost friends and relatives to gun violence. He had graduated from high school and was already enrolled in the local county college. He wanted to transfer to a school in New York City, and also wanted to join the military.

**Leon Benson**—18-year-old African American incarcerated for armed robbery of a liquor store with a gun. He said he had been robbing people since he was 11, but not always with a gun. He also sold heroin, crack, and weed. He lived with his mother, who told his father to leave because he was a "big-time drug dealer" and she disapproved of what he was doing. This happened when Leon was 14, and his father gave him a gun and bullets when he left so Leon could protect the family. Leon was not in a gang. He had shot at people and had been shot at and would rather not say whether he hit anyone he shot at. He wore a bulletproof vest because he worried about retaliation from people he "robbed in the past." He enjoyed different kinds of guns, the different sounds they make, and the feeling of power he got from having a gun. He had been robbed at gunpoint several times. He said his mother was strained for money and that "I feel as if I go get it by myself, that's less I need to get from her." He rejected the idea of violence as a part of masculinity: "No. The image of a man don't come from violence."

**Luke Carter**—18-year-old African American incarcerated for armed robbery that he committed with a friend who wielded a .357. They robbed a young man they targeted because he had nice clothes and jewelry. He had gotten away with similar robberies. Sometimes he was the gunman and sometimes he was alone. Luke was a member of the Bloods, and lived with his mother and younger brother. He had been shot at but not shot, and he had shot at others. He has a child. He liked both the money and the excitement from robberies and would buy clothes, drugs to use, and drugs to sell. He sold cocaine. He liked guns as material objects, the way they made him feel, and all the things he could do with a gun. He didn't like school and "wanted to get money," so he dropped out. He enjoyed both robbing and fighting other gangs. He said he had lost a couple of good friends "to this life." He thought that if he'd had a father figure or been raised in "another environment," things might have been different. He said he didn't rob females. He said his previous charges included other robberies, assault charges, and drug charges. He would also rob people with a knife, or just strong-arm. He compared his need to do robberies to the way a "cokehead" needs to do drugs. He wanted to be a good father to his daughter, not like his own father.

**Mark Tobias**—18-year-old Latino incarcerated for attempted murder with a knife. He came from Mexico with his family when he was six, and first shot a gun in Mexico in the company of his father and grandfather outside their home. He was a gang member, and declined to say whether he had used a gun against opponents in street fights. He said the reason for the stabbing was that someone at school said he wanted to fight Mark's younger brother. He bought his first gun when he was 15. He sold cocaine and other drugs. His gang engaged in street fights using any kind of weapon they had, including fists, chains, bats, bottles, knives, and guns. As his parents had moved to another area, he was hoping to join them and make a "new start" upon his release. He was about to graduate from high school through the Juvenile Justice Commission.

**Naheem Lewis**—19-year-old African American incarcerated for a drug distribution charge, who previously was on probation for a strong-arm robbery. He and a friend beat up a man and took his cell phone and his book bag containing a laptop computer as the man got off the train. Naheem owned a gun, but said he had only fired it to shoo away the kids on the block who would disrupt his drug business. He was not in a gang. He lived with his mother and his brothers. He was expecting a baby, but was not sure the baby was his, as the baby's mother was his Number Two girl, not his Number One girl. He sold coke and heroin. Naheem said the robbery was his first and his last, as he knew he got off "very easy" with probation, and that people could serve a lot of time for robberies. He viewed the gun he had as protection. He was drawn to the money from drug dealing and would give some of it to his mother. He had an argument with "a father figure" in his life and was planning to attempt a reconciliation upon his release.

**Nate Ingram**—19-year-old African American incarcerated for an armed robbery where his female codefendant had the knife. Although Nate said he committed many armed robberies with guns, he said he approached this victim intending to do a strong-arm robbery when the girl he was with came off the porch and joined in on the robbery with a knife. Nate was a member of the Bloods and lived with his aunt. His father had been a drug dealer who died. His mother suffered from alcoholism and a nervous breakdown following his father's death, so at age ten Nate and his brother went to live with their aunt. Nate had been incarcerated for three and a half years, since he was 15. He said his current term included aggravated assault, weapons, car theft, and drug charges in addition to the robbery. He would also sell drugs and would spend the proceeds on clothes, weed, and so on. He said his aunt was quite well off and gave him plenty of food and money, but he preferred returning to the projects and getting in trouble with his friends. He said he "had to go get money," although he described it as more of an emotional need than a financial need. He said he liked the feeling of having power that he got from doing robberies. He liked guns, but said he never shot anyone, although he might hit someone with a gun during a robbery if they didn't comply immediately. He said, "A gun is a key to anything you wanna do."

**Nick Morris**—18-year-old African American incarcerated for a violation of probation on an underlying charge of gun possession, which he denied. He declined to have his interview recorded. Nick said his parents were married, he had two older siblings and one younger one, and he was "the only criminal." He sold crack cocaine, but only smoked marijuana. He showed me multiple scars from gunshot wounds that appeared to be from a shotgun blast, as they extended from one shoulder across his chest and to the other shoulder. He said he still has bullet fragments in his chest. He said his high school was the type of place that would make you want to carry a gun if you didn't already have one, and thought that growing up in a nicer environment might have made a difference for him, but he also said he had made bad choices.

**Norman Nelson**—18-year-old African American incarcerated for a gun charge, which he denied, saying his friend threw the gun away when he saw the police approaching, and Norman was charged with it. He was not in a gang. Norman had a child, and lived with his mother, his daughter, two brothers, a sister, and his girlfriend, who moved between his mother's and her mother's homes. He said he did not sell drugs or have guns, despite his current adjudication. He said he limited his circle of friends to two or three in order to avoid beefs and drama. He was on probation for aggravated assault when he incurred this arrest. He said anger and being quick to fight had been problems for him, and he believed he had benefited from the different anger-management programs he had experienced. He was looking forward to the Fathers on Track program that would be part of his transitional program. He had been granted a requested transfer to his current facility so that he could take advantage of the strong off-site culinary arts program that he had just completed, and he hoped to get a job there upon his release.

**Owen Irving**—21-year-old African American incarcerated for the past three years for an attempted murder with a knife. His home was with his mother, but he had been living with a friend who got him started selling drugs, and the friend's mother. He was not in a gang, nor were his adversaries in the fight that resulted in the attempted murder charge. He sold drugs ("marijuana, ecstasy, crack, whatever"), and usually carried a gun. He said the stabbing was the culmination of a long-running beef that started with a fistfight, and then there was shooting on both sides. On the day of the stabbing, he was caught without his gun and grabbed the knife from his mother's house. He said he actually stabbed about six people during the melee, but was only charged with the serious one. He sold drugs because "it was the money, man," and he used the money to buy clothes, liquor, weed, guns, a car, food, or "whatever." "I wanted my own shit. The money made me feel good!" Sometimes he would give his mother some money, but mostly he just didn't have to ask her for any. When she noticed him wearing clothes she hadn't bought for him, she objected, yelling, "Take that shit off!" He said he had shot at lots of people, usually in crowds, but didn't know if he ever hit anyone because he didn't stand around to see.

**Quinto Navarro**—17-year-old Latino incarcerated for gun possession. He lived with his father, and visited his mother who lived nearby. He was not in a gang. He said his brother was locked up for a long, long time. He had sold crack and marijuana since he was around 14 and had two previous drug charges. When arrested this time, he had just retrieved his gun from the house to ward off some interlopers that "his boys" selling drugs had complained about. He loved guns, and came from a drug-selling family, where guns were in the house. He said he spent most of his drug proceeds on food, and food seemed scarce in his house. He loved guns as material objects, for how they made him feel, and for what they could do. He said he had shot at people but had never hit anybody. He suggested I watch the film *New Jack City* to get a visual picture of what he was describing about needing guns in case of a beef. He described being robbed at gunpoint, and said he doesn't commit robberies.

**Sam Lord**—17-year-old African American incarcerated for armed robbery with a gun. He lived with his grandmother and two cousins. He received his first term of probation for a simple assault, and next was charged with attempted burglary prior to this. He was in a gang. He did not sell drugs, but had done other robberies. He had been robbed twice. He selected this victim, a youngish black male, as the victim came off the light rail train because he had a phone, a book bag, and was walking toward the white section of town, so Sam thought, "Good, he's probably got something in that book bag." He loved guns, and was knowledgeable about different kinds. He would sometimes entertain girls by showing them his gun, and he said they weren't surprised because "what homie don't carry a gun?" He had "shot at a lot of people," and thought he "had a couple people's mothers crying in the hospital a couple of days."

**Thomas Tulane**—African American over 18 (I didn't ask his age) incarcerated for armed robbery with a gun. He was raised by his mother, but had recently come to live with his father, who was a stranger to him, and it didn't work out, so he was living at various places and then with his girlfriend. He was a member of the Bloods, and said he sold drugs and robbed drug dealers. He had been shot even while wearing a bulletproof vest and had shot at a number of people, but he preferred not to say whether he had hit anyone when he shot at them. He has a daughter. He said he was previously incarcerated in New York for gang participation and robbery. The current robbery was of a drug dealer who called the police and reported the robbery. He said he had an abusive stepfather who was a drug dealer, and lived in a dangerous apartment building with bullet holes in the doors. It was there that he saw his first gun. Once he started selling drugs, he used the money to buy "food, clothes, sneakers." He felt that having a real dad might have made a difference for him, and living in a different area. "Yeah, I woulda been perfect. I know I would have been a good kid. I know I would have been in college right now. I would have been that guy, right now, that I look at TV and I see people playing basketball—I would have been that guy on TV." "But . . . I still look at it as this—I think everything happens for a reason. And I really don't know that reason yet, but I'm pretty sure it's gonna come real soon."

**Tim Myers**—19-year-old African American incarcerated since he was 16 for possession of a loaded gun. This gun was the second of two guns that he had found. He lived with his mother "and her boyfriend at the time." He had been a member of the Bloods, but unlike other participants, said he was not anymore. He said he never shot anybody, but was shot at. He said his stepfather, with whom he had been close, was a drug dealer who was shot and killed when Tim was 13. He said his stepfather's public occupation was owning an automobile dealership, but Tim said he eventually figured out that his father sold drugs, and he believes his stepfather was killed as a result of this. Tim sold crack cocaine and also got into lots of fights. He had previously been on probation for aggravated assault (fracturing someone's facial bone in a fight after school), having a stolen car, and other gun charges. He said his gang mainly sold drugs, but said there was also "a lot of beef," "a lot of shootin', a lot of killin'." He'd had many guns, acquired in a variety of ways. Once he saw that I was attempting to trace his acquisition of his various guns, he said, "Like, if I keep telling you how many guns I had, I'm gonna be goin' on all afternoon." He said he was never an "all-out gangster," but was mainly interested in making money. He distinguished between those who needed to sell drugs to live and himself, saying he sold drugs not to live but to "live it up."

**Tony Kenwood**—18-year-old African American incarcerated for possession of a loaded gun. He lived with his mother and little brother, but staff said he had older brothers who were incarcerated. He was not in a gang, he did not sell drugs, and he had no previous history of adjudications. He had never been shot at or robbed, but he knew plenty of people who had been shot. He did not move to the city from the suburbs until he was ten, and was fearful any time he left his house, even in the daytime. He liked to stay out late at night just socializing with his friends, smoking, drinking, and walking around, but felt that he could be a victim of violent crime at any time. After watching the film *Scarface* starring Al Pacino, he thought he could get a gun for protection, and eventually did so. He believed that living in a different neighborhood and having a helpful father to guide him might have made a difference for him. He was concerned about how he would handle his fear of the streets upon his release, as just staying in the house didn't appeal to him either. Tony represented the atypical path to gun acquisition among the study participants.

**Vernon Campion**—19-year-old African American incarcerated for gun possession and conspiracy to distribute crack cocaine. He said he didn't like guns, and that his codefendant, with whom he was selling drugs, was the one who had the gun. He lived with his mother and his father, and was to be released in two weeks. He said he was attracted to the streets and to selling drugs because of the money. He lived in the projects. While on the one hand he said money wasn't that tight at home, on the other hand he said he would "help out as needed" with the household "bills." He thought his parents knew where the money came from. He said he wanted to do things "for myself," to "have my own money" and "buy what I wanted," which was clothes, cars, and jewels. He would have an adult rent cars for him from legitimate car rental companies. He said he didn't drink or use drugs, and was known among his friends to be "antigun"; everyone on his drug set knew that he would not handle any guns.

**Victor Kane**—18-year-old African American incarcerated for armed robbery with a gun, which he said was wielded by his codefendant. He lived with his mother and little sister and was expecting a baby. During his current offense, he robbed a drug dealer on the corner, and the person who was with the victim ran and called the police. He said he was drinking with an adult male and female. When they saw that their money was getting low, they decided to get some money fast by robbing a drug dealer. The female codefendant stayed in the car. He was not in a gang and did not sell drugs. He said he never shot at anyone or pointed a gun at anyone. He had previous adjudications for stealing a car and hitting a school security guard. He said he had stolen a couple of cars, which he drove for a while and then let his friends use, but did not consider himself to be a car thief. He said he'd had other guns before the one that his codefendant used during the robbery. He said he fought a lot, and that nowadays it seemed as though the fight was never over until somebody got shot. Also, he liked guns and said they made him "feel a little more masculine," "kind of like Superman." He had been a lookout for other robberies, but said this was the first one in which he'd participated actively. He said he did it for the money and denied getting any other emotional gratification from robbery.

**Xavier Donovan**—18-year-old African American incarcerated for armed robbery with a gun. He lived with his aunt and cousins, but would also go back and forth between there and his mother's. He was not in a gang. He sold crack cocaine and robbed drug dealers, but the current offense "wasn't supposed to be a robbery." Rather, it began as an attempt to intimidate a drug dealer who was bothering his female cousin, escalated to a fight, and ended with Xavier taking the victim's chain and phone, which ended up on the ground. He helped his aunt pay some of the bills while living with her. He understood that both his mother and his aunt were struggling financially, and he would also spend his money on clothes, stuff for his aunt, and other things. He thought his mother and aunt both "pretty much knew" where his money came from. Having a gun made him feel powerful, protected, and "like Superman, and there's no kryptonite." He said he was "infatuated with guns." He talked about different occasions when he would use his guns, such as when someone disrespected him, his family, his boys, or "tried to take money from us." He first said he didn't want to discuss whether he had shot at anyone, but later described various "valid reasons" he fired at people, such as the time when, after he had robbed somebody, he thought the victim was going to try to run him down with his car. He said he hit the car, not the driver. He expressed concern that people he fired guns at might want to come after him. He talked about people being jealous and wanting to harm him, including a woman who tried to set him up to be robbed. When I asked what he did when he found out, he said, "I don't wanna talk about that."

(Of the 25 completed interviews, only one participant, Ned, is not discussed by name in the data chapters. However, in the interest of completeness, I include a brief sketch of his interview here.)

**Ned Davis**—18-year-old African American incarcerated for armed robbery, allegedly with an unloaded BB gun that the police later recovered from his house. His previous adjudications were for assault (fighting), disorderly conduct (fighting), and criminal mischief. He lived with his mother and older brother. He was not in a gang, and said he never had a real gun. He smoked weed. He declined to have his interview recorded, perhaps because he had a recall hearing coming up and didn't want to take any chances. He committed the robbery with his two adult cousins, a male who assisted him and a female who stayed in the car. His share of the proceeds was two hundred dollars, but they got caught after the female codefendant used one of the stolen credit cards, and his cousins then implicated him. He at one point said he did the robbery for the money, but then said he had no urgent need for money, and he's not sure why he did it. He liked school and did well there, playing basketball on the school team. He earned his high school diploma from his home school district while he was incarcerated. He wanted to go to trade school for auto body work. He did not consider himself to be "in the streets." The armed robbery seemed somewhat aberrational for him, and he seemed to have done it against his better judgment without really knowing why.

# Notes

## Chapter 1

1. Gregory Squires and Charis Kubrin, "Privileged Places: Race, Uneven Development and the Geography of Opportunity in Urban America," *Urban Studies* 42, no. 1 (2005).

2. Edmund Husserl, *The Crisis of European Sciences and Transcendental Phenomenology,* trans. David Carr (Evanston, IL: Northwestern University Press, 1970), 111. The term *life world,* sometimes written *life-world,* especially in translation, is a term often used in discussions of phenomenology to describe the realm of subjective phenomena that make up a person's lived experience.

3. Herbert Blumer, *Symbolic Interactionism: Perspective and Method* (Englewood Cliffs, NJ: Prentice-Hall, 1969), 16.

4. David P. Farrington and Brandon C. Welsh, *Saving Children from a Life of Crime: Early Risk Factors and Effective Interventions* (Oxford: Oxford University Press, 2007), 19.

5. Maurice Merleau-Ponty, *Phenomenology of Perception* (New York: Humanities Press, 1970).

6. See Elijah Anderson, *Code of the Street: Decency, Violence and the Moral Life of the Inner City* (New York: W. W. Norton, 1999).

7. Blumer, *Symbolic Interactionism.*

8. Steinar Kvale and Svend Brinkmann, *InterViews: Learning the Craft of Qualitative Research Interviewing,* 2nd ed. (Los Angeles: Sage, 2009).

9. Michael S. Kimmel, *The Gendered Society* (New York: Oxford University Press, 2000), 5.

10. R. W. Connell, *Masculinities,* 2nd ed. (Berkeley: University of California Press, 2005), 77.

11. C. J. Pascoe, *Dude, You're A Fag: Masculinity and Sexuality in High School,* 2nd ed. (Berkeley: University of California Press, 2012).

12. Connell, *Masculinities,* 111.

13. Federal Bureau of Investigation, "2008 Crime in the United States, Table 33," accessed March 24, 2010, http://www.fbi.gov/ucr/nibrs.

14. Terri Lewis et al., "Maltreatment History and Weapon Carrying among Early Adolescents," *Child Maltreatment* 12 (2007): 263.

15. Pascoe, *Dude, You're a Fag,* 65.

16. Ibid., 8.

17.  James W. Messerschmidt, *Masculinities and Crime: Critique and Reconceptualization of Theory* (Lanham, MD: Rowman and Littlefield, 1993), 27–28; 87.
18.  Ibid., 79, 85.
19.  Michelle Fine, *Framing Dropouts: Notes on the Politics of an Urban Public High School* (Albany, NY: State University of New York Press, 1991); Ann Arnett Ferguson, *Bad Boys: Public Schools in the Making of Black Masculinity* (Ann Arbor: University of Michigan Press, 2000).
20.  Elaine F. Cassidy and Howard C. Stevenson, "They Wear the Mask," *Journal of Aggression, Maltreatment, and Trauma* 11, no. 4 (2005): 55.
21.  Howard C. Stevenson, "Missed, Dissed, and Pissed: Making Meaning of Neighborhood Risk, Fear, and Anger Management in Urban Black Youth," *Cultural Diversity and Mental Health* 3 (1997); Pedro Noguera, "The Trouble with Black Boys," *Urban Education* 38 (2003).
22.  Henry Giroux, *Fugitive Cultures: Race, Violence, and Youth* (New York: Routledge, 1996), 201.
23.  Connell, *Masculinities*.
24.  Richard Slotkin, *Gunfighter Nation: The Myth of the Frontier in Twentieth-Century America* (New York: Harper, 1992).
25.  Ibid., 126.
26.  Ibid., 260.
27.  Ibid., 380.
28.  Joseph A. Maxwell, *Qualitative Research Design: An Interactive Approach* (Thousand Oaks, CA: Sage, 2005).
29.  Robert Emerson, Rachel Fretz, and Linda Shaw, *Writing Ethnographic Fieldnotes* (Chicago: University of Chicago, 1995), 215–16.
30.  Carla L. Barrett, *Courting Kids: Inside an Experimental Youth Court* (New York: New York University, 2013).
31.  Herbert J. Rubin and Irene S. Rubin, *Qualitative Interviewing: The Art of Hearing Data*, 2nd ed. (Thousand Oaks, CA: Sage, 2005), 86.
32.  Jody Miller, "The Impact of Gender When Interviewing 'Offenders on Offending,'" in *Offenders on Offending: Learning about Crime from Criminals*, ed. Wim Bernasco (Portland, OR: Willan, 2010), 161–83.
33.  Readers who wish to read a précis of each participant's story, including the offenses for which he was adjudicated, may refer to Appendix C.
34.  For a snapshot of particular aggregated data and demographic information, see Appendix B.
35.  See David Oswell, *The Agency of Children: From Family to Global Human Rights* (New York: Cambridge University Press, 2013).
36.  Urie Bronfenbrenner, "The Ecology of Cognitive Development: Research Models and Findings," in *Development in Context: Acting and Thinking in Specific Environments*, ed. R. H. Wozniak and K. W. Fischer (Hillsdale, NJ: Lawrence Erlbaum, 1993), 3–44.
37.  Rolf E. Muuss, "Urie Bronfenbrenner's Ecological Perspective of Human Development," in *Theories of Adolescence*, 6th ed. (New York: McGraw-Hill, 1999), 321.

38. George Herbert Mead and Charles W. Morris, *Mind, Self, and Society: From the Standpoint of a Social Behaviorist* (Chicago: University of Chicago Press, 1967).

39. Robert J. Sampson and John H. Laub, *Crime in the Making: Pathways and Turning Points through Life* (Cambridge, MA: Harvard University Press, 1993), 8.

## Chapter 2

1. Margaret Beale Spencer et al., "Identity, Self, and Peers in Context," in *Handbook of Applied Developmental Science: Promoting Positive Child, Adolescent, and Family Development through Research, Policies and Programs,* ed. R. M. Lerner, F. Jacobs, and D. Wertleib, vol. 1 (Thousand Oaks, CA: Sage, 2003), 123–42.

2. Howard S. Becker, "Becoming a Marihuana User," *American Journal of Sociology* 59, no. 3 (1953): 238.

3. Robert Garot, *Who You Claim: Performing Gang Identity in School and on the Streets* (New York: New York University Press, 2010), 112.

4. Erving Goffman, *The Presentation of Self in Everyday Life* (Garden City, NY: Doubleday Anchor Books, 1959).

5. Pierre Bourdieu, *The Weight of the World: Social Suffering in Contemporary Society* (Stanford, CA: Stanford University Press, 1999), 64.

6. Barrie Thorne, "'The Chinese Girls' and 'the Pokémon Kids': Children Negotiating Differences in Urban California," in *Figuring the Future: Globalization and the Temporalities of Children and Youth,* ed. Jennifer Cole and Deborah Durham (Santa Fe, NM: School for Advanced Research Press, 2008), 90; Barrie Thorne, "The Current Economic Crisis and Children's Experiences and Management of Family Shame" (presentation at the 2010 International Conference of the Center for Research on Families and Relationships, University of Edinburgh, June 2010). The term *shame work* includes identity work performed by poor children (or youth, as in the current study) in order "to sustain a sense of dignity" (Thorne, 2008: 90; 2010).

7. Laurie Schaffner, *Girls in Trouble with the Law*, Rutgers Series in Childhood Studies, ed. Myra Bluebond-Langner (New Brunswick, NJ: Rutgers University Press, 2006).

8. Ronald L. Simons et al., "Explaining the Higher Incidence of Adjustment Problems among Children of Divorce Compared with Those in Two-Parent Families," *Journal of Marriage and the Family* 61 (1999): 131–48.

9. Prudence L. Carter, *Keepin' It Real: School Success beyond Black and White* (New York: Oxford University Press, 1999); James W. Messerschmidt, *Masculinities and Crime.*

10. Kjerstin Andersson, *Talking Violence, Constructing Identity: Young Men in Institutional Care* (Linkoping: Linkoping University, 2008), 159. Andersson discovered while researching young Swedish men's talk of violence that young men can "be seen to position themselves in relation to particular discourses of masculinity, based on certain understandings of what it entails to be a man. These discourses call for the man to be in control of the situation, to be able to protect himself and others."

11. Connell, *Masculinities,* 111.

12. Messerschmidt, *Masculinities and Crime.*
13. Sudhir Alladi Venkatesh, *American Project: The Rise and Fall of a Modern Ghetto* (Cambridge, MA: Harvard University Press, 2000), 189; Messerschmidt, *Masculinities and Crime,* 102.
14. Alex Kotlowitz, *There Are No Children Here: The Story of Two Boys Growing Up in the Other America* (New York: Anchor Books, 1991).
15. Rosario Ceballo et al., "Community Violence and Children's Psychological Well-Being: Does Parental Monitoring Matter?" *Journal of Clinical Child and Adolescent Psychology* 32, no. 4 (2003): 586–92; Hammack et al., "Social Support Factors as Moderators of Community Violence Exposure among Inner-City African American Young Adolescents," *Journal of Clinical Child and Adolescent Psychology* 33, no. 3 (2004): 450–62.
16. John Richters and Pedro Martinez, "The NIMH Community Violence Project: Children's Distress Symptoms Associated with Violence Exposure," *Psychiatry* 56 (1993): 22–35.
17. See Adrian Nicole LeBlanc, *Random Family: Love, Drugs, Trouble and Coming of Age in the Bronx* (New York: Scribner, 2003), 343.
18. Allison J. Pugh, *Longing and Belonging: Parents, Children, and Consumer Culture* (Berkeley: University of California Press, 2009), 23.
19. In discussing the dilemmas of low-income parenting, Pugh spoke of the "alchemy of desire into need" (ibid., 123), citing Annette Lareau's *Unequal Childhoods: Class, Race, and Family Life* (Berkeley: University of California Press, 2003) for low-income parents' practice of constructing "good-enough" childhoods for their children. One way in which parents did this was by "instilling in children a sense of 'emerging constraint'" (ibid., 126). Pugh argued that affluent parents sought to check their children's consumer desires for reasons of character-building and seemliness, not wanting their children to be—or seem—overly materialistic. The poor parents, on the other hand, tried to check their children's consumer desires because they could not afford everything the child wanted.
20. Steve Hall, Simon Winlow, and Craig Ancrum, *Criminal Identities and Consumer Culture: Crime, Exclusion, and the New Culture of Narcissism* (Portland, OR: Willan, 2008).
21. Lara Riley, "Neonaticide: A Grounded Theory Study," *Journal of Human Behavior in the Social Environment* 12, no. 4 (2005): 1–42; Cheryl Meyer and Michelle Oberman, *Mothers Who Kill Their Children: Understanding the Acts of Moms from Susan Smith to the "Prom Mom"* (New York: New York University Press, 2001).
22. Mary Lorena Kenny, *Hidden Heads of Households: Child Labor in Urban Northeast Brazil* (Peterborough: Broadview Press, 2007), 72.
23. Tobias Hecht, *At Home in the Street: Street Children of Northeast Brazil* (Cambridge: Cambridge University Press, 1998), 88.
24. Karen Transberg Hansen, *Youth and the City in the Global South: Urban Lives in Brazil, Vietnam, and Zambia* (Bloomington: Indiana University Press, 2008).
25. Nikki Jones, *Between Good and Ghetto: African American Girls and Inner-City Violence,* Rutgers Series in Childhood Studies, ed. Myra Bluebond-Langner (New Brunswick, NJ: Rutgers University Press, 2010), 55.

26. Henry A. Giroux, *Fugitive Cultures: Race, Violence, and Youth* (New York: Routledge, 1996), 5–6.
27. Anderson, *Code of the Street*, 98.
28. Jack Katz, *Seductions of Crime: Moral and Sensual Attractions in Doing Evil* (New York: Basic Books, 1988), 117.

## Chapter 3

1. Hecht, *At Home in the Street*, 22.
2. Blumer, *Symbolic Interactionism*, 11.
3. Arlie Hochschild (1983) conceptualizes emotions, including fear, as being constituted of both interactionist and biological elements and argues that emotion has a "signal" function, warning "us of where we stand vis-à-vis outer or inner events." As such, "what does and does not stand out as a 'signal' presupposes certain culturally taken-for-granted ways of seeing and holding expectations about the world." Arlie Hochschild, *The Managed Heart: Commercialization of Human Feeling* (Berkeley: University of California, 1983), 28. Her observation echoes Maurice Merleau-Ponty's (1970) figure/background schema, which notes that the perceived is shaped by its context (Merleau-Ponty, *Phenomenology of Perception*, 11) because "the perceptual 'something' is always in the middle of something else, it is always part of a 'field'" (ibid., 4).
4. See Deanna Wilkinson and Jeffrey Fagan, "A Theory of Violent Events," in *The Process and Structure of Crime*, edited by Robert F. Meier, Leslie W. Kennedy, and Vincent F. Sacco, vol. 9, 169–95 (New Brunswick, NJ: Transaction, 2001), 179–80.
5. Sheldon Glueck and Eleanor Glueck, *Delinquents in the Making: Paths to Prevention* (New York: Harper and Row, 1952).
6. Sampson and Laub, *Crime in the Making*.
7. Jan Kornelis Dijkstra et al., "Influence and Selection Processes in Weapon Carrying during Adolescence: The Roles of Status, Aggression, and Vulnerability," *Criminology* 48, no. 1 (2010): 187–220.
8. See Oswell, *The Agency of Children*, 159.
9. Following Lee N. Robins, *Deviant Children Grown Up* (Baltimore: Williams and Wilkins, 1966), Sampson and Laub (1993) argue that the insignificant influence of delinquent siblings, relative to other factors, suggests that adolescents tend to select friends who are similar to themselves in behavior and attitudes (Sampson and Laub, *Crime in the Making*, 116–17). They also cite the difficulty of interpreting temporal ordering in searching for the effect of peers on delinquency since, as Farrington noted, most delinquent acts are committed in groups and "those who commit such acts will almost inevitably have delinquent friends" (ibid., 104). Likewise, self-report measurements of offending and delinquent peers, as Gottfredson and Hirschi point out, "may, almost by definition, be measuring the same underlying theoretical construct of delinquent peers" (ibid., 104).
10. Wilkinson and Fagan, "Theory of Violent Events," 179–80.
11. Merleau-Ponty, *Phenomenology of Perception*; Hochschild, *Managed Heart*.

12. Nancy Lesko, "Denaturalizing Adolescence: The Politics of Contemporary Representations," *Youth and Society* 28, no. 2 (1996): 152.
13. Merleau-Ponty, *Phenomenology of Perception*, 143.
14. Daniel W. Webster, Patricia S. Gainer, and Howard R. Champion, "Weapon Carrying among Inner-City Junior High School Students: Defensive Behavior vs. Aggressive Delinquency," *American Journal of Public Health* 83, no. 11 (1993): 1607.
15. Philip J. Cook et al., "Underground Gun Markets," *Economic Journal* 117 (November 2007): 597.
16. Anderson, *Code of the Street*.
17. William Julius Wilson, *The Truly Disadvantaged: The Inner City, the Underclass, and Public Policy* (Chicago: University of Chicago Press, 1987), 7–8.
18. Carter, *Keepin' It Real*, 139.
19. Alfred Blumstein, Frederick Rivara, and Richard Rosenfield, "The Rise and Decline of Homicide—and Why," *Annual Review of Public Health* 21, no. 1 (2000): 529; see also Colin Loftin, "Assaultive Violence as a Contagious Social Process," *New York Academy of Medicine* 62, no. 5 (1986).
20. Kjerstin Andersson, *Talking Violence*, 74.
21. Slotkin, *Gunfighter Nation*.
22. Anderson, *Code of the Street*.
23. Joseph F. Sheley and James D. Wright, "Motivations for Gun Possession and Carrying among Serious Juvenile Offenders," *Behavioral Sciences and the Law* 11 (1993): 382.
24. Ibid., 387.
25. Ibid.
26. Cook et al., "Underground Gun Markets," *Economic Journal* 117 (November 2007).
27. Sheley and Wright, "Motivations for Gun Possession," 386.
28. Ibid., 385.
29. Merleau-Ponty, *Phenomenology of Perception*, 143.
30. Erving Goffman, *Asylums: Essays on the Social Situation of Mental Patients and Other Inmates* (Chicago: Alding, 1968), 61.
31. Connell, *Masculinities;* Messerschmidt, *Masculinities and Crime;* Anderson, *Code of the Street*.
32. Oswell, *Agency of Children*, 70.

## Chapter 4

1. Wilkinson and Fagan, "Theory of Violent Events," 179–80.
2. Farrington and Welsh, *Saving Children*, 19.
3. Hochschild, *Managed Heart;* Thorne, "Chinese Girls,"; Ibid., "Current Economic Crisis."
4. Farrington and Welsh, *Saving Children*, 19.
5. James Paul Gee, "Identity as an Analytic Lens for Research in Education," *Review of Research in Education* 25, no. 1 (2000): 109.
6. Americo Paredes, "On Ethnographic Work among Minority Groups: A Folklorist's Perspective," *New Scholar* 6, no. 1 (1977): 9.

7. Lindsay McCrum, *Chicks with Guns* (New York: Vendome Press, 2011).

8. David Rosen, *Armies of the Young: Child Soldiers in War and Terrorism* (New Brunswick, NJ: Rutgers University Press, 2005).

9. Ronald E. Dahl and Linda Spear, *Adolescent Brain Development: Vulnerabilities and Opportunities,* vol. 1021 (New York: New York Academy of Sciences, 2004).

10. Slotkin, *Gunfighter Nation,* 380.

11. Alford A. Young Jr., *The Minds of Marginalized Black Men: Making Sense of Mobility, Opportunity, and Future Life Chances* (Princeton, NJ: Princeton University Press, 2004).

12. Anderson, *Code of the Street,* 84.

13. Merleau-Ponty, *Phenomenology of Perception,* 364.

14. Philippe I. Bourgois, *In Search of Respect: Selling Crack in El Barrio,* Structural Analysis in the Social Sciences, 2nd ed. (New York: Cambridge University Press, 2003), 15.

15. Howard C. Stevenson, "Missed, Dissed, and Pissed: Making Meaning of Neighborhood Risk, Fear, and Anger Management in Urban Black Youth," *Cultural Diversity and Mental Health* 3 (1997): 50.

16. Paul B. Stretesky et al., "Prisonization and Accounts of Gun Carrying," *Journal of Criminal Justice* 35 (2007): 486.

17. Gresham M. Sykes and David Matza, "Techniques of Neutralization: A Theory of Delinquency," *American Sociological Review* 22, no. 6 (1957), 666–68.

18. Antony Whitehead, "Man to Man Violence: How Masculinity May Work as a Dynamic Risk Factor," *Howard Journal of Criminal Justice* 44, no. 4 (2005): 412.

19. Steven F. Messner and Scott J. South, "Economic Deprivation, Opportunity Structures and Robbery Victimization: Intra- and Interracial Patterns," *Social Forces* 64, no. 4 (1986): 976, 979.

20. Messerschmidt, *Masculinities and Crime,* 107.

21. Arlie Russell Hochschild, "Emotion Work, Feeling Rules," *American Journal of Sociology* 85, no. 3 (1979): 563.

22. Ibid., 566.

23. Paredes, "Ethnographic Work," 1977.

24. Heith Copes and Andy Hochstetler, "Interviewing the Incarcerated: Pitfalls and Promises," in *Offenders on Offending: Learning about Crime from Criminals,* ed. Wim Bernasco (Portland, OR: Willan, 2010), 56.

25. Katz, *Seductions of Crime.*

26. Ibid., 106.

27. Becker, "Becoming a Marihuana User."

28. Katz, *Seductions of Crime,* 10.

29. Anne E. Kelley, Terri Schochet, and Charles Landry, "Risk Taking and Novelty Seeking in Adolescence: Introduction to Part I," in *Adolescent Brain Development: Vulnerabilities and Opportunities,* ed. Ronald E. Dahl and Linda Patia Spear (New York: New York Academy of Sciences, 2004), 28–31.

30. Oswell, *Agency of Children,* 65.

31. Ibid., 66.

32. Elizabeth Chin, *Purchasing Power: Black Kids and American Consumer Culture* (Minneapolis, MN: University of Minnesota Press, 2001), 29.

33. Ibid., 30.

34. Ibid., 60.

35. Anderson, *Code of the Street,* 91.
36. Ibid., 124–25.
37. Hecht, *At Home in the Street,* 214.
38. Stephanie A. Shields, *Speaking from the Heart: Gender and the Social Meaning of Emotion* (Cambridge: Cambridge University Press, 2002), 70.
39. Ibid., 78, quoting from Herbert Spencer, *The Study of Sociology* (New York: D. Appleton, 1902), 342.
40. Hochschild, *Managed Heart;* Shields, *Speaking from the Heart;* Connell, *Masculinities.*
41. Shields, *Speaking from the Heart,* 49.
42. Jones, *Between Good and Ghetto;* Miller, "Impact of Gender."
43. Shields, *Speaking from the Heart,* 95.
44. Messerschmidt, *Masculinities and Crime,* 111.
45. Whitehead, "Man to Man Violence," 2005.
46. Shields, *Speaking from the Heart,* 166.
47. Candace West and Don Zimmerman, "Accounting for Doing Gender," *Gender and Society* 23, no. 1 (2009): 114.
48. LeBlanc, *Random Family,* 343.
49. Philippe Bourgois, "The Moral Economy of Violence in the US Inner Cities: An Ethnography of Friendly Killers" (lecture, Rutgers University, Camden, NJ, April 2012).
50. Edwin H. Sutherland, *Principles of Criminology,* 3rd ed. (Philadelphia: Lippincott, 1939); Albert Bandura and Richard H. Walters, *Social Learning and Personality Development* (New York: Holt, Rhinehart, and Winston, 1963).
51. Jones, *Between Good and Ghetto,* 68.
52. Robert K. Merton, *Social Theory and Social Structure* (Toronto: Free Press, 1964), 178.
53. Stevenson, "Missed, Dissed, and Pissed," 42.
54. Ibid., 45–46.
55. Pedro A. Noguera, "The Trouble with Black Boys," *Urban Education* 38 (2003): 440.
56. Ibid., 454–55.
57. David M. Kennedy, *Don't Shoot: One Man, a Street Fellowship, and the End of Violence in Inner-City America,* 1st ed. (New York: Bloomsbury, 2011).
58. Beatriz Luna and John Sweeney, "The Emergence of Collaborative Brain Function: FMRI Studies of the Development of Response Inhibition," in *Adolescent Brain Development: Vulnerabilities and Opportunities,* ed. Ronald E. Dahl and Linda Patia Spear (New York: New York Academy of Sciences, 2004).
59. Spencer, "Identity, Self, and Peers."

# Chapter 5

1. Deanna Wilkinson, *Guns, Violence, and Identity among African American and Latino Youth* (New York: LFB Scholarly Publishing, 2003), 205.
2. John May et al., "Prior Nonfatal Firearm Injuries in Detainees of a Large Urban Jail," *Journal of Health Care for the Poor and Underserved* 6, no. 2 (1995): 164.
3. Ibid., 163.

4. Rolf Loeber et al., "Gun Injury and Mortality: The Delinquent Backgrounds of Juvenile Victims," *Violence and Victims* 14, no. 4 (Winter 1999): 345.

5. Ibid., 347.

6. Ibid., 349.

7. Michael G. Vaughn, Matthew O. Howard, and Lisa Harper-Chang (2006) also explored the relationship among street activities, weapon carrying, and violent victimization, and found that selling drugs, gang fighting, and drug use, much more than prior victimization, were the best predictors of weapon carrying. Moreover, they found that weapon carrying "increases the risk for interpersonal violence stemming from the use of firearms or other weapons." Michael G. Vaughn, Matthew O. Howard, and Lisa Harper-Chang, "Do Prior Trauma and Victimization Predict Weapon Carrying among Delinquent Youth?" *Youth Violence and Juvenile Justice* 4, no. 4 (October 2006): 324.

8. Dana Peterson, Terrance J. Taylor, and Finn-Aage Esbensen, "Gang Membership and Violent Victimization," *Justice Quarterly* 21, no. 4 (2004), 812.

9. Chris Melde, Terrance J. Taylor, and Finn-Aage Esbensen, "'I Got Your Back': An Examination of the Protective Function of Gang Membership in Adolescence," *Criminology* 47, no. 2 (2009). The gang-involved youth also accurately perceived that their risk of victimization was increased during their time with the gang. The authors therefore found a contradiction between the young men's objective beliefs about their victimization risk and their subjective feelings of being less fearful while in a gang. To help explain this apparent paradox, they pointed to the feelings that young gang members described. The sense that their fellow gang members had their back provided them with peace of mind or emotional protection that more than compensated for their awareness of an increased objective risk of harm. As the authors put it, gang membership may serve a protective function, "albeit in the emotive sense alone." Melde, Taylor, and Esbensen, "I Got Your Back," 58.

10. Chris Melde, "Lifestyle, Rational Choice, and Adolescent Fear: A Test of a Risk-Assessment Framework," *Criminology* 47, no. 3 (2009): 800.

11. See Elijah Anderson, *Code of the Street,* 92; Eric Stewart, Christopher Schreck and Ronald Simons, "'I Ain't Gonna Let no One Disrespect Me': Does the Code of the Street Reduce Or Increase Violent Victimization among African American Adolescents?" *Journal of Research in Crime and Delinquency* 43 (2006); Eric Stewart and Ronald Simons, "The Code of the Street and African-American Adolescent Violence" (research in brief, Washington, DC: National Institute of Justice, 2009).

12. Timothy Brezina, Erdal Tekin, and Volkan Topalli, "'Might Not Be a Tomorrow': A Multimethods Approach to Anticipated Early Death and Youth Crime," *Criminology* 47, no. 4 (2009).

13. Ibid., 1119.

14. Ibid., 1121.

15. Ibid., 1116.

16. Robert Merton, *Social Theory,* 128.

17. Ibid., 421.

18. John U. Ogbu, "Collective Identity and the Burden of 'Acting White' in Black History, Community, and Education," *Urban Review* 36, no. 1 (2004).
19. Melde, "Lifestyle, Rational Choice," 802–3.
20. Young, *Minds of Marginalized Black Men.*
21. Ibid., 174.
22. Jay MacLeod, *Ain't No Makin' It: Leveled Aspirations in a Low-Income Neighborhood* (Boulder, CO: Westview Press, 1995).

## Chapter 6

1. Oswell, *Agency of Children,* 160.
2. Slotkin, *Gunfighter Nation.*
3. Oswell, *Agency of Children,* 146–147.
4. Sampson and Laub, *Crime in the Making,* 3.
5. Bourgois, *In Search of Respect,* 9.
6. Chin, *Purchasing Power,* 60.
7. Bronfenbrenner, "Ecology of Cognitive Development."
8. David Hawkins and Richard F. Catalano, *Communities That Care: Action for Drug Abuse Prevention,* Jossey-Bass Education Series, 1st ed. (San Francisco: Jossey-Bass, 1992).
9. Kennedy, *Don't Shoot.*
10. Philip J. Cook, S. Molliconi, and T. B. Cole, "Regulating Gun Markets," *Journal of Criminal Law and Criminology* 86 (1995); Philip J. Cook and Jens Ludwig, *Gun Violence: The Real Costs,* Studies in Crime and Public Policy, ed. Michael Tonry and Norval Norris (Oxford: Oxford University Press, 2000); Philip J. Cook, Jens Ludwig, Sudhir Venkatesh, and Anthony Braga, "Underground Gun Markets," *Economic Journal* 117 (November 2007).
11. Peter Ash et al., "Gun Acquisition and Use by Juvenile Offenders," *Journal of the American Medical Association* 275 (1996).
12. Webster et al., "Weapon Carrying among Students"; Michael G. Vaughn, Matthew O. Howard, and Lisa Harper-Chang, "Weapon Carrying among Delinquent Youth"; Dijkstra, "Influence and Selection Processes."
13. Joy D. Osofsky, *Children in a Violent Society* (New York: Guilford Press, 1997), 328.
14. Carter, *Keepin' It Real,* 143–53.
15. Oswell, *Agency of Children,* 155.
16. Loeber et al., "Gun Injury and Mortality."
17. See Merton, *Social Theory,* 135.
18. See Marie Rosenkrantz Lindegaard, "Method, Actor and Context Triangulations: Knowing What Happened during Criminal Events and the Motivations for Getting Involved," in *Offenders on Offending: Learning about Crime from Criminals,* ed. Wim Bernasco (Portland, OR: Willan, 2010), 114.

# Bibliography

Anderson, Elijah. *Code of the Street: Decency, Violence and the Moral Life of the Inner City.* New York: W. W. Norton, 1999.

Andersson, Kjerstin. *Talking Violence, Constructing Identity: Young Men in Institutional Care.* Linkoping, Sweden: Linkoping University, 2008.

Ash, Peter, Arthur L. Kellerman, Dawna Fuqua-Whitley, and Arlene Johnson. "Gun Acquisition and Use by Juvenile Offenders." *Journal of the American Medical Association* 275 (1996): 1754–58.

Bandura, Albert, and Richard H. Walters. *Social Learning and Personality Development.* New York: Holt, Rhinehart, and Winston, 1963.

Barrett, Carla L. *Courting Kids: Inside an Experimental Youth Court.* New York: New York University Press, 2013.

Becker, Howard S. "Becoming a Marihuana User." *American Journal of Sociology* 59, no. 3 (1953): 235–42.

Blumer, Herbert. *Symbolic Interactionism: Perspective and Method.* Englewood Cliffs, NJ: Prentice-Hall, 1969.

Blumstein, Alfred, Frederick Rivara, and Richard Rosenfield. "The Rise and Decline of Homicide—and Why." *Annual Review of Public Health* 21, no. 1 (2000): 505–41.

Bourdieu, Pierre. *The Weight of the World: Social Suffering in Contemporary Society.* Stanford, CA: Stanford University Press, 1999.

Bourgois, Philippe I. *In Search of Respect: Selling Crack in El Barrio.* 2nd ed. Structural Analysis in the Social Sciences. New York: Cambridge University Press, 2003.

———. "The Moral Economy of Violence in the US Inner Cities: An Ethnography of Friendly Killers." Lecture given at Rutgers University, Camden, NJ, April 2012.

Brezina, Timothy, Erdal Tekin, and Volkan Topalli. "'Might Not Be a Tomorrow': A Multimethods Approach to Anticipated Early Death and Youth Crime." *Criminology* 47, no. 4 (2009): 1091–1129.

Bronfenbrenner, Urie. "The Ecology of Cognitive Development: Research Models and Findings." In *Development in Context: Acting and Thinking in Specific Environments,* edited by R. H. Wozniak and K. W. Fischer, 3–44. Hillsdale, NJ: Lawrence Erlbaum, 1993.

Carter, Prudence L. *Keepin' It Real: School Success beyond Black and White.* New York: Oxford University Press, 2005.

Cassidy, Elaine F., and Howard C. Stevenson. "They Wear the Mask." *Journal of Aggression, Maltreatment, and Trauma* 11, no. 4 (2005): 53–74.

Ceballo, Rosario, Cynthia Ramirez, Kimberly D. Hearn, and Kelly L. Maltese. "Community Violence and Children's Psychological Well-Being: Does Parental Monitoring Matter?" *Journal of Clinical Child and Adolescent Psychology* 32, no. 4 (2003): 586–92.

Chin, Elizabeth. *Purchasing Power: Black Kids and American Consumer Culture.* Minneapolis: University of Minnesota Press, 2001.

Connell, R. W. *Masculinities.* 2nd ed. Berkeley: University of California Press, 2005.

Cook, Philip J., and Jens Ludwig. *Gun Violence: The Real Costs.* The Studies in Crime and Public Policy series, edited by Michael Tonry and Norval Norris. Oxford: Oxford University Press, 2000.

Cook, Philip J., Jens Ludwig, Sudhir Alladi Venkatesh, and Anthony Braga. "Underground Gun Markets." *Economic Journal* 117 (November 2007): F588–F618.

Cook, Philip J., S. Molliconi, and T. B. Cole. "Regulating Gun Markets." *Journal of Criminal Law and Criminology* 86 (1995): 59–92.

Copes, Heith, and Andy Hochstetler. "Interviewing the Incarcerated: Pitfalls and Promises." In *Offenders on Offending: Learning about Crime from Criminals,* edited by Wim Bernasco, 49–67. Portland, OR: Willan, 2010.

Dahl, Ronald E., and Linda Patia Spear, eds. *Adolescent Brain Development: Vulnerabilities and Opportunities.* Vol. 1021. New York: New York Academy of Sciences, 2004.

Dijkstra, Jan Kornelis, Siegwart Lindenberg, Rene Veenstra, Christian Steglich, Jenny Isaacs, Noel A. Card, and Ernest V. E. Hodges. "Influence and Selection Processes in Weapon Carrying during Adolescence: The Roles of Status, Aggression, and Vulnerability." *Criminology* 48, no. 1 (2010): 187–220.

Emerson, Robert M., Rachel I. Fretz, and Linda L. Shaw. *Writing Ethnographic Fieldnotes.* Chicago: University of Chicago Press, 1995.

Farrington, David P., and Brandon C. Welsh. *Saving Children from a Life of Crime: Early Risk Factors and Effective Interventions.* Oxford: Oxford University Press, 2007.

Federal Bureau of Investigation. "2008 Crime in the United States, Table 33." Accessed March 24, 2010. *http://www.fbi.gov/ucr/nibrs.*

Ferguson, Ann Arnett. *Bad Boys: Public Schools in the Making of Black Masculinity.* Ann Arbor: University of Michigan Press, 2000.

Fine, Michelle. *Framing Dropouts: Notes on the Politics of an Urban Public High School.* Albany, NY: State University of New York Press, 1991.

Garot, Robert. *Who You Claim: Performing Gang Identity in School and on the Streets.* New York: New York University Press, 2010.

Gee, James Paul. "Identity as an Analytic Lens for Research in Education." *Review of Research in Education* 25, no. 1 (2000): 99–125.

Giroux, Henry A. *Fugitive Cultures: Race, Violence, and Youth.* New York: Routledge, 1996.

Glueck, Sheldon, and Glueck Eleanor. *Delinquents in the Making: Paths to Prevention.* New York: Harper and Row, 1952.

Goffman, Erving. *Asylums: Essays on the Social Situation of Mental Patients and Other Inmates.* Chicago: Alding, 1968.

———. *The Presentation of Self in Everyday Life.* Garden City, NY: Doubleday Anchor Books, 1959.

Gottfredson, Michael R. and Travis Hirschi, A *General Theory of Crime,* Stanford, CA: Stanford University Press, 1990.

Hall, Steve, Simon Winlow, and Craig Ancrum. *Criminal Identities and Consumer Culture: Crime, Exclusion, and the New Culture of Narcissism.* Portland, OR: Willan, 2008.

Hammack, Phillip L., Maryse H. Richards, Zupei Luo, Emily S. Edlynn, and Kevin Roy. "Social Support Factors as Moderators of Community Violence Exposure among Inner-City African American Young Adolescents." *Journal of Clinical Child and Adolescent Psychology* 33, no. 3 (2004): 450–62.

Hansen, Karen Transberg. *Youth and the City in the Global South: Urban Lives in Brazil, Vietnam, and Zambia.* Bloomington: Indiana University Press, 2008.

Hawkins, J. David, and Richard F. Catalano. *Communities That Care: Action for Drug Abuse Prevention.* 1st ed. Jossey-Bass Education Series. San Francisco: Jossey-Bass, 1992.

Hecht, Tobias. *At Home in the Street: Street Children of Northeast Brazil.* Cambridge: Cambridge University Press, 1998.

Hochschild, Arlie Russell. "Emotion Work, Feeling Rules, and Social Structure." *American Journal of Sociology* 85, no. 3 (1979): 551–75.

———. *The Managed Heart: Commercialization of Human Feeling.* Berkeley: University of California Press, 1983.

Husserl, Edmund. *The Crisis of European Sciences and Transcendental Phenomenology.* Translated by David Carr. Evanston, IL: Northwestern University Press, 1970.

Jones, Nikki. *Between Good and Ghetto: African American Girls and Inner-City Violence.* Rutgers Series in Childhood Studies, edited by Myra Bluebond-Langner. New Brunswick, NJ: Rutgers University Press, 2010.

Katz, Jack. *Seductions of Crime: Moral and Sensual Attractions in Doing Evil.* New York: Basic Books, 1988.

Kelley, Anne E., Terri Schochet, and Charles E. Landry. "Risk Taking and Novelty Seeking in Adolescence: Introduction to Part I." In *Adolescent Brain Development: Vulnerabilities and Opportunities,* edited by Ronald E. Dahl and Linda Patia Spear, 27–32. New York: New York Academy of Sciences, 2004.

Kennedy, David M. *Don't Shoot: One Man, a Street Fellowship, and the End of Violence in Inner-City America.* 1st ed. New York: Bloomsbury, 2011.

Kenny, Mary Lorena. *Hidden Heads of Households: Child Labor in Urban Northeast Brazil.* Peterborough: Broadview Press, 2007.

Kimmel, Michael S. *The Gendered Society.* New York: Oxford University Press, 2000.

Kotlowitz, Alex. *There Are No Children Here: The Story of Two Boys Growing Up in the Other America.* New York: Anchor Books, 1991.

Kvale, Steinar, and Svend Brinkmann. *InterViews: Learning the Craft of Qualitative Research Interviewing.* 2nd ed. Los Angeles: Sage, 2009.

Lareau, Annette. *Unequal Childhoods: Class, Race, and Family Life.* Berkeley: University of California Press, 2003.

LeBlanc, Adrian Nicole. *Random Family: Love, Drugs, Trouble and Coming of Age in the Bronx.* New York: Scribner, 2003.

Lesko, Nancy. "Denaturalizing Adolescence: The Politics of Contemporary Representations." *Youth and Society* 28, no. 2 (1996): 139–61.

Lewis, Terri, Rebecca Leeb, Jonathan Kotch, Jamie Smith, Richard Thompson, Maureen M. Black, Melissa Pelaez-Merrick, Ernestine Briggs, and Tamera Coyne-Beasley. "Maltreatment History and Weapon Carrying among Early Adolescents." *Child Maltreatment* 12 (2007): 259–68.

Lindegaard, Marie Rosenkrantz. "Method, Actor and Context Triangulations: Knowing What Happened during Criminal Events and the Motivations for Getting Involved." In *Offenders on Offending: Learning about Crime from Criminals,* edited by Wim Bernasco, 109–29. Portland, OR: Willan, 2010.

Loeber, Rolf, Mary DeLamatre, George Tita, Jaqueline Cohen, Magda Stouthamer-Loeber, and David P. Farrington. "Gun Injury and Mortality: The Delinquent Backgrounds of Juvenile Victims." *Violence and Victims* 14, no. 4 (Winter 1999): 339–52.

Loftin, Colin. "Assaultive Violence as a Contagious Social Process." *New York Academy of Medicine* 62, no. 5 (1986): 550–55.

Luna, Beatriz, and John Sweeney. "The Emergence of Collaborative Brain Function: FMRI Studies of the Development of Response Inhibition." In *Adolescent Brain Development: Vulnerabilities and Opportunities,* edited by Ronald E. Dahl and Linda Patia Spear, 296–309. New York: New York Academy of Sciences, 2004.

MacLeod, Jay. *Ain't No Makin' It: Leveled Aspirations in a Low-Income Neighborhood.* Boulder, CO: Westview Press, 1995.

Maxwell, Joseph A. *Qualitative Research Design: An Interactive Approach.* Thousand Oaks, CA: Sage, 2005.

May, John P., Martha G. Ferguson, Richard Ferguson, and Karen Cronin. "Prior Nonfatal Firearm Injuries in Detainees of a Large Urban Jail." *Journal of Health Care for the Poor and Underserved* 6, no. 2 (1995): 162–76.

McCrum, Lindsay. *Chicks with Guns.* New York: Vendome Press, 2011.

Mead, George Herbert, and Charles W. Morris. *Mind, Self, and Society: From the Standpoint of a Social Behaviorist.* 1967. Reprint, Chicago: University of Chicago Press, 1962.

Melde, Chris. "Lifestyle, Rational Choice, and Adolescent Fear: A Test of a Risk-Assessment Framework." *Criminology* 47, no. 3 (2009): 781–812.

Melde, Chris, Terrance J. Taylor, and Finn-Aage Esbensen. "'I Got Your Back': An Examination of the Protective Function of Gang Membership in Adolescence." *Criminology* 47, no. 2 (2009): 565–94.

Merleau-Ponty, Maurice. *Phenomenology of Perception.* New York: Humanities Press, 1970.

Merton, Robert K. *Social Theory and Social Structure.* Toronto: Free Press, 1964.

Messerschmidt, James W. *Masculinities and Crime: Critique and Reconceptualization of Theory.* Lanham, MD: Rowman and Littlefield, 1993.

Messner, Steven F., and Scott J. South. "Economic Deprivation, Opportunity Structures and Robbery Victimization: Intra- and Interracial Patterns." *Social Forces* 64, no. 4 (1986): 975–91.

Meyer, Cheryl L., and Michelle Oberman. *Mothers Who Kill Their Children: Understanding the Acts of Moms from Susan Smith to the "Prom Mom."* New York: New York University Press, 2001.

Miller, Jody. "The Impact of Gender When Interviewing 'Offenders on Offending.'" In *Offenders on Offending: Learning about Crime from Criminals,* edited by Wim Bernasco, 161–83. Portland, OR: Willan, 2010.

Muuss, Rolf E. "Urie Bronfenbrenner's Ecological Perspective of Human Development." In *Theories of Adolescence,* by Rolf E. Muuss. 6th ed., 321–35. New York: McGraw-Hill, 1999.

Noguera, Pedro A. "The Trouble with Black Boys." *Urban Education* 38 (2003): 431–59.

Ogbu, John U. "Collective Identity and the Burden of 'Acting White' in Black History, Community, and Education." *Urban Review* 36, no. 1 (2004): 1–35.

Osofsky, Joy D. *Children in a Violent Society.* New York: Guilford Press, 1997.

Oswell, David. *The Agency of Children: From Family to Global Human Rights.* New York: Cambridge University Press, 2013.

Paredes, Americo. "On Ethnographic Work among Minority Groups: A Folklorist's Perspective." *New Scholar* 6, no. 1 (1977): 1–53.

Pascoe, C. J. *Dude, You're a Fag: Masculinity and Sexuality in High School.* Berkeley: University of California Press, 2012.

Peterson, Dana, Terrance J. Taylor, and Finn-Aage Esbensen. "Gang Membership and Violent Victimization." *Justice Quarterly* 21, no. 4 (2004): 793–815.

Pugh, Allison J. *Longing and Belonging: Parents, Children, and Consumer Culture.* Berkeley: University of California Press, 2009.

Richters, John E., and Pedro Martinez. "The NIMH Community Violence Project: Children's Distress Symptoms Associated with Violence Exposure." *Psychiatry* 56 (1993): 22–35.

Riley, Lara. "Neonaticide: A Grounded Theory Study." *Journal of Human Behavior in the Social Environment* 12, no. 4 (2005): 1–42.

Robins, Lee N. *Deviant Children Grown Up: A Sociological and Psychiatric Study of Sociopathic Personality.* Baltimore: Williams and Wilkins, 1966.

Rosen, David. *Armies of the Young: Child Soldiers in War and Terrorism.* New Brunswick, NJ: Rutgers University Press, 2005.

Rubin, Herbert J., and Irene S. Rubin. *Qualitative Interviewing: The Art of Hearing Data.* 2nd ed. Thousand Oaks, CA: Sage, 2005.

Sampson, Robert J., and John H. Laub. *Crime in the Making: Pathways and Turning Points through Life.* Cambridge, MA: Harvard University Press, 1993.

Schaffner, Laurie. *Girls in Trouble with the Law.* The Rutgers Series in Childhood Studies, edited by Myra Bluebond-Langner. New Brunswick, NJ: Rutgers University Press, 2006.

Sheley, Joseph F., and James D. Wright. "Motivations for Gun Possession and Carrying among Serious Juvenile Offenders." *Behavioral Sciences and the Law* 11 (1993): 375–88.

Shields, Stephanie A. *Speaking from the Heart: Gender and the Social Meaning of Emotion.* Cambridge: Cambridge University Press, 2002.

Simons, Ronald L., Kuei-Hsiu Lin, Leslie Gordon, Rand Conger, and Frederick Lorenz. "Explaining the Higher Incidence of Adjustment Problems among Children of Divorce Compared with Those in Two-Parent Families." *Journal of Marriage and the Family* 61 (1999): 131–48.

Slotkin, Richard. *Gunfighter Nation: The Myth of the Frontier in Twentieth-Century America.* New York: Harper, 1992.

Spencer, Herbert. *The Study of Sociology.* New York: D. Appleton, 1902.

Spencer, Margaret Beale, Vinay Harpalani, Suzanne Fegley, Tabitha Dell'Angelo, and Gregory Seaton. "Identity, Self, and Peers in Context." In *Handbook of Applied Developmental Science: Promoting Positive Child, Adolescent, and Family Development through Research, Policies and Programs,* edited by R. M. Lerner, F. Jacobs, and D. Wertleib, vol. 1, 123–42. Thousand Oaks, CA: Sage, 2003.

Squires, Gregory, and Charis Kubrin. "Privileged Places: Race, Uneven Development and the Geography of Opportunity in Urban America." *Urban Studies* 42, no. 1 (2005): 47–68.

Stevenson, Howard C. "Missed, Dissed, and Pissed: Making Meaning of Neighborhood Risk, Fear, and Anger Management in Urban Black Youth." *Cultural Diversity and Mental Health* 3 (1997): 37–52.

Stewart, Eric A., Christopher J. Schreck, and Ronald L. Simons. "'I Ain't Gonna Let No One Disrespect Me': Does the Code of the Street Reduce or Increase Violent Victimization among African American Adolescents?" *Journal of Research in Crime and Delinquency* 43 (2006): 427–58.

Stewart, Eric A., and Ronald L. Simons. "The Code of the Street and African-American Adolescent Violence." Research in Brief. Washington, DC: National Institute of Justice, 2009.

Stretesky, Paul B., Mark Pogrebin, N. Prabha Unnithan, and Gerry Venor. "Prisonization and Accounts of Gun Carrying." *Journal of Criminal Justice* 35 (2007): 485–97.

Sutherland, Edwin H. *Principles of Criminology.* 3rd ed. Philadelphia: Lippincott, 1939.

Sykes, Gresham M., and David Matza. "Techniques of Neutralization: A Theory of Delinquency." *American Sociological Review* 22, no. 6 (1957): 664–60.

Thornberry, Terence P., Alan J. Lizotte, Marvin D. Krohn, Margaret Farnworth, and S. J. Jang. "Delinquent Peers, Beliefs, and Delinquent Behavior: A Longitudinal Test of Interactional Theory." *Criminology* 32 (1994): 47–84.

Thorne, Barrie. "'The Chinese Girls' and 'the Pokemon Kids': Children Negotiating Differences in Urban California." In *Figuring the Future: Globalization and the Temporalities of Children and Youth,* edited by Jennifer Cole and Deborah Durham, 73–97. Santa Fe, NM: School for Advanced Research Press, 2008.

———. "The Current Economic Crisis and Children's Experiences and Management of Family Shame." Presentation at the 2010 International Conference of the Center for Research on Families and Relationships. Accessed May 16, 2012. *http://www.crfr.ac.uk/events/intconference10/presentations-thurs/Barrie%20Thorne.pdf.*

Vaughn, Michael G., Matthew O. Howard, and Lisa Harper-Chang. "Do Prior Trauma and Victimization Predict Weapon Carrying among Delinquent Youth?" *Youth Violence and Juvenile Justice* 4, no. 4 (October 2006): 314–27.

Venkatesh, Sudhir Alladi. *American Project: The Rise and Fall of a Modern Ghetto.* Cambridge, MA: Harvard University Press, 2000.

Webster, Daniel W., Patricia S. Gainer, and Howard R. Champion. "Weapon Carrying among Inner-City Junior High School Students: Defensive Behavior vs. Aggressive Delinquency." *American Journal of Public Health* 83, no. 11 (1993): 1604–8.

West, Candace, and Sarah Fenstermaker. "Doing Difference." *Gender and Society* 9 (1995): 8–37.

West, Candace, and Don Zimmerman. "Accounting for Doing Gender." *Gender and Society* 23, no. 1 (2009): 112–22.

Whitehead, Antony. "Man to Man Violence: How Masculinity May Work as a Dynamic Risk Factor." *Howard Journal of Criminal Justice* 44, no. 4 (2005): 411–22.

Wilkinson, Deanna. *Guns, Violence, and Identity among African American and Latino Youth.* New York: LFB Scholarly Publishing, 2003.

Wilkinson, Deanna, and Jeffrey Fagan. "A Theory of Violent Events." In *The Process and Structure of Crime,* edited by Robert F. Meier, Leslie W. Kennedy, and Vincent F. Sacco, vol. 9, 169–95. New Brunswick, NJ: Transaction, 2001.

Wilson, William J. *The Truly Disadvantaged: The Inner City, the Underclass, and Public Policy.* Chicago: University of Chicago Press, 1987.

Young, Alford A., Jr. *The Minds of Marginalized Black Men: Making Sense of Mobility, Opportunity, and Future Life Chances.* Princeton, NJ: Princeton University Press, 2004.

# Index

actor-network theory, 83
agency, 107
  in choosing street life, 120
  constraints on, 30–35
  guns and, 83–84, 91, 146–47
  in male identity, 8–10
  passage to, 16, 52
  vulnerability and, 15, 31, 48, 64,
    83–84, 139, 149–50
alienation, 104–5, 121–23
  anger and, 121–23
  in armed robbery, 104–5, 112
  from police and criminal justice
    system, 130
American gun tradition, 150
*American Project,* 34–35
Anderson, Elijah, 50, 69, 82–83
Andersson, Kjerstin, 72, 187n10
anger, 119
  alienation and, 121–23
  with armed robbery, 105–6
  at victimization, 26
armed robbery, 24, 26, 32, 67
  addiction to, 106–7, 155–56
  adrenaline rush with, 109
  for excitement, 100–102
  motivations and subjective experience
    of, 103–7
  protection from, 70
  purpose of, 98–99
  selecting appropriate targets for, 97–98
  suppressing guilty feelings for, 99–100
Ash, Peter, 160
aspirations
  athletic, 144–45
  leveled, 145

athletic career, dreams of, 144–45
*At Home in the Street,* 57
autonomy
  adolescent, 154
  desire for things and, 43–44
  in male identity, 8–9
  as motive for robbery, 106
  from street identity, 34–35
  *See also* agency

Becker, Howard, 23, 106
"being mean," 104
*Between Good and Ghetto,* 49, 120
Blumer, Herbert, 2, 57
Blumstein, Alfred, 72
bonding activities, 100–101
Bourdieu, Pierre, 29–30
Bourgois, Philippe, 96, 119–20, 151
Braga, Anthony A., 67
brain, immature adolescent, 123–24
Brazil, street children of, 48, 112
Brezina, Timothy, 137–38, 139–40
Bronfenbrenner, Urie, 16–17, 156–57

capability, 30–31
  defining masculinity, 10
  financial, 52–53
career aspirations, 144–46
Carter, Prudence, 33, 161
Cassidy, Elaine, 9
Catalano, Richard F., 156–57
Champion, Howard, 65
*Chicks with Guns,* 94
child abuse, 20–21
childhood, "good-enough," 188n19

children, income-earning, 44–49, 53,
153–54
Chin, Elizabeth, 108, 154
class
  juvenile gun use and, 95
  in street violence, 121–22
"Communities That Care" model,
156–57
community violence, 119–20
"connect," 68–69
Connell, Raewyn W., 7, 34, 82–83
consumers
  "combat," 108–9
  pathological, 154
consumption, 10–11, 161–62
  guns as symbols of, 74–75
  lure of money and, 41–44
  in popular culture, 39–50
  as social process, 108–9
contagion theory, 72, 78
Cook, Philip J., 67, 160
Copes, Heith, 102
Cox, Robert, 138
*Crime in the Making,* 189n9
crossing boundaries, 14

death, anticipated early, 136–41
DeLamatre, Mary, 131–32
delinquency
  aggressive, 65
  fearfulness and, 134–35
  friendship networks and, 59–60
  male identity and, 8
  peer influences on, 189n9
  poverty and, 10
  social roots of, 150–51
dependence, 5, 146–47, 154
destiny effect, 29–30
dignity, 82, 89–92
Dijkstra, Jan Kornelis, 59
domestic violence, 20–21, 36, 153
dominance, 110–12
*Don't Shoot,* 123, 159
drug selling, 3, 31–32
  consumer-driven culture and, 41–44
  gun accessibility with, 68–69

gun acquisition and, 66
lure of, 40–41
for money, 98–99
violence and, 21–22, 118
vulnerability and, 61–62
duels, 96

ecological systems theory, 16–17, 156–57
  phenomenological variant of, 20
education, 145
efficacy, defining masculinity, 10
Emerson, Robert, 13
emic perspective, 123–24
emotions
  doing, 113–14
  gendered nature of, 112–13
  in lure of gangs and street, 49–50
  in shooting event, 90–92
  signal function of, 189n3
  about violent events, 100–103
empathy, suppression of, 96, 99–100,
  109, 111–12, 113–14
employment aspirations, 145–46
environment
  criminogenic, 141, 143
  framing of, 56–59
  in identity, 16–17, 20
  nurturing gun possession and use,
    151–52
Esbensen, Finn-Aage, 133–34
etic perspective, 123–24
excitement, 27–28
  of armed robbery, 103–5
  of consumption, 108–9
  in gangs and streets, 49–50
  lure of, 40
  violence as, 100–102

Fagan, Jeffrey, 60, 88, 90
family
  dynamics of, 12
  empty, 31
  financially stressed, 16, 31–35
  group denial dynamic in, 45–46
  gun acquisition from, 66–67
  honor of, 47, 96, 155

interventions focused on, 158–59
producing violence for, 114–16
son's illegal economic contributions
    to, 44–49
violent tradition in, 40
*See also* fathers; mothers
Farrington, David, 88, 90
fatalism, 135, 139–40
fatherless homes, 31–32
fathers
    absence of, 31–32, 35–39
    gun acquisition from, 66–67
    imagined "good," 36–38
    lack of support from, 3
    as positive figure, 141–42
    teenage, 38
father-son relationship, imagined, 36–38
fear
    anticipated early death and, 138–39
    delinquency and, 134–35
    downplaying, 39
    of friends and associates, 135–36
fearlessness, 80–81, 137–38, 149
feeling rules, 101–3, 109
feelings
    about armed robbery, 103–7
    about violent offending, 109–12
    *See also* emotions
female-headed households, 3, 31–32, 52,
    132, 155
    provider role in, 154–55
fights
    lethal weapons in, 77–79
    protection from, 73–74
financial independence, 16
Fretz, Rachel, 13
friends
    versus associates, 135–36
    in gangs, 49–50
    influence of, 59–61
    selection of, 189n9
    selling drugs, 43
friendship networks, 59–60
*Fugitive Cultures,* 50
future, uncertain, 128
futurelessness, sense of, 136–38

Gainer, Patricia, 65
gangbanging, 121
gang membership
    interventions to divert, 157
    for protection, 133–35
    victimization risk of, 133–35, 139–41,
        193n9
gangs
    in constructing social identity, 51–52
    emotional and social attractions of,
        49–50
    ethnic minority, 7
    guns and, 57–58
    loyalty ties in, 119
    rival, 135
    weapons in fights of, 77–79
gangsters/"gangstas," 11, 35, 150
gang violence, 92–94, 117–19
gender
    criminal offending and, 7–8
    doing, 113–14
gendered studies, 6–7
Giroux, Henry, 10, 50
Glueck, Sheldon and Eleanor, 59
Goffman, Erving, 8, 28, 82
good life, lure of, 39–50
Gottfredson, Michael R., 189n9
greed, 43–44
guilty feelings, suppressing, 99–100,
    109
gun acquisition, 1–2
    initial, 61–70
    lifestyle and, 65–70
    negative outcomes of, 2
    pathways to, 55–56
    vulnerability and, 13–14
gun carrying, feeling of safety with,
    134–35
*Gunfighter Nation,* 11, 150
gunfighter nation, United States as, 72,
    150
gun possession
    ecologies that nurture, 151–52
    transformative, 83–84
    violent victimization and, 193n7
gun preferences, 74–76

guns
    aversion to, 77
    as consumer symbols, 74–75
    early encounters with, 21–22
    easy access to, 67–68
    fear of and attraction to, 22–23
    fetishized, 12
    group, 68
    as iconic, 95
    incorporation of, 80–81
    instrumental role of, 96–97
    masculine identity and, 7–9
    multiple meanings of, 2–5, 152–53
    offensive potential of, 87–88
    in popular culture, 11–12
    for protection, 57–58
    reducing availability of, 160
    sensual pleasures of, 76
    in settling personal disputes,
        95–96
    significance of, 146–47
    as solution to problems, 3
    spread of, 72
    street lifestyle and, 57
    symbolic meaning of, 120
    unreliable, 78–79
gunshot wounds
    events leading to, 128–30
    meaning of, 24
gun use
    by adults versus children, 95
    defensive to aggressive, 155–56
    gender differences in, 7–9
    race and class issues of, 95
    responsible, 94–95
    socially approved, 94
    by urban versus rural youth, 95
gun violence
    chance of being killed by, 132–33
    changing image of, 160–61
    etic view of, 94–97
    male gender and, 7–9
    negative outcomes of, 147
    participants' perspectives on, 97–99
    poverty and, 9–10
    race and, 9

    random, 130
    retaliatory, 128–31

Harper-Chang, Lisa, 193n7
Hawkins, J. David, 156–57
Hecht, Tobias, 48, 57, 112
hegemonic man archetype, 6
Hirschi, Travis, 189n9
Hochschild, Arlie, 101–13, 189n3
Hochstetler, Andy, 102
honor, 47, 73, 90, 95–96, 125, 155
Hopeworks 'N Camden, 158
Howard, Matthew O., 193n7

identity
    environment and, 16–17, 20
    guns in, 80–84
    multidimensional, 10–11
illegal activities
    as bonding behavior, 100–101
    financial hardship and, 31–35
    gun acquisition and, 66–70
    lure of, 103–7
    peer and environmental influences on,
        59–61
illegal economic contributions, 44–49
impression management theory, 28, 102
independence, 154
    criminal activities and, 32–35
    drug dealing and, 41
    guns and, 60
    passage to, 52
    risk-taking and, 107
institutional ethos, 60–61
insults, 89–90
    protection from, 72–73
    retaliation against, 115–16, 151
interdependence, in family dynamics,
    12, 48
interventions, 156
    antigun, 160
    community-based, 156–57
    family-focused, 158–59
    individual, 157
    media, 160–61
    school-based, 159

invincibility, feeling of, 80, 138
irresponsibility, 48, 52, 154

jobs programs, 157–58
Jones, Nikki, 49, 120
juvenile courts, 13
juvenile institutional ethos, 102–3
juvenile offender participants
   background information on, 171–83
   demographics of, 169–70

Katz, Jack, 51, 104, 106
Kelley, Ann, 107
Kennedy, David, 123, 159
Kenny, Mary Lorena, 48
Kimmel, Michael S., 6
"knock-out," 113
Kotlowitz, Alex, 35

Lacan, Jacques, 107
Landry, Charles, 107
Laub, John, 59, 150, 189n9
LeBlanc, Adrian Nicole, 116
legal employment
   limited access to, 32–33
   to support family, 34–35
Lesko, Nancy, 64
life worlds, 2, 4, 15–16, 19, 185n2
   capability in, 30–31, 52–53, 64
   dangerous, 39–40, 69–70
      factors making difference in, 141–44
      guns in, 83–84
      participants' views on, 135–36
   money in, 107–8
Loeber, Rolf, 131–32, 161
*Longing and Belonging*, 41
loyalty, 49–51, 117, 119, 135–36
Ludwig, Jens, 67
Luna, Beatriz, 123–24

MacLeod, Jay, 145
maladaptive behaviors, 39
males
   gun violence and, 7–9
   hegemonic, 6, 8
   nonhegemonic, 7–8

manhood
   concept of, 111–12
   demonstrating, 100
   guns and, 149
man of the house, 3, 48, 153–55
   de facto role of, 35–36
   responsibilities of, 31–35, 39, 43
Martinez, Pedro, 39
masculinity, 153
   absent fathers and, 35–39
   collective performance of, 7
   constructing, 6–7
   discourses of, 187n10
   greed and, 43–44
   guns and, 7–9, 80–84, 110–12
   hegemonic and nonhegemonic, 6–8
   multidimensional identities and, 10–11
   power to protect and, 21
   proving, 100
   violence and, 7–9, 110–13
Matza, David, 99
May, John, 131
McCrum, Lindsay, 94
Mead, George Herbert, 17, 23
Melde, Chris, 134–35
Merleau-Ponty, Maurice, 96, 189n3
Merton, Robert, 139
Messerschmidt, James, 8, 33, 34, 82–83,
   101, 113
Meyer, Cheryl, 45–46
Miller, Jody, 14
money, 161–62
   dangers of having, 61–62
   emotional and symbolic meaning of,
      105–6
   "fast," 41–43, 48–49, 151–52, 157
   gun acquisition and, 16
   illegal activities to make, 31–35, 98–99
   lure of, 40, 41–44, 59, 147, 151–52
   need for, 30
   power of, 107–9
   protecting, 70
   shortage of, 31–32
mothers
   dependence on, 3
   financial independence from, 40–41

mothers (*continued*)
  financially struggling, 10, 32
  negotiating son's illegal economic
    contributions, 44–49
  organized against street violence, 123
  positive influence of, 142
  as provider, 43
  *See also* female-headed households
multisystemic therapy, 158–59
murder, 24–25
Muuss, Rolf, 16–17

neighborhoods
  criminogenic, 141, 143
  experience of, 56–57
  framing of, 56–59
  unsafe, 62–65
  *See also* environment; life worlds
*New Jack City*, 11, 40
New Jersey Juvenile Justice Commission,
  14
Noguera, Pedro, 121–22

Oberman, Michelle, 45–46
offenders, victimization among, 131–33
Ogbu, John, 139
"old heads"
  grooming young men, 69–70, 119–20
  guns from, 66, 69, 85, 155
Osofsky, Joy, 160–61
Oswell, David, 107, 161

Paredes, Americo, 92, 102
parent-child dependency relationship,
  154–55
parents
  low-income, 16, 29, 188n19
  neglectful, 30–31, 34
  *See also* fathers; mothers
Pascoe, C. J., 7–8
peer pressure, 59–61
penitent reconstruction, 102, 118
personal disputes, 95–96
Peterson, Dana, 133–34
phenomenology, 2, 4–5, 16–17, 81, 162
  ecological systems theory and, 20

popular culture
  consumption and, 39–50
  guns and, 11–12
poverty, 161–62
  pathway out of, 87–88
  shame of, 3
  structural violence of, 28–30
  symbolic violence of, 19
  *See also* money
power, 153
  versus "being mean," 104
  defining masculinity, 10
  feelings of, 80–83
  to purchase, 107–9
  in street identity, 34–35
powerlessness, 10, 82–33
  pathway out of, 87–88
power structures, male behavior and, 7–8
pre-gun offending, 20, 23–24
presentation, 3–4, 30, 39–41, 115, 135,
  138, 153
protection, 96–97, 149–50, 152–53, 156
  from armed robbery, 70
  broad definition of, 79–80
  in drug selling, 25, 62
  of family, 38, 66–67, 114–16
  from fights, 73–74
  of friends, 25–27, 91
  of gang members, 77–78, 79, 133–35,
    193n9
  from insults, 72–73
  from known others, 4
  masculinity and, 8, 10, 21
  from personal violence, 71
  power and, 81–83
  reasons for needing, 70–74
  from retaliation, 24
  in school, 70–71
  from street violence, 57–58, 62–65,
    77–78, 83–84, 87–88
protector role, 8–9, 114–16, 124
provider-children, 44–49
provider role, 124, 153–55
  defining masculinity, 10
  invisibility of, 154–55
  of man, 8–9, 142–43

psychological addiction, to robbery, 106–7, 124, 125, 155–56
public policies, 156–62
public service announcements, anti–gun violence, 160–61
public spaces, victimization and violence exposure in, 22–28
Pugh, Allison, 41, 188n19
*Purchasing Power,* 108

qualitative research, 13
    future direction of, 162–63
    limitations on, 162
qualitative research interview, 1–2, 4–5
    protocol for, 165–67

race, 13–14
    gun violence and, 9
    juvenile gun use and, 95
    in street violence, 121–22
racism, 9
    structural, 19
    vulnerability and, 10
*Random Family,* 116
rap music, 11–12
recognition, unsuccessful bids for, 90–91
reflexivity, 13
respect, 4, 73, 82–83
    violence and, 115–16
responsibility, 60–61, 154
    as man of the house, 31–35
    passage to, 52
retaliation, 115–16, 128–31, 151
    escalating, 90–91
reward-seeking behaviors, 107
Richters, John, 39
Riley, Lara, 45–46
risk-taking behaviors, 107
Rivara, Frederick, 72
robbery. *See* armed robbery
Rosenfield, Richard, 72
Rubin, Herbert, 14
Rubin, Irene, 14
rural youth, gun use by, 95

Sampson, Robert, 59, 150, 189n9
*Scarface,* 11, 63

Schaffner, Laurie, 31
Schochet, Terri, 107
school, 8, 34, 161
    interventions based in, 159
    need for protection in, 65, 70–71
    versus street life, 49, 155
    violence in, 159–60
*Seductions of Crime,* 106
shamework, 31, 43, 187n6
Shaw, Linda, 13
Sheley, Joseph, 73–74, 79
Shields, Stephanie, 112–13, 114
shootings
    accounts of, 89–94
    retaliation for, 128–31
Slotkin, Richard, 11, 12, 150
snitching, 129–30
"social doing," 114
social identity, 3–4
    constructing, 51–52
    stigmatized, 28–30
social learning theory, 120, 142–43
social problems, 150–51
social relegation, sites of, 29
Spencer, Herbert, 112–13
Spencer, Margaret Beale, 20
sports aspirations, 144–45
stepfathers, abusive, 36
Stevenson, Howard, 9, 96, 121
street
    constructing social identity on, 51–52
    emotional and social attractions of, 49–50, 155
    lure of, 50–52
    "manhood" on, 111–12
    nonmaterial rewards of, 53
    protection from, 62–65
    "stickiness" of, 50–51, 141
    vulnerability on, 52–53
street elites, 51
street fighting, 153, 155–56
street lifestyle, 57, 59–61, 155–56
    anticipated early death and, 136–41
    danger of, 133–35
    gun acquisition and, 57–58, 65–70
    negative outcomes of, 147

street lifestyle (*continued*)
    participants' views on, 135–36
    violent victimization and, 193n7
strong-arm robbery, 23–24
Sweeney, John, 123–24
Sykes, Gresham, 99
symbolic interactionism, 1–2, 4

Taylor, Terrance, 133–34
Tekin, Erdal, 137–38, 139–40
testosterone, building up, 110–12
*There Are No Children Here,* 35
Tita, George, 131–32
Topalli, Volkan, 137–38, 139–40
top-down cognitive behavior control,
    123–24

urban youth, gun use by, 95

Vaughn, Michael G., 193n7
Venkatesh, Sudhir, 34–35, 67
victimization, 4–5, 19
    gang membership and, 193n9
    of juvenile offenders, 131–33
    levels of exposure to, 130–31
    risk of, 139–41
    violence exposure and, 20–28
    weapon carrying and, 193n7
victimology, 2
violence
    with and on behalf of others, 114–19
    consumption of, 5–6, 24
    dangerous adaptations to, 39
    doing, 112–14
    emotional experience of, 112–14
    etic versus emic perspectives on,
        123–24
    excitement of, 27–28
    exposure to, 19, 20–28
    moral economy of, 119–20

multiple roles of, 119–23
    negative outcomes of, 127–28
    normalized, 155
    producing, 87–88
    routinized, 26–27
    social situation in, 60
    structural, 28–30
    symbolic, 19
    victimization and, 20–28
    *See also* domestic violence; gun
        violence
violent events
    emotions about, 100–103
    unfolding of, 89–94
violent offending, bad feelings about,
    109–12
vocational training, 145
vulnerability, 5, 12, 13–14, 61–62,
    83–84
    agency and, 139
    childhood, 149–50
    pathway out of, 87–88
    poverty and, 10
    on the street, 52–53

Webster, Daniel W., 65
Welsh, Brandon, 88, 90–91
West, Candace, 114
Western films, 11, 12
Western outlaws, 11
Whitehead, Antony, 100
Wild West mythology, 11, 96, 150
Wilkinson, Deanna, 60, 88, 90–91, 131
women, compassion for, 113–14
Wright, James, 73–74, 79

Young, Alford, 144

Zimmerman, Don, 114